Compiled by RONNIE CULLY and PHILIP JOYCE

Published by SMG Newspapers Ltd.,

200 Renfield Street, Glasgow, G2 3PR.

ISBN: 0-903-21605-1

# BIG GAME DATES

## EUROPEAN CHAMPIONSHIP QUALIFIERS

Faroe Islands v SCOTLAND ...... Saturday, September 7, 2002
Iceland v SCOTLAND ............. Saturday, October 12, 2002
SCOTLAND v Iceland ............... Saturday, March 29, 2003
Lithuania v SCOTLAND ............. Wednesday, April 2, 2003
SCOTLAND v Germany ................ Saturday, June 7, 2003
SCOTLAND v Faroe Islands ...... Saturday, September 6, 2003
Germany v SCOTLAND ........ Wednesday, September 10, 2003
SCOTLAND v Lithuania ............ Saturday, October 11, 2003

## INTERNATIONAL CHALLENGE MATCHES

SCOTLAND v Denmark ........... Wednesday, August 21, 2002
Scotland home match ................... Tuesday, October 15 , 2002
Scotland home match ...................... Wednesday, November 20, 2002
Scotland away match ....................... Wednesday, February 12, 2002
SCOTLAND v Republic of Ireland ................. Wednesday, April 30, 2003

## EUROPEAN UNDER-21 CHAMPIONSHIP QUALIFIERS

Iceland v. SCOTLAND ..................................... Friday, October 11, 2002
SCOTLAND v Iceland .......................................... Friday, March 28, 2003
Lithuania v SCOTLAND ..................................... Tuesday, April 1, 2003
SCOTLAND v Germany ........................................... Friday, June 6, 2003
Germany v SCOTLAND ............................. Tuesday, September 9, 2003
SCOTLAND v Lithuania ...................................... Friday, October 10, 2003

## UNDER-21 INTERNATIONAL CHALLENGE MATCHES

SCOTLAND v Denmark ................................... Tuesday, August 20, 2002
SCOTLAND v Israel (TBC) .................. Wednesday, September 4, 2002

## UNDER-20 MATCHES

### Northern Ireland Milk Cup Tournament, Elite Section

SCOTLAND v Rep of Ireland ............ Tuesday, July 23, 2002 (Coleraine)
SCOTLAND v Denmark .......... Wednesday, July 24, 2002 (Ballymoney)
Final or play-off match .................... Thursday, July 25, 2002 (Coleraine)

## CIS LEAGUE CUP

FIRST ROUND ..................... Tuesday/Wednesday, September 10/11, 2002
SECOND ROUND ................ Tuesday/Wednesday, September 24/25, 2002
THIRD ROUND .................... Tuesday/Wednesday, October 15/16, 2002
QUARTER-FINALS .............. Tuesday/Wednesday, November 5/6, 2002
SEMI-FINALS ..................... Tuesday/Wednesday, February 4/5, 2003
FINAL ................................................................... Sunday, March 16, 2003

## BELL'S CHALLENGE CUP

FIRST ROUND .......................................................... Tuesday, August 6, 2002
SECOND ROUND ..................................................... Tuesday, August 13, 2002
THIRD ROUND .......................................................... Tuesday, August 20, 2002
SEMI-FINALS .......................................................... Tuesday, August 27, 2002
FINAL ..................................................................... Sunday, October 20, 2002

## TENNENT'S SCOTTISH CUP

FIRST ROUND ................................................ Saturday, December 7, 2002
SECOND ROUND ............................................. Saturday, January 4, 2003
THIRD ROUND ................................................ Saturday, January 25, 2003
FOURTH ROUND ............................................ Saturday, February 22, 2003
QUARTER-FINALS ........................................... Saturday, March 22, 2003
SEMI-FINALS ................................................ Saturday, April 19, 2003
FINAL ............................................................. Saturday, May 31, 2003

## EUROPEAN CHAMPIONS LEAGUE
### (Tuesdays/Wednesdays)

FIRST QUALIFYING ROUND....................................July 17 and 24, 2002
SECOND QUALIFYING ROUND ....................July 31 and August 7, 2002
THIRD QUALIFYING ROUND...................August 13/14 and 27/28, 2002
FIRST GROUP PHASE (32 clubs, eight groups, six matches each)
.... September 17/18, 24/25, October 1/2, 22/23, 29/30, November 12/13
SECOND GROUP PHASE (16 clubs, four groups, six matches each)
...November 26/27, December 10/11, February 18/19, 25/26, March 11/12, 18/19
QUARTER-FINALS ..............................................April 8/9 and 22/23, 2003
SEMI-FINALS .......................................................May 6/7 and 13/14, 2003
FINAL .................Wednesday, May 28, 2003 (at Old Trafford, Manchester)

## UEFA CUP
### (Thursdays, apart from the final)

QUALIFYING ROUND.............................................August 15 and 29, 2002
FIRST ROUND.............................September 19 and October 3, 2002
SECOND ROUND..........................October 31 and November 14, 2002
THIRD ROUND................................November 28 and December 12, 2002
FOURTH ROUND...............................................February 20 and 27, 2003
QUARTER-FINALS .................................................March 13 and 20, 2003
SEMI-FINALS .........................................................April 10 and 24, 2003
FINAL..........................................May 21, 2003 (at Olimpico Stadium, Seville)

# FINAL LEAGUE TABLES 2001-2002

## BANK OF SCOTLAND PREMIER LEAGUE

|  | P | W | D | L | F | A | Pt |
|---|---|---|---|---|---|---|---|
| Celtic | 38 | 33 | 4 | 1 | 94 | 18 | 103 |
| Rangers | 38 | 25 | 10 | 3 | 82 | 27 | 85 |
| Livingston | 38 | 16 | 10 | 12 | 50 | 47 | 58 |
| Aberdeen | 38 | 16 | 7 | 15 | 51 | 49 | 55 |
| Hearts | 38 | 14 | 6 | 18 | 52 | 57 | 48 |
| Dunfermline | 38 | 12 | 9 | 17 | 41 | 64 | 45 |
| Kilmarnock | 38 | 13 | 10 | 15 | 44 | 54 | 49 |
| Dundee Utd | 38 | 12 | 10 | 16 | 38 | 59 | 46 |
| Dundee | 38 | 12 | 8 | 18 | 41 | 55 | 44 |
| Hibernian | 38 | 10 | 11 | 17 | 51 | 56 | 41 |
| Motherwell | 38 | 11 | 7 | 20 | 49 | 69 | 40 |
| St J'nstone | 38 | 5 | 6 | 27 | 24 | 62 | 21 |

## BELL'S DIVISION ONE

|  | P | W | D | L | F | A | Pt |
|---|---|---|---|---|---|---|---|
| Partick | 36 | 19 | 9 | 8 | 61 | 38 | 66 |
| Airdrie | 36 | 15 | 11 | 10 | 59 | 40 | 56 |
| Ayr | 36 | 13 | 13 | 10 | 53 | 44 | 52 |
| Ross Co | 36 | 14 | 10 | 12 | 51 | 43 | 52 |
| Clyde | 36 | 13 | 10 | 13 | 51 | 56 | 49 |
| Inverness | 36 | 13 | 9 | 14 | 60 | 51 | 48 |
| Arbroath | 36 | 14 | 6 | 16 | 42 | 59 | 48 |
| St Mirren | 36 | 11 | 12 | 13 | 43 | 53 | 45 |
| Falkirk | 36 | 10 | 9 | 17 | 49 | 73 | 39 |
| Raith | 36 | 8 | 11 | 17 | 50 | 62 | 35 |

## BELL'S DIVISION TWO

|  | P | W | D | L | F | A | Pt |
|---|---|---|---|---|---|---|---|
| QoS | 36 | 20 | 7 | 9 | 64 | 42 | 67 |
| Alloa | 36 | 15 | 14 | 7 | 55 | 33 | 59 |
| Forfar | 36 | 15 | 8 | 13 | 51 | 47 | 53 |
| Clydebank | 36 | 14 | 9 | 13 | 44 | 45 | 51 |
| Hamilton | 36 | 13 | 9 | 14 | 49 | 44 | 48 |
| Berwick | 36 | 12 | 11 | 13 | 44 | 52 | 47 |
| Stranraer | 36 | 10 | 15 | 11 | 48 | 51 | 45 |
| C'denbeath | 36 | 11 | 11 | 14 | 49 | 51 | 44 |
| Sten'muir | 36 | 8 | 12 | 16 | 33 | 57 | 36 |
| Morton | 36 | 7 | 14 | 15 | 48 | 63 | 35 |

## BELL'S DIVISION THREE

|  | P | W | D | L | F | A | Pt |
|---|---|---|---|---|---|---|---|
| Brechin | 36 | 22 | 7 | 7 | 67 | 38 | 73 |
| Dumbarton | 36 | 18 | 7 | 11 | 59 | 48 | 61 |
| Albion | 36 | 16 | 11 | 9 | 51 | 42 | 59 |
| Peterhead | 36 | 17 | 5 | 14 | 63 | 52 | 56 |
| Montrose | 36 | 16 | 7 | 13 | 43 | 39 | 55 |
| Elgin | 36 | 13 | 8 | 15 | 45 | 47 | 47 |
| E Stirling | 36 | 12 | 4 | 20 | 51 | 58 | 40 |
| East Fife | 36 | 11 | 7 | 18 | 39 | 56 | 40 |
| Stirling Alb | 36 | 9 | 10 | 17 | 45 | 68 | 37 |
| Queen's Pk | 36 | 9 | 8 | 19 | 38 | 53 | 35 |

## ABERCORN CENTRAL LEAGUE 2001-2002

### PREMIER DIVISION

| | P | W | D | L | F | A | Pts |
|---|---|---|---|---|---|---|---|
| Johnstone | 22 | 12 | 6 | 4 | 36 | 27 | 42 |
| Larkhall | 22 | 12 | 3 | 7 | 39 | 30 | 39 |
| Pollok | 22 | 12 | 2 | 8 | 39 | 30 | 38 |
| Neilston | 22 | 12 | 2 | 8 | 41 | 36 | 38 |
| Benburb | 22 | 10 | 5 | 7 | 34 | 20 | 35 |
| Maryhill | 22 | 9 | 5 | 8 | 39 | 31 | 32 |
| Arthurlie | 22 | 9 | 4 | 9 | 33 | 29 | 31 |
| Cambuslang | 22 | 9 | 4 | 9 | 26 | 28 | 31 |
| Cumbernauld | 22 | 6 | 7 | 9 | 24 | 38 | 25 |
| Renfrew | 22 | 6 | 4 | 12 | 26 | 34 | 22 |
| Petershill | 22 | 6 | 4 | 12 | 29 | 41 | 22 |
| Lanark | 22 | 3 | 6 | 13 | 20 | 41 | 15 |

### FIRST DIVISION

| | P | W | D | L | F | A | Pts |
|---|---|---|---|---|---|---|---|
| Shettleston | 26 | 16 | 5 | 5 | 59 | 27 | 53 |
| Shotts | 26 | 14 | 8 | 4 | 50 | 30 | 50 |
| Bellshill | 26 | 14 | 7 | 5 | 52 | 32 | 49 |
| Glencairn | 26 | 13 | 8 | 5 | 53 | 34 | 47 |
| E Kilbride | 26 | 12 | 7 | 7 | 43 | 32 | 43 |
| Greenock | 26 | 10 | 10 | 6 | 40 | 37 | 40 |
| Blantyre V | 26 | 10 | 7 | 9 | 57 | 52 | 37 |
| Kilsyth | 26 | 10 | 7 | 9 | 55 | 52 | 37 |
| Rob Roy | 26 | 10 | 5 | 11 | 43 | 44 | 35 |
| Vale of Leven | 26 | 7 | 5 | 14 | 44 | 52 | 26 |
| Lesmahagow | 26 | 6 | 8 | 12 | 41 | 55 | 26 |
| Dunipace | 26 | 7 | 4 | 15 | 33 | 56 | 25 |
| St Anthony's | 26 | 5 | 3 | 18 | 33 | 70 | 18 |
| Carluke | 26 | 3 | 6 | 17 | 24 | 54 | 15 |

### SECOND DIVISION

| | P | W | D | L | F | A | Pts |
|---|---|---|---|---|---|---|---|
| Perthshire | 22 | 13 | 6 | 3 | 50 | 32 | 45 |
| St Roch's | 22 | 13 | 3 | 6 | 36 | 28 | 42 |
| Vale of Clyde | 22 | 13 | 0 | 9 | 42 | 31 | 39 |
| Pt Glasgow | 22 | 11 | 5 | 6 | 52 | 42 | 38 |
| Thorniewood | 22 | 10 | 5 | 7 | 43 | 35 | 35 |
| Baillieston | 22 | 9 | 7 | 6 | 41 | 29 | 34 |
| Yoker | 22 | 8 | 8 | 6 | 33 | 31 | 32 |
| Forth Wands | 22 | 7 | 5 | 10 | 32 | 35 | 26 |
| Stonehouse | 22 | 8 | 2 | 12 | 32 | 39 | 26 |
| Royal Albert | 22 | 7 | 5 | 10 | 29 | 43 | 26 |
| Ashfield | 22 | 4 | 8 | 10 | 33 | 40 | 20 |
| Coltness | 22 | 0 | 4 | 18 | 23 | 61 | 4 |
| Wishaw | ...withdrawn |

## WESTERN SCOTTISH LEAGUE 2001-2002

### FIRST DIVISION

| | P | W | D | L | F | A | Pts |
|---|---|---|---|---|---|---|---|
| Glenafton | 18 | 15 | 1 | 2 | 49 | 13 | 46 |
| Cumnock | 18 | 11 | 3 | 4 | 40 | 22 | 36 |
| Kilwinning | 18 | 11 | 2 | 5 | 38 | 27 | 35 |
| Auchinleck | 18 | 7 | 3 | 8 | 23 | 26 | 24 |
| Irvine M'dow | 18 | 6 | 3 | 9 | 33 | 33 | 21 |
| Kilbirnie L'de | 18 | 5 | 4 | 9 | 22 | 28 | 19 |
| Lugar | 18 | 0 | 0 | 18 | 10 | 66 | 0 |

### SECOND DIVISION

| | P | W | D | L | F | A | Pts |
|---|---|---|---|---|---|---|---|
| Largs Th | 21 | 15 | 3 | 3 | 58 | 17 | 48 |
| Hurlford | 21 | 14 | 3 | 4 | 39 | 19 | 45 |
| Beith | 21 | 13 | 4 | 4 | 40 | 24 | 43 |
| Troon | 21 | 13 | 2 | 6 | 38 | 27 | 41 |
| Irvine Vics | 21 | 6 | 3 | 12 | 42 | 59 | 21 |
| Muirkirk | 21 | 3 | 6 | 12 | 26 | 44 | 15 |
| Kello Rovs | 21 | 4 | 3 | 14 | 23 | 53 | 15 |
| Craigmark | 21 | 3 | 2 | 16 | 22 | 45 | 11 |

**Renfrew boss Mick Dunlop**

### THIRD DIVISION

| | P | W | D | L | F | A | Pts |
|---|---|---|---|---|---|---|---|
| Dalry Th | 21 | 15 | 2 | 4 | 49 | 25 | 47 |
| Maybole | 21 | 13 | 5 | 3 | 56 | 26 | 44 |
| Ardrossan | 21 | 10 | 4 | 7 | 43 | 41 | 34 |
| Saltcoats | 21 | 10 | 3 | 8 | 50 | 38 | 33 |
| Whitletts | 21 | 10 | 2 | 9 | 50 | 43 | 32 |
| Ardeer Th | 21 | 6 | 4 | 11 | 35 | 56 | 22 |
| Annbank | 21 | 4 | 4 | 13 | 36 | 54 | 16 |
| Darvel | 21 | 2 | 4 | 15 | 25 | 59 | 10 |

## BANK OF SCOTLAND
## SCOTTISH PREMIER LEAGUE 2002-2003

*FIXTURES SUBJECT TO CHANGE FOR LIVE TV COVERAGE*

**Saturday, 3 August, 2002**
Celtic v Dunfermline
Dundee v Hearts
Hibernian v Aberdeen
Kilmarnock v Rangers
Livingston v Motherwell
Partick v Dundee Utd

**Saturday, 10 August**
Aberdeen v Celtic
Dundee Utd v Kilmarnock
Dunfermline v Livingston
Hearts v Hibernian
Motherwell v Partick
Rangers v Dundee

**Saturday, 17 August**
Celtic v Dundee Utd
Dunfermline v Dundee
Hibernian v Rangers
Kilmarnock v Motherwell

**Sunday, 18 August**
Aberdeen v Hearts
Partick v Livingston

**Saturday, 24 August**
Dundee v Hibernian
Hearts v Dunfermline
Livingston v Kilmarnock
Partick v Celtic

**Sunday, 25 August**
Dundee Utd v Motherwell
Rangers v Aberdeen

**Saturday, 31 August**
Dundee Utd v Dundee
Dunfermline v Rangers
Hearts v Kilmarnock
Motherwell v Hibernian

**Sunday, 1 September**
Aberdeen v Partick
Celtic v Livingston

**Wednesday, 11 September**
Aberdeen v Dundee Utd
Dundee v Livingston
Hibernian v Dunfermline
Kilmarnock v Partick
Motherwell v Celtic
Rangers v Hearts

**Saturday, 14 September**
Celtic v Hibernian
Dundee Utd v Dunfermline
Hearts v Motherwell
Kilmarnock v Aberdeen
Livingston v Rangers
Partick v Dundee

**Saturday, 21 September**
Dundee v Celtic
Dunfermline v Motherwell
Hearts v Dundee Utd
Hibernian v Kilmarnock
Livingston v Aberdeen

**Sunday, 22 September**
Rangers v Partick

**Saturday, 28 September**
Aberdeen v Dunfermline
Celtic v Kilmarnock
Dundee Utd v Rangers
Hibernian v Livingston
Motherwell v Dundee
Partick v Hearts

**Saturday, 5 October**
Dundee v Kilmarnock
Dunfermline v Partick
Hibernian v Dundee Utd
Livingston v Hearts
Motherwell v Aberdeen

**Sunday, 6 October**
Celtic v Rangers

**Saturday, 19 October**
Aberdeen v Dundee
Dundee Utd v Livingston
Hearts v Celtic
Kilmarnock v Dunfermline
Partick v Hibernian
Rangers v Motherwell

**Saturday, 26 October**
Aberdeen v Hibernian
Dundee Utd v Partick
Dunfermline v Celtic
Hearts v Dundee
Motherwell v Livingston
Rangers v Kilmarnock

**Saturday, 2 November**
Celtic v Aberdeen
Dundee v Rangers
Hibernian v Hearts
Kilmarnock v Dundee Utd
Livingston v Dunfermline
Partick v Motherwell

**Saturday, 9 November**
Dundee Utd v Celtic
Hearts v Aberdeen
Livingston v Partick
Motherwell v Kilmarnock
Rangers v Hibernian

**Sunday, 10 November**
Dundee v Dunfermline

**Saturday, 16 November**
Aberdeen v Rangers
Celtic v Partick
Dunfermline v Hearts
Hibernian v Dundee
Kilmarnock v Livingston
Motherwell v Dundee Utd

**Saturday, 23 November**
Dundee v Dundee Utd
Hibernian v Motherwell
Kilmarnock v Hearts
Livingston v Celtic
Partick v Aberdeen
Rangers v Dunfermline

**Saturday, 30 November**
Celtic v Motherwell
Dundee Utd v Aberdeen
Dunfermline v Hibernian
Hearts v Rangers
Livingston v Dundee
Partick v Kilmarnock

**Wednesday, 4 December**
Aberdeen v Kilmarnock
Dundee v Partick
Dunfermline v Dundee Utd
Hibernian v Celtic
Motherwell v Hearts
Rangers v Livingston

**Saturday, 7 December**
Aberdeen v Motherwell
Dundee Utd v Hibernian
Hearts v Livingston
Kilmarnock v Dundee
Partick v Dunfermline
Rangers v Celtic

**Saturday, 14 December**
Dundee v Motherwell
Dunfermline v Aberdeen
Hearts v Partick
Kilmarnock v Celtic
Livingston v Hibernian
Rangers v Dundee Utd

**Saturday, 21 December**
Aberdeen v Livingston
Celtic v Dundee
Dundee Utd v Hearts
Kilmarnock v Hibernian
Motherwell v Dunfermline
Partick v Rangers

**Thursday, 26 December**
Celtic v Hearts
Dundee v Aberdeen
Dunfermline v Kilmarnock
Hibernian v Partick
Livingston v Dundee Utd
Motherwell v Rangers

**Sunday, 29 December**
Celtic v Dunfermline
Dundee v Hearts
Hibernian v Aberdeen
Kilmarnock v Rangers
Livingston v Motherwell
Partick v Dundee Utd

**Thursday, 2 January 2003**
Aberdeen v Celtic
Dundee Utd v Kilmarnock
Dunfermline v Livingston
Hearts v Hibernian
Motherwell v Partick
Rangers v Dundee

**Tuesday, 28 January**
Partick v Livingston

**Wednesday, 29 January**
Aberdeen v Hearts
Celtic v Dundee Utd
Dunfermline v Dundee
Hibernian v Rangers
Kilmarnock v Motherwell

**Saturday, 1 February**
Dundee v Hibernian
Hearts v Dunfermline
Livingston v Kilmarnock
Partick v Celtic

**Sunday, 2 February**
Dundee Utd v Motherwell
Rangers v Aberdeen

**Saturday, 8 February**
Aberdeen v Partick
Celtic v Livingston
Dundee Utd v Dundee
Dunfermline v Rangers
Hearts v Kilmarnock
Motherwell v Hibernian

**Saturday, 15 February**
Aberdeen v Dundee Utd

Dundee v Livingston
Hibernian v Dunfermline
Kilmarnock v Partick
Motherwell v Celtic
Rangers v Hearts

**Saturday, 1 March**
Celtic v Hibernian
Dundee Utd v Dunfermline
Hearts v Motherwell
Kilmarnock v Aberdeen
Livingston v Rangers
Partick v Dundee

**Saturday, 8 March**
Celtic v Rangers
Dundee v Kilmarnock
Dunfermline v Partick
Hibernian v Dundee Utd
Livingston v Hearts
Motherwell v Aberdeen

**Saturday, 15 March**
Aberdeen v Dundee
Dundee Utd v Livingston
Hearts v Celtic
Kilmarnock v Dunfermline
Partick v Hibernian
Rangers v Motherwell

**Saturday, 5 April**
Dundee v Celtic
Dunfermline v Motherwell
Hearts v Dundee Utd
Kilmarnock v Hibernian
Livingston v Aberdeen
Rangers v Partick

**Saturday, 12 April**
Aberdeen v Dunfermline
Celtic v Kilmarnock
Dundee Utd v Rangers
Hibernian v Livingston
Motherwell v Dundee
Partick v Hearts

*LEAGUE WILL NOW SPLIT IN TWO FOR FINAL FIVE GAMES.*
*DATES TO BE ARRANGED.*

# BELL'S LEAGUE DIVISION ONE 2002-2003

**Saturday, 3 August 2002**
Arbroath v Ross County
Ayr v Falkirk
Inverness CT v Alloa
QoS v Clyde
St Mirren v St Johnstone

**Saturday, 10 August**
Alloa v Arbroath
Clyde v Ayr
Falkirk v St Mirren
Ross County v QoS
St Johnstone v Inverness CT

**Saturday, 17 August**
Arbroath v Clyde
Ayr v Ross County
Inverness CT v Falkirk
QoS v St Johnstone
St Mirren v Alloa

**Saturday, 24 August**
Alloa v Falkirk
Arbroath v St Johnstone
Clyde v St Mirren
Inverness CT v Ross County
QoS v Ayr

**Saturday, 31 August**
Ayr v Arbroath
Falkirk v QoS
Ross County v Clyde
St Johnstone v Alloa
St Mirren v Inverness CT

**Saturday, 14 September**
Arbroath v St Mirren
Ayr v St Johnstone
Clyde v Alloa
QoS v Inverness CT
Ross County v Falkirk

**Saturday, 21 September**
Alloa v Ayr
Falkirk v Clyde
Inverness CT v Arbroath
St Johnstone v Ross County
St Mirren v QoS

**Saturday, 28 September**
Ayr v St Mirren
Clyde v Inverness CT
Falkirk v St Johnstone
QoS v Arbroath
Ross County v Alloa

**Saturday, 5 October**
Alloa v QoS
Arbroath v Falkirk
Inverness CT v Ayr
St Johnstone v Clyde
St Mirren v Ross County

**Saturday, 19 October**
Alloa v Inverness CT
Clyde v QoS
Falkirk v Ayr
Ross County v Arbroath
St Johnstone v St Mirren

**Saturday, 26 October**
Arbroath v Alloa
Ayr v Clyde
Inverness CT v St Johnstone
QoS v Ross County
St Mirren v Falkirk

**Saturday, 2 November**
Alloa v St Johnstone
Arbroath v Ayr
Clyde v Ross County
Inverness CT v St Mirren
QoS v Falkirk

**Saturday, 9 November**

Ayr v QoS
Falkirk v Alloa
Ross County v Inverness CT
St Johnstone v Arbroath
St Mirren v Clyde

**Saturday, 16 November**

Alloa v Clyde
Falkirk v Ross County
Inverness CT v QoS
St Johnstone v Ayr
St Mirren v Arbroath

**Saturday, 23 November**

Arbroath v Inverness CT
Ayr v Alloa
Clyde v Falkirk
QoS v St Mirren
Ross County v St Johnstone

**Saturday, 30 November**

Alloa v Ross County
Arbroath v QoS
Inverness CT v Clyde
St Johnstone v Falkirk
St Mirren v Ayr

**Saturday, 7 December**

Ayr v Inverness CT
Clyde v St Johnstone
Falkirk v Arbroath
QoS v Alloa
Ross County v St Mirren

**Saturday, 14 December**

Alloa v St Mirren
Clyde v Arbroath
Falkirk v Inverness CT
Ross County v Ayr
St Johnstone v QoS

**Saturday, 21 December**

Arbroath v Ross County
Ayr v Falkirk
Inverness CT v Alloa
QoS v Clyde
St Mirren v St Johnstone

**Saturday, 28 December**

Ayr v Arbroath
Falkirk v QoS
Ross County v Clyde
St Johnstone v Alloa
St Mirren v Inverness CT

**Wednesday, 1 January 2003**

Alloa v Falkirk
Arbroath v St Johnstone
Clyde v St Mirren
Inverness CT v Ross County
QoS v Ayr

**Saturday, 4 January**

Arbroath v St Mirren
Ayr v St Johnstone
Clyde v Alloa
QoS v Inverness CT
Ross County v Falkirk

**Saturday, 11 January**

Alloa v Ayr
Falkirk v Clyde
Inverness CT v Arbroath
St Johnstone v Ross County
St Mirren v QoS

**Saturday, 18 January**

Alloa v QoS
Arbroath v Falkirk
Inverness CT v Ayr
St Johnstone v Clyde
St Mirren v Ross County

**Saturday, 1 February**
Ayr v St Mirren
Clyde v Inverness CT
Falkirk v St Johnstone
QoS v Arbroath
Ross County v Alloa

**Saturday, 8 February**
Arbroath v Clyde
Ayr v Ross County
Inverness CT v Falkirk
QoS v St Johnstone
St Mirren v Alloa

**Saturday, 15 February**
Alloa v Arbroath
Clyde v Ayr
Falkirk v St Mirren
Ross County v QoS
St Johnstone v Inverness CT

**Saturday, 1 March**
Alloa v St Johnstone
Arbroath v Ayr
Clyde v Ross County
Inverness CT v St Mirren
QoS v Falkirk

**Saturday, 8 March**
Ayr v QoS
Falkirk v Alloa
Ross County v Inverness CT
St Johnstone v Arbroath
St Mirren v Clyde

**Saturday, 15 March**
Arbroath v Inverness CT
Ayr v Alloa
Clyde v Falkirk
QoS v St Mirren
Ross County v St Johnstone

**Saturday, 5 April**
Alloa v Clyde
Falkirk v Ross County
Inverness CT v QoS
St Johnstone v Ayr
St Mirren v Arbroath

**Saturday, 12 April**
Alloa v Ross County
Arbroath v QoS
Inverness CT v Clyde
St Johnstone v Falkirk
St Mirren v Ayr

**Saturday, 19 April**
Ayr v Inverness CT
Clyde v St Johnstone
Falkirk v Arbroath
QoS v Alloa
Ross County v St Mirren

**Saturday, 26 April**
Alloa v Inverness CT
Clyde v QoS
Falkirk v Ayr
Ross County v Arbroath
St Johnstone v St Mirren

**Saturday, 3 May**
Arbroath v Alloa
Ayr v Clyde
Inverness CT v St Johnstone
QoS v Ross County
St Mirren v Falkirk

**Saturday, 10 May**
Alloa v St Mirren
Clyde v Arbroath
Falkirk v Inverness CT
Ross County v Ayr
St Johnstone v QoS

## BELL'S LEAGUE
## DIVISION TWO 2002-2003

**Saturday, 3 August 2002**
Brechin v Berwick
Clydebank v Forfar
Cowdenbeath v Hamilton
Raith v Stranraer
Stenhousemuir v Dumbarton

**Saturday, 10 August**
Berwick v Raith
Dumbarton v Brechin
Forfar v Stenhousemuir
Hamilton v Clydebank
Stranraer v Cowdenbeath

**Saturday, 17 August**
Brechin v Hamilton
Clydebank v Stranraer
Cowdenbeath v Forfar
Raith v Dumbarton
Stenhousemuir v Berwick

**Saturday, 24 August**
Brechin v Forfar
Cowdenbeath v Raith
Dumbarton v Clydebank
Hamilton v Berwick
Stenhousemuir v Stranraer

**Saturday, 31 August**
Berwick v Dumbarton
Clydebank v Cowdenbeath
Forfar v Hamilton
Raith v Stenhousemuir
Stranraer v Brechin

**Saturday, 14 September**
Berwick v Stranraer
Brechin v Cowdenbeath
Dumbarton v Forfar
Raith v Clydebank
Stenhousemuir v Hamilton

**Saturday, 21 September**
Clydebank v Brechin
Cowdenbeath v
Stenhousemuir
Forfar v Berwick
Hamilton v Raith
Stranraer v Dumbarton

**Saturday, 28 September**
Berwick v Cowdenbeath
Dumbarton v Hamilton
Raith v Brechin
Stenhousemuir v Clydebank
Stranraer v Forfar

**Saturday, 5 October**
Brechin v Stenhousemuir
Clydebank v Berwick
Cowdenbeath v Dumbarton
Forfar v Raith
Hamilton v Stranraer

**Saturday, 19 October**
Brechin v Dumbarton
Clydebank v Hamilton
Cowdenbeath v Stranraer
Raith v Berwick
Stenhousemuir v Forfar

**Saturday, 26 October**
Berwick v Brechin
Dumbarton v
Stenhousemuir
Forfar v Clydebank
Hamilton v Cowdenbeath
Stranraer v Raith

**Saturday, 2 November**
Brechin v Stranraer
Cowdenbeath v Clydebank

Dumbarton v Berwick
Hamilton v Forfar
Stenhousemuir v Raith

**Saturday, 9 November**
Berwick v Hamilton
Clydebank v Dumbarton
Forfar v Brechin
Raith v Cowdenbeath
Stranraer v Stenhousemuir

**Saturday, 16 November**
Clydebank v Raith
Cowdenbeath v Brechin
Forfar v Dumbarton
Hamilton v Stenhousemuir
Stranraer v Berwick

**Saturday, 23 November**
Berwick v Forfar
Brechin v Clydebank
Dumbarton v Stranraer
Raith v Hamilton
Stenh'semuir v Cowdenb'th

**Saturday, 30 November**
Berwick v Clydebank
Dumbarton v Cowdenbeath
Raith v Forfar
Stenhousemuir v Brechin
Stranraer v Hamilton

**Saturday, 14 December**
Brechin v Raith
Clydebank v Stenhousemuir
Cowdenbeath v Berwick
Forfar v Stranraer
Hamilton v Dumbarton

**Saturday, 21 December**
Brechin v Berwick
Clydebank v Forfar
Cowdenbeath v Hamilton
Raith v Stranraer
Stenhousemuir v Dumbarton

**Saturday, 28 December**
Berwick v Stenhousemuir
Dumbarton v Raith
Forfar v Cowdenbeath
Hamilton v Brechin
Stranraer v Clydebank

**Wednesday, 1 January 2003**
Brechin v Forfar
Cowdenbeath v Raith
Dumbarton v Clydebank
Hamilton v Berwick
Stenhousemuir v Stranraer

**Saturday, 11 January**
Berwick v Dumbarton
Clydebank v Cowdenbeath
Forfar v Hamilton
Raith v Stenhousemuir
Stranraer v Brechin

**Saturday, 18 January**
Berwick v Stranraer
Brechin v Cowdenbeath
Dumbarton v Forfar
Raith v Clydebank
Stenhousemuir v Hamilton

**Saturday, 1 February**
Clydebank v Brechin
Cowdenb'th v Stenh'semuir
Forfar v Berwick
Hamilton v Raith
Stranraer v Dumbarton

**Saturday, 8 February**
Berwick v Cowdenbeath
Dumbarton v Hamilton
Raith v Brechin
Stenhousemuir v Clydebank
Stranraer v Forfar

**Saturday, 15 February**
Brechin v Stenhousemuir
Clydebank v Berwick
Cowdenbeath v Dumbarton
Forfar v Raith
Hamilton v Stranraer

**Saturday, 22 February**
Berwick v Raith
Dumbarton v Brechin
Forfar v Stenhousemuir
Hamilton v Clydebank
Stranraer v Cowdenbeath

**Saturday, 1 March**
Brechin v Hamilton
Clydebank v Stranraer
Cowdenbeath v Forfar
Raith v Dumbarton
Stenhousemuir v Berwick

**Saturday, 8 March**
Berwick v Hamilton
Clydebank v Dumbarton
Forfar v Brechin
Raith v Cowdenbeath
Stranraer v Stenhousemuir

**Saturday, 15 March**
Brechin v Stranraer
Cowdenbeath v Clydebank
Dumbarton v Berwick
Hamilton v Forfar
Stenhousemuir v Raith

**Saturday, 22 March**
Berwick v Forfar
Brechin v Clydebank
Dumbarton v Stranraer
Raith v Hamilton
Stenhousemuir v Cowdenbeath

**Saturday, 5 April**
Clydebank v Raith
Cowdenbeath v Brechin
Forfar v Dumbarton
Hamilton v Stenhousemuir
Stranraer v Berwick

**Saturday, 12 April**
Berwick v Clydebank
Dumbarton v Cowdenbeath
Raith v Forfar
Stenhousemuir v Brechin
Stranraer v Hamilton

**Saturday, 19 April**
Brechin v Raith
Clydebank v Stenhousemuir
Cowdenbeath v Berwick
Forfar v Stranraer
Hamilton v Dumbarton

**Saturday, 26 April**
Berwick v Brechin
Dumbarton v Stenhousemuir
Forfar v Clydebank
Hamilton v Cowdenbeath
Stranraer v Raith

**Saturday, 3 May**
Brechin v Dumbarton
Clydebank v Hamilton
Cowdenbeath v Stranraer
Raith v Berwick
Stenhousemuir v Forfar

**Saturday, 10 May**
Berwick v Stenhousemuir
Dumbarton v Raith
Forfar v Cowdenbeath
Hamilton v Brechin
Stranraer v Clydebank

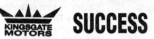

# BELL'S LEAGUE
## DIVISION THREE 2002-2003

**Saturday, 3 August 2002**
East Stirling v Montrose
Gretna v Morton
Peterhead v East Fife
Queen's Park v Elgin
Stirling v Albion

**Saturday, 10 August**
Albion v Peterhead
East Fife v East Stirling
Elgin v Gretna
Montrose v Queen's Park
Morton v Stirling

**Saturday, 17 August**
East Stirling v Albion
Gretna v Montrose
Peterhead v Morton
Queen's Park v East Fife
Stirling v Elgin

**Saturday, 24 August**
East Fife v Montrose
Elgin v Peterhead
Morton v Queen's Park
Gretna v Albion
Stirling v East Stirling

**Saturday, 31 August**
Albion v East Fife
East Stirling v Morton
Montrose v Elgin
Peterhead v Stirling
Queen's Park v Gretna

**Saturday, 14 September**
Elgin v East Fife
Morton v Albion
Gretna v Peterhead
Queen's Park v East Stirling
Stirling v Montrose

**Saturday, 21 September**
Albion v Elgin
East Fife v Stirling
East Stirling v Gretna
Montrose v Morton
Peterhead v Queen's Park

**Saturday, 28 September**
East Stirling v Elgin
Montrose v Peterhead
Morton v East Fife
Gretna v Stirling
Queen's Park v Albion

**Saturday, 5 October**
Albion v Montrose
East Fife v Gretna
Elgin v Morton
Peterhead v East Stirling
Stirling v Queen's Park

**Saturday, 19 October**
East Stirling v East Fife
Gretna v Elgin
Peterhead v Albion
Queen's Park v Montrose
Stirling v Morton

**Saturday, 26 October**
Albion v Stirling
East Fife v Peterhead
Elgin v Queen's Park
Montrose v East Stirling
Morton v Gretna

**Saturday, 2 November**
East Fife v Albion
Elgin v Montrose
Morton v East Stirling
Gretna v Queen's Park
Stirling v Peterhead

**Saturday, 9 November**
Albion v Gretna
East Stirling v Stirling
Montrose v East Fife
Peterhead v Elgin
Queen's Park v Morton

**Saturday, 16 November**
Albion v Morton
East Fife v Elgin
East Stirling v Queen's Park
Montrose v Stirling
Peterhead v Gretna

**Saturday, 23 November**
Elgin v Albion
Morton v Montrose
Gretna v East Stirling
Queen's Park v Peterhead
Stirling v East Fife

**Saturday, 30 November**
East Stirling v Peterhead
Montrose v Albion
Morton v Elgin
Gretna v East Fife
Queen's Park v Stirling

**Saturday, 14 December**
Albion v Queen's Park
East Fife v Morton
Elgin v East Stirling
Peterhead v Montrose
Stirling v Gretna

**Saturday, 21 December**
East Stirling v Montrose
Gretna v Morton
Peterhead v East Fife
Queen's Park v Elgin
Stirling v Albion

**Saturday, 28 December**
Albion v East Stirling

East Fife v Queen's Park
Elgin v Stirling
Montrose v Gretna
Morton v Peterhead

**Wednesday, 1 January 2003**
East Fife v Montrose
Elgin v Peterhead
Morton v Queen's Park
Gretna v Albion
Stirling v East Stirling

**Saturday, 11 January**
Albion v East Fife
East Stirling v Morton
Montrose v Elgin
Peterhead v Stirling
Queen's Park v Gretna

**Saturday, 18 January**
Elgin v East Fife
Morton v Albion
Gretna v Peterhead
Queen's Park v East Stirling
Stirling v Montrose

**Saturday, 1 February**
Albion v Elgin
East Fife v Stirling
East Stirling v Gretna
Montrose v Morton
Peterhead v Queen's Park

**Saturday, 8 February**
East Stirling v Elgin
Montrose v Peterhead
Morton v East Fife
Gretna v Stirling
Queen's Park v Albion

**Saturday, 15 February**
Albion v Montrose
East Fife v Gretna

Elgin v Morton
Peterhead v East Stirling
Stirling v Queen's Park

**Saturday, 22 February**
Albion v Peterhead
East Fife v East Stirling
Elgin v Gretna
Montrose v Queen's Park
Morton v Stirling

**Saturday, 1 March**
East Stirling v Albion
Gretna v Montrose
Peterhead v Morton
Queen's Park v East Fife
Stirling v Elgin

**Saturday, 8 March**
Albion v Gretna
East Stirling v Stirling
Montrose v East Fife
Peterhead v Elgin
Queen's Park v Morton

**Saturday, 15 March**
East Fife v Albion
Elgin v Montrose
Morton v East Stirling
Gretna v Queen's Park
Stirling v Peterhead

**Saturday, 22 March**
Elgin v Albion
Morton v Montrose
Gretna v East Stirling
Queen's Park v Peterhead
Stirling v East Fife

**Saturday, 5 April**
Albion v Morton

East Fife v Elgin
East Stirling v Queen's Park
Montrose v Stirling
Peterhead v Gretna

**Saturday, 12 April**
East Stirling v Peterhead
Montrose v Albion
Morton v Elgin
Gretna v East Fife
Queen's Park v Stirling

**Saturday, 19 April**
Albion v Queen's Park
East Fife v Morton
Elgin v East Stirling
Peterhead v Montrose
Stirling v Gretna

**Saturday, 26 April**
Albion v Stirling
East Fife v Peterhead
Elgin v Queen's Park
Montrose v East Stirling
Morton v Gretna

**Saturday, 3 May**
East Stirling v East Fife
Gretna v Elgin
Peterhead v Albion
Queen's Park v Montrose
Stirling v Morton

**Saturday, 10 May**
Albion v East Stirling
East Fife v Queen's Park
Elgin v Stirling
Montrose v Gretna
Morton v Peterhead

# WORLD CUP FINALS 2002

## Group A
France 0 Senegal 1, Uruguay 1 Denmark 2, Denmark 1 Senegal 1, France 0 Uruguay 0, Denmark 2 France 0, Senegal 3 Uruguay 3.
**Points:** Denmark 7, Senegal 5, Uruguay 2, France 1.

## Group B
Spain 3 Slovenia 1, Paraguay 2 South Africa 2, Spain 3 Paraguay 1, South Africa 1 Slovenia 0, South Africa 2 Spain 3, Slovenia 1 Paraguay 3.
**Points:** Spain 9, Paraguay 4, South Africa 4, Slovenia 0.

## Group C
Brazil 2 Turkey 1, China 0 Costa Rica 2, Brazil 4 China 0, Costa Rica 1 Turkey 1, Costa Rica 2 Brazil 5, Turkey 3 China 0.
**Points:** Brazil 9, Turkey 4, Costa Rica 4, China 0.

## Group D
South Korea 2 Poland 0, USA 3 Portugal 2, South Korea 1 USA 1, Portugal 4 Poland 0, Portugal 0 South Korea 1, Poland 3 USA 1.
**Points:** South Korea 7, USA 4, Portugal 3, Poland 3.

## Group E
Rep of Ireland 1 Cameroon 1, Germany 8 Saudi Arabia 0, Cameroon 1 Saudi Arabia 0, Germany 1 Rep of Ireland 1, Cameroon 0 Germany 2, Saudi Arabia 0 Rep of Ireland 3.
**Points:** Germany 7, Rep of Ireland 5, Cameroon 4, Saudi Arabia 0.

## Group F
Argentina 1 Nigeria 0, England 1 Sweden 1, Sweden 2 Nigeria 1, Argentina 0 England 1, Sweden 1 Argentina 1, Nigeria 0 England 0.
**Points:** Sweden 5, England 5, Argentina 4, Nigeria 1.

## Group G
Croatia 0 Mexico 1, Italy 2 Ecuador 0, Italy 1 Croatia 2, Mexico 2 Ecuador 1, Mexico 1 Italy 1, Ecuador 1 Croatia 0.
**Points:** Mexico 7, Italy 4, Croatia 3, Ecuador 3.

## Group H
Japan 2 Belgium 2, Russia 2 Tunisia 0, Japan 1 Russia 0, Tunisia 1 Belgium 1, Tunisia 0 Japan 2, Belgium 3 Russia 2.
**Points:** Japan 7, Belgium 5, Russia 3, Tunisia 1.

## Round of the Last 16
Germany 1 Paraguay 0, Denmark 0 England 3, Sweden 1 Senegal 2 (golden goal), Spain 1 Rep of Ireland 1 (Spain won 3-2 on penalties),

Mexico 0 USA 2, Brazil 2 Belgium 0, Japan 0 Turkey 1, South Korea 2 Italy 1 (golden goal).

**Quarter-finals**
England 1 Brazil 2, Germany 1 USA 0, Spain 0 South Korea 0 (South Korea won 5-3 on penalties) , Senegal 0 Turkey 1 (golden goal).

**Semi-finals**
Germany 1 South Korea 0, Brazil 1 Turkey 0.

**Third place play-off**
South Korea 2 Turkey 3.

**Final**
Brazil  2 Germany 0.
BRAZIL: Marcos, Edmilson, Lucio, Roque Junior, Cafu, Kleberson, Gilberto, Carlos, Ronaldinho (Juninho 85), Rivaldo, Ronaldo (Denilson 89).
GERMANY: Kahn, Linke, Ramelow, Metzelder, Frings, Schneider, Jeremies (Asamoah 77), Hamann, Bode (Ziege 84), Neuville, Klose (Bierhoff 73).

---

# PREVIOUS WORLD CUP WINNERS

| Year | Winners | Runners-up | Venue |
|---|---|---|---|
| 1930 | URUGUAY............4 | Argentina..........2 | Uruguay |
| 1934 | ITALY .................2 | Czechosl'kia.....1 | Italy |
| | | (After extra time) | |
| 1938 | ITALY .................4 | Hungary ..........2 | France |
| 1950 | URUGUAY......2 | Brazil ................1 | Brazil |
| 1954 | W GERMANY......3 | Hungary ..........2 | Switzerland |
| 1958 | BRAZIL................5 | Sweden ...........2 | Sweden |
| 1962 | BRAZIL................3 | Czechosl'kia....1 | Chile |
| 1966 | ENGLAND............4 | W Germany......2 | Wembley |
| | | (After extra time) | |
| 1970 | BRAZIL................4 | Italy .................1 | Mexico |
| 1974 | W GERMANY......2 | Holland.............1 | W Germany |
| 1978 | ARGENTINA.........3 | Holland.............1 | Argentina |
| | | (After extra time) | |
| 1982 | ITALY ..................3 | W Germany......1 | Spain |
| 1986 | ARGENTINA.........3 | W Germany......2 | Mexico |
| 1990 | W GERMANY......1 | Argentina..........0 | Italy |
| 1994 | BRAZIL................0 | Italy ..................0 | America |
| | (After extra time) | Brazil won 3-2 on | penalties |
| 1998 | FRANCE..............3 | Brazil ................0 | France |

## 2001-2002 REVIEW OF THE SEASON

### JUNE

**14:** Bobo Balde holds talks at Parkhead with Martin O'Neill over move from Toulouse.

**16:** Dundee draw 0-0 at Dens against Sartid, of Yugoslavia, in InterToto Cup.

**20:** Giovanni van Bronckhorst joins Arsenal from Rangers for £8.5m.

**22:** Rangers sign Christian Nerlinger from Borussia Dortmund for £2.5million.

**23:** Dundee lose 5-2 in return against Sartid to go out of Inter-Toto Cup. Caballero sent off.

**25:** Rangers report back for training at new £12m complex at Auchenhowie, later named Murray Park.

### JULY

**4:** Russell Latapy joins Rangers on free from Hibs.

**24:** Celtic beat Sunderland 1-0 in friendly at Parkhead.

**25:** Rangers win 3-0 away to NK Maribor in Champions League second qualifying round. Double from Tore Andre Flo and one from Nerlinger.

**28:** SPL season kicks off with champions Celtic winning 3-0 at home to St Johnstone. Rangers win by same score at Aberdeen with three new signings, Claudio Caniggia, Latapy and Nerlinger, on the mark.

### AUGUST

**1:** Rangers 1-0 down v NK Maribor before goals from Caniggia (2) and Flo see them through 6-1 on aggregate. Celtic win 4-3 in Ryan Giggs

Testimonial at Old Trafford.

**2:** John Hartson joins Celtic from Coventry, £4m down-payment with further £2.5m in installments. Momo Sylla also signs from St Johnstone for £750,000 and Steve Guppy joins from Leicester for £600,000.

**4:** Livingston draw 0-0 at Ibrox. Rangers without Latapy, who is caught in traffic after losing licence for drink driving.

**8:** Celtic beat Ajax 3-1 in Amsterdam ArenA with goals from Bobby Petta, Didier Agathe and Chris Sutton (Shota Arveladze hitting late consolation for Dutch) in Champions League third qualifying round first leg. In same competition, Rangers held 0-0 by Fenerbahce, with Michael Mols sent off.

**9:** Chris Innes' injury-time goal gives Kilmarnock 1-0 away win against Glenavon in Uefa Cup qualifying round first leg.

**10:** Agathe signs new contract to keep him a Celt until 2006.

**17:** Rangers pay Everton £6.5m for 21-year-old Michael Ball, despite knee injury.

**18:** Celtic drop first points as Javier Sanchez Broto saves Henrik Larsson penalty to ensure 0-0 draw at Livingston. Gary Bollan sent off.

**22:** Rangers fail to make it into Champions League, losing 2-1 at Fenerbahce. Fernando Ricksen goal too little too late after Haim Revivo and Serhat Akin put Turks ahead. Celtic reach group stages on 3-2

## 2001-2002 REVIEW OF THE SEASON

aggregate, despite losing 1-0 to Wamberto goal for Ajax.

**23:** Ally Mitchell goal gives Kilmarnock 1-0 victory for 2-0 aggregate win over Glenavon. Larsson receives Golden Shoe award in Monaco.

**24:** Mark Burchill joins Portsmouth from Celtic for £600,000. Wolves sign Colin Cameron from Hearts for £2m.

**25:** St Johnstone grab first point with 1-1 draw against Aberdeen.

**29:** Rangers sign Arveladze from Ajax for £3m as former target Don Hutchison joins West Ham United.

**31:** Allan Johnston joins Middlesbrough from Rangers for £600,000.

### SEPTEMBER

**1:** Scotland held 0-0 at Hampden by Croatia to leave Craig Brown's side third in World Cup qualifying group.

**5:** Belgium defeat Scotland 2-0 in Brussels to all-but kill off hopes of reaching finals. Nico Van Kerckhoven and Bart Goor score. Billy Dodds, Paul Lambert and Tom Boyd announce retirement from international football.

**6:** Rangers' Kenny Miller joins Wolves on three-month loan.

**8:** Balde makes debut for Celtic in 3-1 win over Dunfermline.

**11:** Uefa order Rangers to play Uefa Cup first round tie against Anzhi Makhachkala in Dagestan, despite safety fears. Rangers take case to Council for Arbitration in Sport, but lose.

**12:** Celtic's Champions League tie against Rosenborg called off as a result of New York terrorist attacks 24 hours earlier. Uefa also postpone all other games.

**15:** Stilian Petrov scores first goal since leg break in March in Celtic's 4-0 win at Dens. Shaun Maloney gets first senior goal.

**17:** Sutton flies to Turin to face Juventus, despite birth of baby son 11 weeks premature at weekend.

**18:** Celtic lose 3-2 in Stadio Del Alpe after late penalty awarded for dive by Nicola Amoruso, who scored from spot. David Trezeguet scores Juve's other two, with Petrov and Larsson bringing Celtic back into match. O'Neill sent to stand by German ref Helmut Krug after protests about penalty decision. Ref also sent off Edgar Davids in his first game back after drugs ban. In other group game, Porto win 2-1 at Rosenborg. Motherwell sack boss Billy Davies. John Philliben and Mio Krivokapic take interim control of team.

**19:** Uefa order Rangers to play Anzhi in one-off match in Poland.

**20:** Celtic lodge appeals with Uefa against O'Neill's sending off and booking for Joos Valgaeren at late penalty incident in Turin. In Uefa Cup first round first leg, Craig

## 2001-2002 REVIEW OF THE SEASON

Dargo goal gives Kilmarnock 1-1 draw at Rugby Park against Viking Stavanger, but Hibs go down 2-0 at AEK Athens.

**21:** Uefa ban O'Neill for one game. Lorenzo Amoruso signs two-year extension to Ibrox contract.

**22:** Flo hat-trick the highlight of Rangers' 6-1 win over Dundee United at Tannadice. Motherwell get first league win of season, 2-0 v Hearts.

**24:** Sandy Clark sacked as manager of St Johnstone, Billy Kirkwood takes over temporarily. Celtic lodge appeals with Court of Arbitration in Sport against Uefa's ban on O'Neill and Valgaeren's booking v Juventus. Both thrown out.

**25:** O'Neill in stand as Celtic beat Porto 1-0 with Larsson goal. Rosenborg draw 1-1 with Juventus. Hearts out of CIS Cup after a penalty shoot-out with Ross County at Tynecastle. At same stage, Airdrie beat Motherwell 2-1.

**27:** Bert Konterman scores late winner to see Rangers past Anzhi in controversial winner-takes-all Uefa Cup tie in Warsaw. But Hibs go out 4-3 on aggregate after leading 2-0 after 90 minutes against AEK Athens. Killie also crash out, losing 2-0 at Viking Stavanger, 3-1 on aggregate.

**30:** Celtic win 2-0 at Ibrox to go seven points clear of Rangers. Mistake by Stefan Klos allows Petrov to open the scoring. In second half,

Amoruso sent off for foul on Larsson in the box, but Klos saves his penalty. Alan Thompson scores wonder second goal to wrap up points.

### OCTOBER

**5:** Billy Stark appointed boss of St Johnstone after Tommy Burns turned down the job.

**6:** Craig Brown resigns after watching Scotland win 2-1 against Latvia at Hampden, but go out of the World Cup. Goals from David Weir and Dougie Freedman ensure victory after Andrejs Rubins opened scoring. Croatia qualify after beating Belgium, who go into a play-off v Czech Republic.

**9:** Arveladze scores a double on debut as Rangers knock Airdrie out of the CIS Cup at the third-round stage with 3-0 win at Ibrox. Ayr send Killie crashing in penalty shoot-out.

**10:** Thompson free-kick gives Celtic 1-0 home win over Rosenborg. They go top of Champions League group after Porto beat Juventus 1-0.

**12:** Petrov named Player of Month for September.

**16:** Eric Black and Terry Butcher unveiled as Motherwell's new management team. Temuri Ketsbaia joins Dundee from Wolves.

**17:** Porto thrash Celtic 3-0 with two goals from Clayton and one from Mario Silva. Juventus go back to top of group after beating Rosenborg 1-0 in Turin.

**18:** Rangers beat Moscow Dynamo 3-1 in first leg of Uefa Cup second round at Ibrox with goals from Amoruso, Ball and Ronald de Boer.

**20:** Hartson hits first Celtic hat-trick in 5-1 SPL romp against Dundee United.

**24:** Harald Brattbakk comes back to haunt Celtic with two goals as Rosenborg win 2-0 in Trondheim. Rab Douglas saves Bent Skammelsrud's penalty, but O'Neill's side can't find their shooting boots. Juve move into the next round of Champions League with 3-1 win over Porto.

**27:** Danish keeper Peter Kjaer makes debut for Aberdeen in 3-2 win over Hearts.

**31:** Celtic win seven-goal thriller against Juventus, but left agonisingly one point short of qualifying for next stage of Champions League after Porto win 1-0 against Rosenborg. Packed Parkhead watches as goals from Valgaeren, Sutton (2) and a Larsson penalty hold off Juve, who score first through Alessandro del Piero and add a double from Trezeguet.

### NOVEMBER

**1:** Rangers win 4-1 in Moscow against Dynamo to go through to third round of Uefa Cup 7-2 on aggregate. Goals from de Boer, Flo, Peter Lovenkrands and an own goal from goalkeeper Vasily Khomutovsky make it a comfortable night.

**3:** SFA to investigate after air horn thrown at ref Stuart Dougal during Dundee derby which ended 1-1 after Dens defender Fan Zhiyi is sent off.

**5:** Larsson named Glasgow Sports Person of the Year.

**6:** Wieghorst plays first game since April 2000, as Celtic hammer Stirling Albion 8-0 in CIS Cup third round. Maloney scores four.

**7:** Motherwell sign Eric Deloumeaux from Le Havre for £100,000. John McClelland steps up from director to vice-chairman of Rangers.

**9:** Europe's elite group of clubs, G14, knock back Old Firm's application for entry.

**10:** St Johnstone record first league win of season after 14 games, Willie Falconer giving them 1-0 victory at Killie.

**13:** Dick Advocaat named Manager of Month.

**17:** Flo double makes it 17 goals in 19 games for Rangers as they beat Dunfermline 4-0. Larsson scores only goal as Celtic beat Hearts at Tynecastle, a win marred by knee injury to Agathe.

**22:** Celtic go down to a Vicente goal as Valencia win Uefa Cup third round first leg tie in Mestalla Stadium. Sutton misses game after baby son rushed to hospital seriously ill. Rangers held 0-0 at home against PSG, with Ricksen sent off for two yellow cards.

**25:** Celtic win second Old Firm game of season 2-1 at Parkhead to go 10 points

## 2001-2002 REVIEW OF THE SEASON

clear. Goals from Valgaeren and a Larsson penalty before Lovenkrands hits late consolation. Advocaat has public slanging match with Ball as defender is substituted. Player later fined £10,000, with cash donated to charity.

**26:** Real Madrid's Belgian teenager, Kevin Franck, arrives for trial with Celtic.

**27:** Bayern Munich beat Boca Juniors 1-0 in Japan to win Toyota Cup.

**28:** Livingston v Celtic CIS Cup quarter-final postponed after floodlight failure before kick-off. Rangers win 2-1 at Dingwall against Ross County, but Amoruso sent off conceding late penalty taken by Ian Maxwell and saved by Klos. Arveladze and Claudio Reyna score for Gers, Steven Mackay for County. Ayr reach semi-finals with 5-1 win over Inverness.

**30:** Rab Douglas Player of the Month for November.

### DECEMBER

**1:** Celtic 12 points clear in SPL after 3-0 win against Hibs, while Rangers held 0-0 at Dens Park.

**3:** Bell's sign three-year extension worth £3m to continue sponsorship of three SFL divisions through to 2006. Challenge Cup also part of package, renamed the Bell's Cup. The Observer newspaper agrees to pay O'Neill 'substantial damages' after admitting report his advisors met Manchester United had no basis in truth.

**6:** Rangers win penalty shoot-out 4-3 to beat PSG in Uefa Cup after game finished goalless. De Boer had chance to seal it with penalty in final minute of extra time, but missed. Celtic beat Valencia with Larsson goal at Parkhead to take tie into extra time. But no further scoring and they lose penalty shoot-out 5-4 with Douglas saving twice, but Valgaeren missing twice after ref ordered penalty re-take. Larsson and Petrov also failed from spot. Larsson now club's all-time top scorer in Europe with 17.

**7:** Reyna joins Sunderland from Rangers for £4m. Motherwell sign Yann Soloy from France on a free.

**8:** Gala Fairydean beat Stirling Albion 1-0 to go into third round of Scottish Cup.

**11:** Alex McLeish appointed manager of Rangers on 18-month contract, with assistant Andy Watson joining him in move from Hibs, who demand compensation as both are under contract. Dick Advocaat steps up to director of football. Peter Hetherston resigns as boss of Raith Rovers.

**12:** Advocaat's last game in charge of Rangers sees them draw 1-1 at home to Hibs, who have Donald Park in temporary charge.

**13:** Miller joins Wolves in £3m move from Ibrox. Despite

## 2001-2002 REVIEW OF THE SEASON

Alloa and Celtic wanting to play Scottish Cup tie at Fir Park, SFA demand it must go on at Brockville as Recreation Park not suitable.

**14:** Franck Sauzee appointed manager of Hibs. At 36, hangs up boots after picking up Achilles injury.

**15:** McLeish's first game in charge of Rangers ends in 2-2 draw at Motherwell. Fan Zhiyi gives Dundee shock lead at Parkhead, but Celtic hit back to win 3-1 and extend lead at top of SPL to 13 points. Hibs lose 1-0 at Dunfermline in Sauzee's first game as boss.

**17:** Real Madrid's Luis Figo named world Player of Year. Larsson voted into 14th spot.

**19:** Celtic chairman Brian Quinn admits youth academy and new training complex put on ice due to club's finances.

**20:** Jocky Scott appointed manager of Raith Rovers.

**21:** Tommy Johnson joins Kilmarnock on free from Sheffield Wednesday.

**22:** Celtic suffer first domestic defeat of season, losing 2-0 at snowy Pittodrie. Dons skipper Derek Whyte sent off, but goals from Robbie Winters (pen) and Darren Mackie secure win. Rangers close gap to 10 points with 3-2 win over Dundee United at Ibrox.

**26:** Celtic need last-minute Larsson goal to beat Livi 3-2 at Parkhead. His second of day takes total with Hoops to 101. But Valgaeren first Celt of season to get red card and

Sutton carried off with ankle injury. Hibs have Ulrik Laursen and Tom McManus sent off late on as Rangers win 3-0 at Easter Road. Motherwell to contest red card shown to Greg Strong, sent off by referee John Rowbotham, along with St Johnstone's Ross Forsyth, for violent conduct as Saints win 2-1 at Fir Park.

**28:** SFA revoke Strong's red card after video review.

**29:** Mols marks return to action after months injured by scoring for Rangers inside two minutes for only goal of game v St Johnstone.

### JANUARY

**1:** Celtic 13 points clear again with 2-0 win over Motherwell as Rangers' game at Rugby Park is frozen off. Partick Thistle go top of Division One with 2-1 win over Clyde.

**5:** Rangers' cup tie at Berwick and Celtic v Alloa frozen off. Falkirk get 1-1 draw at Dens Park, Hibs held 0-0 at Stranraer and Killie knock out Airdrie 3-0.

**7:** SFA announce £25m TV deal with Sky and BBC for internationals and Scottish Cup ties for next four years.

**8:** Wieghorst scores first competitive goal for almost two years and Sylla gets first for club as Celtic demolish Alloa 5-0. Lennon fined by club after reports he had been thrown out of Glasgow night club following altercation. Albion

## 2001-2002 REVIEW OF THE SEASON

Rovers v Livingston cup tie abandoned goalless at half-time due to lights failure.

**9:** Former boss and chairman Jim McLean on new Dundee United board that takes control to find buyer for club.

**15:** Berwick hold Rangers to goalless draw in Scottish Cup third round. Hibs get first win under Sauzee, 4-0 v Stranraer in cup replay. SPL to push ahead with plans for own TV channel. David Kelly's contract ended by Motherwell after argument with boss Eric Black at Dunfermline.

**16:** Dundee win 1-0 in cup replay at Falkirk.

**19:** Amoruso grabs only goal as Rangers win 1-0 at Aberdeen. But game marred by crowd trouble. Players taken off for 17 minutes by ref McCurry after Winters struck on head by coin while taking corner. Coins also thrown at ref Young during Dundee United's 1-0 win over Dundee.

**21:** Rangers beat Berwick 3-0 in cup replay.

**24:** Colin Healy joins Coventry on loan from Celtic.

**25:** Advocaat named as part-time boss of Holland.

**26:** Inverness Caley win 3-1 at Tynecastle to knock Hearts out of Scottish Cup in fourth round. Ayr United dump Dunfermline 3-0, and Partick hold Dundee 1-1. Lights failure delays start of Celtic's tie at Kilmarnock for 47 minutes before Hoops go on to win 2-0. Rangers make light work of

Hibs, winning 4-1 at Ibrox.

**29:** Lambert accepts deal to keep him at Celtic until 2005.

**30:** Rangers surrender 2-0 lead at Killie to finish 2-2, while Celtic stretch lead to 15 points by coming from behind at Livingston to win 3-1.

### FEBRUARY

**2:** Balde caught on TV using forearm against Hibs' Fenwick off the ball during Celtic's 1-1 draw at Easter Road. Missed by ref Freeland, but O'Neill announces he'll fine his player and SFA start investigation using video. Rangers close gap after coming from behind to beat Dundee 2-1 at Ibrox. Thistle stay three clear of Airdrie after 1-1 draw at Firhill.

**5:** Rangers defeat Celtic 2-1 in CIS Cup semi-final. Lovenkrands opens scoring, Balde equalises before Konterman blasts home winner in extra time after Arveladze penalty miss.

**6:** Eddie Annand penalty in extra time gives Ayr 1-0 CIS Cup semi-final win over Hibs. Partick Thistle knock Dundee out of Scottish Cup with 2-1 replay win at Dens. SFA announce four-year £5.1m sponsorship deal with Safeway. Amoruso named Player of Month.

**7:** Clyde boss Allan Maitland, assistant Denis McDaid and general manager George Fairley resign over youth development finance dispute.

**13:** Rangers send Mario

## 2001-2002 REVIEW OF THE SEASON

Espartero back to Metz after he rejects loan deal.

**14:** SPL chief executive Roger Mitchell upsets Partick Thistle by claiming anyone who thinks Jags can survive in SPL must be smoking dope.

**15:** New Scotland boss unveiled and says: "Call me Berti McVogts".

**19:** Balde handed one-game ban for striking Fenwick. Will miss second game as 12 points takes him through disciplinary barrier. Celtic to appeal on procedural grounds.

**21:** Hibs sack Sauzee after just two months and one win during his 15 games in charge. Rangers held 1-1 at home by Feyenoord in Uefa Cup fourth round first leg. Ferguson penalty equalises Shinji Ono's opener.

**23:** In Scottish Cup quarter-finals, Ayr draw 2-2 at Tannadice while Partick and Inverness draw 2-2 at Firhill.

**24:** Forfar crash 6-0 at home to Rangers in cup with Dodds grabbing hat-trick.

**25:** Celtic book remaining cup semi-final place with a 2-0 win at Aberdeen. Hartson opens scoring before being sent off for aiming kick at McAllister. Lennon spoken to by police for gesture made as he left field. Bobby Williamson appointed Hibs boss on five-year contract. Assistant Gerry McCabe also moves from Killie.

**28:** Rangers out of Uefa Cup after losing 3-2 in Rotterdam, (4-3 on aggregate). Pierre van Hooijdonk scores two and sets up third for Kalouf. McCann (later sent off, as was Pauwwe) opened scoring and Ferguson penalty kept Gers' hopes alive to end. Jim Jefferies named boss of Kilmarnock with Billy Brown as assistant.

### MARCH

**1:** Alan Kernaghan named manager of Clyde.

**2:** Thompson and Hicham Zerouali sent off after scuffling during Celtic's 1-0 win over Dons. Both clubs appeal red cards, Zerouali's reduced to yellow, but Thompson's stands.

**5:** Partick win 1-0 Inverness to book cup semi-final spot.

**6:** Ayr beat Dundee United 2-0 at Somerset Park in cup replay.

**8:** James McFadden signs deal to keep him at Fir Park until 2005.

**10:** Rangers and Celtic draw 1-1 at Ibrox, Numan equalising Petrov's opener, to keep Hoops' lead at 10 points.

**12:** Independent Tribunal upholds SFA ban on Balde. Bob Malcolm rejects £200,000 move to Dundee United.

**14:** McLeish Manager of Month, with skipper Ferguson Player of Month. Valgaeren has hernia operation. Peter Cormack quits as Morton boss.

**15:** Lambert agrees to return to Scotland squad as captain.

**17:** Rangers lift CIS Cup after

## 2001-2002 REVIEW OF THE SEASON

4-0 win over Ayr, with goals from Flo, Caniggia (2) and a Ferguson penalty.

**18:** Tommy Burns accepts post as No.2 to Vogts. SFA reveal Agathe's booking in recent cup tie v Dons not reported. Caution removed from record at later meeting.

**22:** Tebily leaves Celtic for Birmingham in £750,000 deal.

**23:** Celtic beat Ayr 3-0 in Scottish Cup semi-final.

**24:** Rangers beat Partick 3-0 to reach Scottish Cup final.

**26:** Hamilton players threaten strike action over unpaid wages.

**27:** Scotland trounced 5-0 in Paris by France on Vogts' debut as boss. First-half goals from Zinedine Zidane, Trezeguet (2) and Thierry Henry followed after break by one from Steve Marlet. Bust-up at airport on way home between Vogts and Rab Douglas after Celt failed to win first cap.

**30:** Partick Thistle open new 1414-seater stand to bring ground up to SPL standard, but can only draw 1-1 with Ross County. Brechin the first club in Britain to win promotion after 1-1 draw with Peterhead.

#### APRIL

**4:** Jimmy Calderwood named Manager of Month.

**6:** Celtic crowned champions after 5-1 demolition of Livingston in first game after split. St Johnstone relegated

after 1-1 draw with second-bottom Motherwell.

**8:** Rangers and Celtic vote against SPL TV channel, claiming it is not viable. Celtic beat Leicester 1-0 in friendly at Filbert Street.

**11:** Balde undergoes surgery on knee.

**13:** Partick Thistle clinch First Division title with 2-0 win at Love Street. Queen of the South promoted to Division One.

**14:** Stenhousemuir part company with boss Jimmy Bone.

**16:** Ten clubs outwith Old Firm give notice of intention to resign from SPL over voting structure.

**17:** Scotland lose friendly 2-1 to Nigeria at Pittodrie. Christian Dailly opens scoring, but Julius Aghahowa hits back with double.

**20:** Alloa win promotion to First Division after draw at Cappielow.

**21:** Final Old Firm league game of season finishes 1-1 after Thompson equalises Lovenkrands opener. Mjallby, Ricksen and Hartson sent off by ref Clarke after late goal-mouth scuffle. On appeal, Hartson's card removed.

**24:** Motherwell call in interim administrators after chairman John Boyle admits £3m loss for year takes his personal losses in four years since took over to £11m. Manager Black and chief executive Nevin resign. Butcher in charge of team temporarily.

## 2001-2002 REVIEW OF THE SEASON

**27:** Ayr v Airdrie match abandoned after 20 minutes with home side leading 1-0. Pitch invasion by visiting fans protesting against Ayr chairman Bill Barr leaves cross bar broken. SFL decree result stands. Livingston clinch Uefa Cup place with 4-1 win over Dunfermline.

**29:** Administrators make 10 Motherwell players redundant, release nine others and offer reduced contracts to four more. Raith Rovers sack Jocky Scott. John McVeigh resigns from Albion Rovers and takes over as boss of Stenhousemuir. Stirling Albion release boss Ray Stewart.

### MAY

**1:** After being in receivership for 27 months, Airdrie go into full liquidation.

**4:** Rangers win Scottish Cup final 3-2 with last-minute winner from Lovenkrands. Celtic had opened scoring through Hartson, Lovenkrands equalised, Balde put Hoops 2-1 up before Ferguson made it 2-2.

**6:** Ian McCall new coach of Falkirk with Alex Totten becoming director of football.

**7:** Celtic beat Leeds 4-1 in Gary Kelly's testimonial.

**8:** Barry Ferguson announces he is staying with Rangers, despite offers to move to England and Spain. Feyenoord beat Borussia Dortmund 3-2 to lift Uefa Cup.

**9:** Airdrie officially leave the SFL – first club to do so since

Third Lanark folded in 1967. As a consequence, Falkirk will no longer be relegated, and Stenhousemuir will not go down from Division Two.

**10:** Stephen Hughes signs new five-year deal with Rangers, who also announce they are signing Mikel Arteta from Barcelona and Kevin Muscat from Wolves.

**12:** Celtic finish 18 points clear in SPL after 1-0 win at Pittodrie, while Rangers end with draw at Dunfermline.

**13:** Celtic and Arsenal draw 1-1 in Tony Adams testimonial.

**15:** Hampden hosts Champions League Final between Real Madrid and Bayer Leverkusen. Raul opens scoring for Spanish club, but Lucio equalises. Game won by spectacular goal from Zidane.

**16:** Scotland tour of Far East starts with 4-1 hammering from South Korea in Busan. Scott Dobie scores on debut.

**20:** Scotland lose 2-0 to South Africa in Hong Kong's Reunification Cup.

**23:** Scotland beat Hong Kong League Select 4-0 with goals from Kevin Kyle, Steven Thompson, Dailly and Scott Gemmill. Rangers boss McLeish signs two-year extension to contract.

### JUNE

**18:** Gretna admitted to SFL ahead of six others including Airdrie United.

**30:** Brazil beat Germany 2-0 to win the World Cup Final.

# LEADING EXECUTIVES/SECRETARIES

**SCOTTISH FA** – D. Taylor, Chief Executive, Hampden Park, Glasgow, G42 9AY. Tel: 0141 616 6000. Website: scottishfa.co.uk

**SCOTTISH PREMIER LEAGUE** – R Mitchell, Chief Executive, Hampden Park, Glasgow, G42 9DE. 0141 620 4140. Website: scotprem.com

**SCOTTISH FOOTBALL LEAGUE** – P. Donald, Secretary, Hampden Park, Glasgow, G42 9EB. Tel: 0141 620 4160. Website: scottishfootball.com

**ENGLISH FA** – A. Crozier, Chief Executive, 25 Soho Square, London, W1D 4FA. Tel: 0207 262 4542. Website: thefa.com

**ENGLISH PREMIER LEAGUE** – R. Scudamore, Chief Executive, 11 Connaught Place, London, W2 2ET. Tel: 0207 298 1600. Website: 4thegame.com

**ENGLISH FOOTBALL LEAGUE** – D. Burns, Chief Executive, Edward VII Quay, Navigation Way, Preston, PR2 2YF. Tel: 01772 325800. Website: football-league.co.uk

**FA OF WALES** – D. Collins, Chief Executive, 3 Westgate Street, Cardiff, CF10 1DP. Tel: 02920 372325. Website: faw.org.uk

**NORTHERN IRELAND FA** – D. I. Bowen, General Secretary, 20 Windsor Avenue, Belfast, BT9 6EE. Tel: 02890 669458. Website: irishfa.com

**IRISH LEAGUE** – H. Wallace, Secretary, 96 University Street, Belfast, BT7 1HE. Tel: 02890 242888. Website: irish-league.co.uk

**FA OF IRELAND** – B. Menton, General Secretary, 80 Merrion Square, Dublin 2, Eire. Tel: 00 353 1 6766864. Website: fai.ie

**FOOTBALL LEAGUE OF IRELAND** – M. Hyland, Secretary, 80 Merrion Square, Dublin 2, Eire. Tel: 00 353 1 6765120. Website: fai.ie

**FIFA** – S. Blatter, President, FIFA House, PO Box 85, 8030, Zurich, Switzerland. 00 411 384 9595. Website: fifa.com

**UEFA** – G. Aigner, Chief Executive, Route de Geneve 46, CH-1260 Nyon 2, Switzerland. Tel: 00 41 22 994 4444. Website: uefa.com

**SCOTTISH PROFESSIONAL FOOTBALLERS' ASSOCIATION** – A. Higgins, Secretary, Fountain House, 1/3 Woodside Crescent, Glasgow, G3 7UJ. 0141 332 8641.

**SCOTTISH JUNIOR FA** – T. Johnston, Secretary, Hampden Park, Glasgow, G42 9DD. Tel: 0141 620 4560.

**CENTRAL REGIONAL LEAGUE** – J. Scott Robertson, Secretary. Tel: 01698 266725.

**WEST OF SCOTLAND JUNIOR FA** – M. Spiers, Secretary. Tel: 01563 527408.

**SCOTTISH WOMEN'S FA** – Ms M McGonigle, Executive Administrator. Hampden Park, Glasgow G42. Tel: 0141 620 4580.

# ABERDEEN

| | |
|---|---|
| **NICKNAME:** | The Dons |
| **COLOURS:** | Red and white |
| **GROUND:** | Pittodrie |
| **TELEPHONE:** | 01224 650400 |
| **FAX:** | 01224 644173 |
| **WEBSITE:** | afc.co.uk |
| **CAPACITY:** | 22,199 |
| **RECORD ATT:** | 45,061 (v Hearts, 1954) |
| **RECORD VICTORY:** | 13-0 (v Peterhead, 1923) |
| **RECORD DEFEAT:** | 0-8 (v Celtic, 1965) |
| **MANAGER:** | Ebbe Skovdahl |
| **CHIEF EXECUTIVE:** | Keith Wyness |
| **CHAIRMAN:** | Stewart Milne |
| **MOST LEAGUE** | |
| **GOALS (1 SEASON):** | 38, Benny Yorston, 1929-30 |
| **GOALS (OVERALL):** | 199, Joe Harper |

## HONOURS

**LEAGUE CHAMPIONSHIP (4):** Division 1 – 1954-55. Premier Division – 1979-80, 1983-84, 1984-85. **SCOTTISH CUP (7):** 1947, 1970, 1982, 1983, 1984, 1986, 1990. **LEAGUE CUP (5):** 1955-56, 1976-77, 1985-86, 1989-90, 1995-96. **EUROPEAN CUP-WINNERS' CUP:** 1983. **EUROPEAN SUPER CUP:** 1983-84.

### LEAGUE RESULTS 2001-2002

| | |
|---|---|
| Aberdeen 0 Rangers 3 | Aberdeen 0 Dundee 0 |
| Hearts 1 Aberdeen 0 | Dunfermline 1 Aberdeen 0 |
| Hibernian 2 Aberdeen 0 | Aberdeen 0 Livingston 3 |
| Aberdeen 4 Motherwell 2 | Hearts 3 Aberdeen 1 |
| St Johnstone 1 Aberdeen 1 | Aberdeen 0 Rangers 1 |
| Aberdeen 2 Kilmarnock 0 | Hibernian 3 Aberdeen 4 |
| Aberdeen 2 Dundee Utd 1 | Aberdeen 1 Motherwell 5 |
| Celtic 2 Aberdeen 0 | St Johnstone 0 Aberdeen 1 |
| Dundee 1 Aberdeen 4 | Aberdeen 1 Kilmarnock 1 |
| Livingston 2 Aberdeen 2 | Aberdeen 4 Dundee Utd 0 |
| Aberdeen 3 Dunfermline 2 | Celtic 1 Aberdeen 0 |
| Aberdeen 3 Hearts 2 | Dundee 2 Aberdeen 3 |
| Rangers 2 Aberdeen 0 | Aberdeen 1 Dunfermline 0 |
| Aberdeen 2 Hibernian 0 | Livingston 0 Aberdeen 0 |
| Motherwell 3 Aberdeen 2 | Dunfermline 1 Aberdeen 0 |
| Aberdeen 1 St Johnstone 0 | Aberdeen 2 Hearts 3 |
| Kilmarnock 3 Aberdeen 1 | Aberdeen 3 Livingston 0 |
| Dundee Utd 1 Aberdeen 1 | Rangers 2 Aberdeen 0 |
| Aberdeen 2 Celtic 0 | Aberdeen 0 Celtic 1 |

# ALBION ROVERS

| | |
|---|---|
| *NICKNAME:* | The Rovers |
| *COLOURS:* | Yellow and black |
| *GROUND:* | Cliftonhill Stadium |
| *TELEPHONE No:* | 01236 606334 |
| *FAX No:* | 01236 606334 |
| *CAPACITY:* | 2,496 |
| *RECORD ATT:* | 27,381 |
| | (v Rangers, 1936) |
| *RECORD VICTORY:* | 12-0 (v Airdriehill, 1887) |
| *RECORD DEFEAT:* | 1-11 (v Partick Thistle, 1993) |
| *MANAGER:* | Peter Hetherston |
| *CHAIRMAN:* | Andrew Dick |
| *MOST LEAGUE* | |
| *GOALS (1 SEASON):* | 41, Jim Renwick, 1932-33 |

## HONOURS

LEAGUE CHAMPIONSHIP: Division II – 1933-34. Second Division – 1988-89.

## LEAGUE RESULTS 2001-2002

| | |
|---|---|
| East Fife 0 Albion 0 | East Fife 2 Albion 3 |
| Albion 1 Stirling 3 | Albion 2 Queen's Park 0 |
| Elgin 2 Albion 0 | Brechin 0 Albion 0 |
| Brechin 4 Albion 1 | Albion 5 East Stirling 1 |
| Albion 2 Queen's Park 1 | Dumbarton 2 Albion 0 |
| Dumbarton 1 Albion 1 | Albion 2 Peterhead 1 |
| Albion 0 East Stirling 4 | Montrose 2 Albion 0 |
| Montrose 1 Albion 2 | Albion 2 Stirling 0 |
| Albion 1 Peterhead 0 | Elgin 0 Albion 0 |
| | |
| Albion 3 East Fife 0 | Albion 0 Brechin 1 |
| Stirling 2 Albion 2 | Queen's Park 0 Albion 3 |
| Queen's Park 1 Albion 2 | Albion 1 Dumbarton 1 |
| Albion 1 Brechin 2 | East Stirling 1 Albion 2 |
| Albion 0 Dumbarton 2 | Albion 0 Montrose 0 |
| East Stirling 1 Albion 2 | Peterhead 0 Albion 2 |
| Albion 0 Montrose 0 | Albion 2 East Fife 1 |
| Peterhead 0 Albion 0 | Stirling 0 Albion 3 |
| Albion 4 Elgin 4 | Albion 2 Elgin 2 |

# ALLOA

| | |
|---|---|
| *NICKNAME:* | The Wasps |
| *COLOURS:* | Gold and black |
| *GROUND:* | Recreation Park |
| *TELEPHONE No:* | 01259 722695 |
| *FAX No:* | 01259 210886 |
| *CAPACITY:* | 3,142 |
| *RECORD ATT:* | 13,000 (v Dunfermline, 1939) |
| *RECORD VICTORY:* | 9-2 (v Forfar, 1933) |
| *RECORD DEFEAT:* | 0-10 (v Dundee, 1937) |
| *MANAGER:* | Terry Christie |
| *CHAIRMAN:* | Ewen Cameron |
| *MOST LEAGUE GOALS (1 SEASON):* | 49, William Crilley, 1921-22 |

## HONOURS

LEAGUE CHAMPIONS: Division II – 1921-22. Third Division – 1997-98. BELL'S CHALLENGE CUP: 1999-00.

## LEAGUE RESULTS 2001-2002

Berwick 0 Alloa 4
Alloa 1 Morton 1
Stranraer 1 Alloa 1
Cowdenbeath 1 Alloa 2
Alloa 0 Stenhousemuir 1
Alloa 1 Clydebank 0
Forfar 0 Alloa 1
Alloa 2 Hamilton 1
QoS 2 Alloa 1

Alloa 2 Berwick 2
Morton 1 Alloa 1
Stenhousemuir 1 Alloa 1
Alloa 5 Cowdenbeath 1
Clydebank 1 Alloa 0
Alloa 1 Forfar 2
Hamilton 1 Alloa 0
Alloa 2 QoS 0
Alloa 2 Stranraer 2

Berwick 0 Alloa 1
Alloa 4 Stenhousemuir 0
Cowdenbeath 1 Alloa 2
Forfar 4 Alloa 1
Alloa 2 Clydebank 2
QoS 0 Alloa 1
Alloa 2 Hamilton 2
Alloa 4 Morton 0
Stranraer 0 Alloa 2

Alloa 0 Cowdenbeath 0
Stenhousemuir 1 Alloa 0
Clydebank 1 Alloa 1
Alloa 2 Forfar 1
Hamilton 1 Alloa 1
Alloa 4 QoS 1
Alloa 1 Berwick 1
Morton 0 Alloa 0
Alloa 0 Stranraer 0

# ARBROATH

| | |
|---|---|
| NICKNAME: | The Red Lichties |
| COLOURS: | Maroon and white |
| GROUND: | Gayfield Park |
| TELEPHONE No: | 01241 872157 |
| FAX No: | 01241 431125 |
| WEBSITE: | arbroathfc.co.uk |
| CAPACITY: | 6,488 |
| RECORD ATT: | 13,510 |
| | (v Rangers, 1952) |
| RECORD VICTORY: | 36-0 (v Bon Accord, 1885) |
| RECORD DEFEAT: | 1-9 (v Celtic, 1993) |
| FOUNDED: | 1878 |
| MANAGER: | John Brownlie |
| CHAIRMAN: | John D Christison |
| MOST LEAGUE | |
| GOALS (1 SEASON): | 45, Dave Easson, 1958-59 |

## LEAGUE RESULTS 2001-2002

Ross Co 0 Arbroath 2
Arbroath 0 Airdrie 6
Clyde 1 Arbroath 0
Arbroath 1 Partick 3
Inverness CT 5 Arbroath 1
Raith 3 Arbroath 1
Arbroath 3 Ayr 2
Arbroath 1 Falkirk 0
St Mirren 1 Arbroath 0

Arbroath 2 Ross Co 1
Airdrie 3 Arbroath 1
Arbroath 3 Inverness CT 2
Partick 4 Arbroath 1
Ayr 0 Arbroath 1
Arbroath 1 Raith 1
Arbroath 0 St Mirren 3
Falkirk 3 Arbroath 2
Arbroath 2 Clyde 1

Ross Co 0 Arbroath 1
Inverness CT 3 Arbroath 2
Arbroath 1 Partick 0
Raith 0 Arbroath 0
Arbroath 0 Ayr 2
Arbroath 0 Falkirk 1
St Mirren 2 Arbroath 3
Clyde 1 Arbroath 0
Arbroath 2 Airdrie 1

Partick 2 Arbroath 2
Arbroath 1 Inverness CT 0
Ayr 0 Arbroath 0
Arbroath 2 Raith 2
Falkirk 1 Arbroath 3
Arbroath 0 St Mirren 3
Arbroath 1 Ross Co 1
Airdrie 2 Arbroath 0
Arbroath 2 Clyde 0

# AYR UNITED

| | |
|---|---|
| *NICKNAME:* | The Honest Men |
| *COLOURS:* | White and black |
| *GROUND:* | Somerset Park |
| *TELEPHONE No:* | 01292 263435 |
| *FAX No:* | 01292 281314 |
| *CAPACITY:* | 9,949 |
| *RECORD ATT:* | 25,225 |
| | (v Rangers, 1969) |
| *RECORD VICTORY:* | 11-1 (v Dumbarton, 1952) |
| *RECORD DEFEAT:* | 0-9 (v Rangers, 1929; v Hearts, 1931; v Third Lanark, 1954) |
| *MANAGER:* | Gordon Dalziel |
| *CHAIRMAN:* | William Barr |
| *MOST LEAGUE GOALS (1 SEASON):* | 66, Jimmy Smith, 1927-28 |
| *GOALS (OVERALL):* | 213, Peter Price, 1955-61 |

## HONOURS

**LEAGUE CHAMPIONS:** Division II (6) – 1911-12, 1912-13, 1927-28, 1936-37, 1958-59, 1965-66. Second Division (2) – 1987-88, 1996-97.

Falkirk 1 Ayr 2
Ayr 2 Ross Co 0
Airdrie 2 Ayr 1
Ayr 1 Raith 1
Partick 2 Ayr 1
Ayr 4 St Mirren 2
Arbroath 3 Ayr 2
Ayr 2 Clyde 1
Inverness CT 3 Ayr 1

Ayr 2 Falkirk 2
Ross Co 3 Ayr 2
Ayr 0 Partick 2
Raith 1 Ayr 1
Ayr 0 Arbroath 1
St Mirren 0 Ayr 1
Ayr 3 Inverness CT 0
Clyde 2 Ayr 2
Ayr 1 Airdrie 3

Falkirk 0 Ayr 2
Partick 2 Ayr 1
Ayr 3 Raith 1
Ayr 4 St Mirren 1
Arbroath 0 Ayr 2
Ayr 0 Clyde 1
Inverness CT 1 Ayr 1
Airdrie 1 Ayr 2
Ayr 0 Ross Co 0

Raith 3 Ayr 3
Ayr 1 Partick 1
Ayr 0 Arbroath 0
St Mirren 1 Ayr 1
Clyde 2 Ayr 2
Ayr 1 Inverness CT 0
Ayr 0 Falkirk 0
Ross Co 1 Ayr 1
Ayr 1 Airdrie 0

# BERWICK RANGERS

| | |
|---|---|
| NICKNAME: | The Borderers |
| COLOURS: | Black and gold |
| GROUND: | Shielfield Park |
| TELEPHONE No: | 01289 307424 |
| FAX No: | 01289 309424 |
| WEBSITE: | berwickrangers.com |
| CAPACITY: | 4,131 |
| RECORD ATT: | 13,365 (v Rangers, 1967) |
| RECORD VICTORY: | 8-1 (v Forfar Athletic, 1965; |
| | Vale of Leithen, 1966) |
| RECORD DEFEAT: | 1-9 (v Hamilton, 1980) |
| MANAGER: | Paul Smith |
| CHAIRMAN: | James G Curle |
| MOST LEAGUE | |
| GOALS (1 SEASON): | 38, Ken Bowron, 1963-64 |

## HONOURS

LEAGUE CHAMPIONSHIP: Second Division – 1978-79

## LEAGUE RESULTS 2001-2002

| | |
|---|---|
| Berwick 0 Alloa 4 | Berwick 0 Alloa 1 |
| Cowdenbeath 2 Berwick 1 | Berwick 2 Hamilton 0 |
| Berwick 0 Clydebank 2 | Stenhousemuir 1 Berwick 3 |
| Stenhousemuir 3 Berwick 0 | Berwick 0 Morton 0 |
| Berwick 0 Hamilton 2 | Stranraer 2 Berwick 2 |
| Stranraer 0 Berwick 2 | Forfar 0 Berwick 0 |
| Berwick 2 Morton 0 | Berwick 1 QoS 0 |
| Berwick 0 QoS 4 | Cowdenbeath 1 Berwick 1 |
| Forfar 2 Berwick 1 | Berwick 1 Clydebank 2 |
| | |
| Alloa 2 Berwick 2 | Berwick 2 Stenhousemuir 1 |
| Berwick 2 Cowdenbeath 5 | Hamilton 3 Berwick 1 |
| Hamilton 0 Berwick 1 | Berwick 4 Stranraer 1 |
| Berwick 1 Stenhousemuir 1 | Morton 3 Berwick 2 |
| Berwick 2 Stranraer 2 | QoS 0 Berwick 0 |
| Morton 1 Berwick 2 | Berwick 0 Forfar 2 |
| QoS 2 Berwick 2 | Alloa 1 Berwick 1 |
| Berwick 1 Forfar 1 | Berwick 1 Cowdenbeath 0 |
| Clydebank 0 Berwick 2 | Clydebank 1 Berwick 2 |

# BRECHIN CITY

| | |
|---|---|
| NICKNAME: | The City |
| COLOURS: | Red and white |
| GROUND: | Glebe Park |
| TELEPHONE No: | 01356 622856 |
| FAX No: | 01356 625667 |
| WEBSITE: | brechincity.co.uk |
| CAPACITY: | 3,960 |
| RECORD ATT: | 8,122 |
| | (v Aberdeen, 1973) |
| RECORD VICTORY: | 12-1 (v Thornhill, 1926) |
| RECORD DEFEAT: | 0-10 (v Airdrie, Albion Rovers, |
| | Cowdenbeath, all 1937-38) |
| MANAGER: | Dick Campbell |
| CHAIRMAN: | David Birse |
| MOST LEAGUE | |
| GOALS (1 SEASON): | 26, W McIntosh, 1959-60 |

## HONOURS

LEAGUE CHAMPIONSHIP: Second Division (2) – 1982-83, 1989-90. Third Division – 2001-02. C Division – 1953-54.

## LEAGUE RESULTS 2001-2002

| | |
|---|---|
| Dumbarton 1 Brechin 2 | Dumbarton 2 Brechin 1 |
| Brechin 6 East Fife 0 | Montrose 0 Brechin 0 |
| Stirling 1 Brechin 3 | Brechin 0 Albion 0 |
| Brechin 4 Albion 1 | Brechin 1 Elgin 0 |
| Montrose 0 Brechin 1 | Queen's Park 0 Brechin 0 |
| Queen's Park 1 Brechin 3 | Brechin 2 East Stirling 0 |
| Brechin 1 Elgin 0 | Peterhead 1 Brechin 3 |
| Peterhead 4 Brechin 2 | Brechin 1 East Fife 1 |
| Brechin 1 East Stirling 2 | Stirling 1 Brechin 3 |
| Brechin 3 Dumbarton 2 | Albion 0 Brechin 1 |
| East Fife 3 Brechin 1 | Brechin 2 Montrose 0 |
| Brechin 0 Montrose 0 | Brechin 5 Queen's Park 0 |
| Albion 1 Brechin 2 | Elgin 3 Brechin 0 |
| Brechin 2 Queen's Park 1 | Brechin 1 Peterhead 1 |
| Elgin 0 Brechin 1 | East Stirling 2 Brechin 0 |
| Brechin 4 Peterhead 3 | Brechin 0 Dumbarton 1 |
| East Stirling 3 Brechin 4 | East Fife 1 Brechin 1 |
| Brechin 3 Stirling 1 | Brechin 2 Stirling 1 |

# CELTIC

| | |
|---|---|
| *NICKNAME:* | The Bhoys |
| *COLOURS:* | Green and white |
| *GROUND:* | Celtic Park |
| *TELEPHONE No:* | 0141 556 2611 |
| *FAX No:* | 0141 551 8106 |
| *WEBSITE:* | celticfc.co.uk |
| *CAPACITY:* | 60,506 |
| *RECORD ATT:* | 92,000 |
| | (v Rangers, 1954) |
| *RECORD VICTORY:* | 11-0 (v Dundee, 1895) |
| *RECORD DEFEAT:* | 0-8 (v Motherwell, 1937) |
| *MANAGER:* | Martin O'Neill |
| *CHIEF EXECUTIVE:* | Ian MacLeod |
| *MOST LEAGUE* | |
| *GOALS (1 SEASON):* | 50, Jimmy McGrory, 1935-36 |

## HONOURS

**LEAGUE CHAMPIONS (38):** 1892-93, 1893-94, 1895-96, 1897-98, 1904-05, 1905-06, 1906-07, 1907-08, 1908-09, 1909-10, 1913-14, 1914-15, 1915-16, 1916-17, 1918-19, 1921-22, 1925-26, 1935-36, 1937-38, 1953-54, 1965-66, 1966-67, 1967-68, 1968-69, 1969-70, 1970-71, 1971-72, 1972-73, 1973-74, 1976-77, 1978-79, 1980-81, 1981-82, 1985-86, 1987-88, 1997-98, 2000-01, 2001-02.

**SCOTTISH CUP WINNERS (31):** 1892, 1899, 1900, 1904, 1907, 1908, 1911, 1912, 1914, 1923, 1925, 1927, 1931, 1933, 1937, 1951, 1954, 1965, 1967, 1969, 1971, 1972, 1974, 1975, 1977, 1980, 1985, 1988, 1989, 1985, 2001.

**LEAGUE CUP WINNERS (12):** 1956-57, 1957-58, 1965-66, 1966-67, 1967-68, 1968-69, 1969-70, 1974-75, 1982-83, 1997-98, 1999-00, 2000-01.

**EUROPEAN CUP WINNERS:** 1966-67.

**JOOS VALGAEREN**

**STEPHEN CRAINEY**

## LEAGUE RESULTS 2001-2002

Celtic 3 St Johnstone 0
Kilmarnock 0 Celtic 1
Celtic 2 Hearts 0
Livingston 0 Celtic 0
Hibernian 1 Celtic 4
Celtic 3 Dunfermline 1
Dundee 0 Celtic 4
Celtic 2 Aberdeen 0
Rangers 0 Celtic 2
Motherwell 1 Celtic 2
Celtic 5 Dundee Utd 1
Celtic 1 Kilmarnock 0
St Johnstone 1 Celtic 2
Hearts 0 Celtic 1
Celtic 2 Rangers 1
Celtic 3 Hibernian 0
Dunfermline 0 Celtic 4
Celtic 3 Dundee 1
Aberdeen 2 Celtic 0

Celtic 3 Livingston 2
Dundee Utd 0 Celtic 4
Celtic 2 Motherwell 0
Kilmarnock 0 Celtic 2
Celtic 2 St Johnstone 1
Celtic 2 Hearts 0
Livingston 1 Celtic 3
Hibernian 1 Celtic 1
Celtic 5 Dunfermline 0
Dundee 0 Celtic 3
Celtic 1 Aberdeen 0
Rangers 1 Celtic 1
Celtic 1 Dundee Utd 0
Motherwell 0 Celtic 4
Celtic 5 Livingston 1
Celtic 5 Dunfermline 0
Celtic 1 Rangers 1
Hearts 1 Celtic 4
Aberdeen 0 Celtic 1

# CLYDE

| | |
|---|---|
| **NICKNAME:** | The Bully Wee |
| **COLOURS:** | White and red |
| **GROUND:** | Broadwood Stadium |
| **TELEPHONE No:** | 01236 451511 |
| **FAX No:** | 01236 733490 |
| **CAPACITY:** | 8,029 |
| **RECORD ATT:** | 52,000 (v Rangers, 1908, at Shawfield) |
| **RECORD VICTORY:** | 11-1 (v Cowdenbeath, 1951) |
| **RECORD DEFEAT:** | 0-11 (v Dumbarton 1879, Rangers, 1880) |
| **FOUNDED:** | 1878 |
| **MANAGER:** | Alan Kernaghan |
| **CHIEF EXECUTIVE:** | Vacant |
| **CHAIRMAN:** | William B. Carmichael |
| **MOST LEAGUE GOALS (1 SEASON):** | 32, Bill Boyd, 1932-33 |

## HONOURS

**LEAGUE CHAMPIONS:** Division II (5) – 1904-05, 1951-52, 1956-57, 1961-62, 1972-73. Second Division (4) – 1977-78, 1981-82, 1992-93, 1999-00. SCOTTISH CUP (3): 1939, 1955, 1958.

## LEAGUE RESULTS 2001-2002

| | |
|---|---|
| Clyde 1 Inverness CT 1 | Clyde 1 Inverness CT 0 |
| St Mirren 4 Clyde 1 | Clyde 0 Ross Co 0 |
| Clyde 1 Arbroath 0 | Falkirk 1 Clyde 6 |
| Falkirk 1 Clyde 1 | Partick 2 Clyde 1 |
| Clyde 3 Ross Co 0 | Clyde 0 Airdrie 1 |
| Partick 3 Clyde 0 | Ayr 0 Clyde 1 |
| Clyde 0 Airdrie 3 | Clyde 1 Raith 2 |
| Ayr 2 Clyde 1 | Clyde 1 Arbroath 0 |
| Clyde 3 Raith 2 | St Mirren 2 Clyde 2 |
| | |
| Inverness CT 5 Clyde 1 | Clyde 2 Falkirk 3 |
| Clyde 1 St Mirren 1 | Ross Co 2 Clyde 1 |
| Ross Co 4 Clyde 0 | Airdrie 2 Clyde 2 |
| Clyde 1 Falkirk 1 | Clyde 2 Partick 1 |
| Airdrie 1 Clyde 2 | Clyde 2 Ayr 2 |
| Clyde 3 Partick 1 | Raith 0 Clyde 1 |
| Raith 1 Clyde 2 | Inverness CT 1 Clyde 1 |
| Clyde 2 Ayr 2 | Clyde 3 St Mirren 1 |
| Arbroath 2 Clyde 1 | Arbroath 2 Clyde 0 |

# CLYDEBANK

| | |
|---|---|
| *NICKNAME:* | The Bankies |
| *COLOURS:* | Red and white |
| *GROUND:* | To be announced |
| *TELEPHONE No:* | – |
| *FAX No:* | – |
| *CAPACITY:* | – |
| *RECORD ATT:* | 14,900 (v Hibs, 1965, New Kilbowie) |
| *RECORD VICTORY:* | 8-1 (v Arbroath, 1977) |
| *RECORD DEFEAT:* | 1-9 (v Gala Fairydean, 1965) |
| *FOUNDED:* | 1965 |
| *MANAGER:* | Vacant |
| *CHAIRMAN:* | Vacant |
| *MOST LEAGUE GOALS (1 SEASON):* | 29, Ken Eadie, 1990-91 |

**HONOURS**
LEAGUE CHAMPIONS: Second Division – 1975-76.

## LEAGUE RESULTS 2001-2002

Forfar 1 Clydebank 2
Clydebank 3 Hamilton 2
Berwick 0 Clydebank 2
QoS 1 Clydebank 0
Clydebank 3 Morton 2
Alloa 1 Clydebank 0
Clydebank 3 Cowdenb'th 2
Stenh'semuir 2 Clydebank 2
Clydebank 1 Stranraer 3

Clydebank 1 Forfar 0
Hamilton 3 Clydebank 0
Morton 0 Clydebank 2
Clydebank 3 QoS 0
Clydebank 1 Alloa 0
Cowdenb'th 1 Clydebank 1
Clydebank 3 Stenh'semuir 2
Stranraer 0 Clydebank 1
Clydebank 0 Berwick 2

Forfar 1 Clydebank 2
Clydebank 1 Morton 2
QoS 1 Clydebank 0
Clydebank 1 Cowdenb'th 0
Alloa 2 Clydebank 2
Clydebank 1 Stranraer 2
Stenh'semuir 0 Clydebank 0
Clydebank 1 Hamilton 1
Berwick 1 Clydebank 2

Clydebank 0 QoS 1
Morton 3 Clydebank 1
Clydebank 1 Alloa 1
Cowdenb'th 2 Clydebank 1
Clydebank 0 Stenh'semuir 0
Stranraer 1 Clydebank 1
Clydebank 1 Forfar 0
Hamilton 2 Clydebank 0
Clydebank 1 Berwick 2

# COWDENBEATH

**NICKNAME:** The Blue Brazil
**COLOURS:** Royal blue and white
**GROUND:** Central Park
**TELEPHONE No:** 01383 610166
**FAX No:** 01383 512132
**WEBSITE:** www.bluebrazil@cowdenbeathfc.com
**CAPACITY:** 4,370
**RECORD ATT:** 25,586 (v Rangers, 1949)
**RECORD VICTORY:** 12-0 (v Johnstone, 1928)
**RECORD DEFEAT:** 1-11 (v Clyde, 1951)
**FOUNDED:** 1881
**MANAGER:** Keith Wright
**CHAIRMAN:** Gordon McDougall
**MOST LEAGUE GOALS (1 SEASON):** 54, Rab Walls 1938-39

## HONOURS

LEAGUE CHAMPIONSHIP: Division II (3) – 1913-14, 1914-15, 1938-39.

## LEAGUE RESULTS 2001-2002

| | |
|---|---|
| Stranraer 3 Cowdenbeath 0 | Stranraer 2 Cowdenbeath 1 |
| Cowdenbeath 2 Berwick 1 | Forfar 0 Cowdenbeath 0 |
| Hamilton 1 Cowdenbeath 0 | Cowdenbeath 1 Alloa 2 |
| Cowdenbeath 1 Alloa 2 | Clydebank 1 Cowdenbeath 0 |
| Forfar 2 Cowdenbeath 1 | Cowdenbeath 1 QoS 2 |
| Cowdenbeath 1 QoS 1 | Cowdenb'th 2 Stenh'semuir 4 |
| Clydebank 3 Cowdenbeath 2 | Morton 0 Cowdenbeath 0 |
| Morton 0 Cowdenbeath 2 | Cowdenbeath 1 Berwick 1 |
| Cowdenb'th 1 Stenh'semuir 1 | Hamilton 0 Cowdenbeath 2 |
| | |
| Cowdenbeath 2 Stranraer 2 | Alloa 0 Cowdenbeath 0 |
| Berwick 2 Cowdenbeath 5 | Cowdenbeath 1 Forfar 2 |
| Cowdenbeath 3 Forfar 2 | QoS 2 Cowdenbeath 1 |
| Alloa 5 Cowdenbeath 3 | Cowdenb'th 2 Clydebank 1 |
| QoS 1 Cowdenbeath 3 | Cowdenbeath 2 Morton 2 |
| Cowdenb'th 1 Clydebank 1 | Stenh'semuir 0 Cowdenb'th 1 |
| Cowdenbeath 1 Morton 0 | Cowdenbeath 1 Stranraer 1 |
| Stenh'semuir 0 Cowdenb'th 3 | Berwick 1 Cowdenbeath 0 |
| Cowdenbeath 2 Hamilton 1 | Cowdenbeath 2 Hamilton 1 |

# DUMBARTON

| | |
|---|---|
| *NICKNAME:* | The Sons |
| *COLOURS:* | White, black and gold |
| *GROUND:* | Strathclyde Homes Stadium |
| *TELEPHONE No:* | 01389 762569 |
| *FAX No:* | 01389 762629 |
| *CAPACITY:* | 2,020 |
| *RECORD ATT:* | 18,000 (v Raith Rovers, 1957) |
| *RECORD VICTORY:* | 13-1 (v Kirkintilloch, 1888) |
| *RECORD DEFEAT:* | 1-11 (v Albion Rovers, 1926; v Ayr United, 1952) |
| *FOUNDED:* | 1872 |
| *MANAGER:* | David Winnie |
| *CHAIRMAN:* | Douglas Dalgleish |
| *GOALS (1 SEASON):* | 38, Kenny Wilson, 1971-72 |

## HONOURS

LEAGUE CHAMPIONS: Division I (2) – 1890-91 (shared with Rangers), 1891-92. Division II (2) – 1910-11, 1971-72. Second Division – 1991-92. SCOTTISH CUP: 1883.

## LEAGUE RESULTS 2001-2002

| | |
|---|---|
| Dumbarton 1 Brechin 2 | Dumbarton 2 Brechin 1 |
| Peterhead 0 Dumbarton 3 | East Stirling 1 Dumbarton 0 |
| Dumbarton 2 Queen's Park 1 | Dumbarton 0 Montrose 5 |
| Dumbarton 0 Montrose 1 | Stirling 2 Dumbarton 1 |
| East Stirling 2 Dumbarton 4 | Dumbarton 2 Albion 0 |
| Dumbarton 1 Albion 1 | East Fife 1 Dumbarton 0 |
| Stirling 4 Dumbarton 5 | Dumbarton 3 Elgin 1 |
| Dumbarton 2 Elgin 2 | Peterhead 4 Dumbarton 0 |
| East Fife 4 Dumbarton 1 | Dumbarton 1 Queen's Park 1 |
| Brechin 3 Dumbarton 2 | Montrose 1 Dumbarton 1 |
| Dumbarton 0 Peterhead 3 | Dumbarton 2 East Stirling 1 |
| Dumbarton 2 East Stirling 2 | Albion 1 Dumbarton 1 |
| Montrose 1 Dumbarton 3 | Dumbarton 2 Stirling 0 |
| Albion 0 Dumbarton 2 | Elgin 2 Dumbarton 0 |
| Dumbarton 4 Stirling 1 | Dumbarton 2 East Fife 0 |
| Elgin 0 Dumbarton 3 | Brechin 0 Dumbarton 1 |
| Dumbarton 1 East Fife 0 | Dumbarton 3 Peterhead 0 |
| Queen's Park 0 Dumbarton 0 | Queen's Park 0 Dumbarton 2 |

# DUNDEE

**NICKNAME:** The Dark Blues
**COLOURS:** Dark blue, red and white

**GROUND:** Dens Park
**TELEPHONE No:** 01382 826104
**FAX No:** 01382 832284
**WEBSITE:** dfc@dundeefc.co.uk

**CAPACITY:** 11,200
**RECORD ATT:** 43,024 (v Rangers, 1953)
**RECORD VICTORY:** 10-0 (v Alloa, 1957; v Dunfermline, 1957)

**RECORD DEFEAT:** 0-11 (v Celtic, 1895)
**MANAGER:** Ivano Bonetti
**CHIEF EXECUTIVE:** Peter Marr
**CHAIRMAN:** Jim Marr
**MOST LEAGUE GOALS (1 SEASON):** 38, Dave Halliday, 1923-24
**GOALS (OVERALL):** 113, Alan Gilzean

## HONOURS

LEAGUE CHAMPIONS: 1961-62. First Division (3) – 1978-79, 1991-92, 1997-98. Division II – 1946-47. SCOTTISH CUP: 1910. LEAGUE CUP WINNERS (3): 1951-52, 1952-53, 1973-74.

## LEAGUE RESULTS 2001-2002

| | |
|---|---|
| Dundee Utd 2 Dundee 2 | Aberdeen 0 Dundee 0 |
| Dundee 2 Hibernian 1 | Motherwell 4 Dundee 2 |
| Dundee 1 Livingston 0 | Dundee 2 Dunfermline 2 |
| Hearts 3 Dundee 1 | Dundee 1 Hibernian 0 |
| Rangers 2 Dundee 0 | Dundee Utd 1 Dundee 0 |
| Dundee 1 St Johnstone 1 | Dundee 2 Livingston 0 |
| Dundee 0 Celtic 4 | Hearts 2 Dundee 0 |
| Kilmarnock 0 Dundee 1 | Rangers 2 Dundee 1 |
| Dundee 1 Aberdeen 4 | Dundee 1 St Johnstone 0 |
| Dunfermline 1 Dundee 0 | Dundee 0 Celtic 3 |
| Dundee 3 Motherwell 1 | Kilmarnock 3 Dundee 2 |
| Hibernian 1 Dundee 2 | Dundee 2 Aberdeen 3 |
| Dundee 1 Dundee Utd 1 | Dundee 2 Motherwell 0 |
| Livingston 1 Dundee 0 | Dunfermline 2 Dundee 0 |
| Dundee 1 Hearts 1 | Dundee 2 Kilmarnock 0 |
| Dundee 0 Rangers 0 | St Johnstone 0 Dundee 1 |
| St Johnstone 0 Dundee 2 | Dundee 0 Dundee Utd 1 |
| Celtic 3 Dundee 1 | Hibernian 2 Dundee 2 |
| Dundee 1 Kilmarnock 2 | Motherwell 2 Dundee 1 |

# DUNDEE UNITED

**NICKNAME:** The Terrors
**COLOURS:** Tangerine
and black
**GROUND:** Tannadice Park
**TELEPHONE No:** 01382 833166
**FAX No:** 01382 889398
**WEBSITE:** dundeeunitedfc.co.uk
**CAPACITY:** 14,209
**RECORD ATT:** 28,000 (v Barcelona, 1966)
**RECORD VICTORY:** 14-0 (v Nithsdale, 1931)
**RECORD DEFEAT:** 1-12 (v Motherwell, 1954)
**MANAGER:** Alex Smith
**CHAIRMAN:** Scott Carnegie
**MOST LEAGUE**
**GOALS (1 SEASON):** 41, John Coyle, 1955-56
**GOALS (OVERALL):** 158, Peter Mackay

## HONOURS

LEAGUE CHAMPIONS: 1982-83. Division 2 (2) – 1924-25,
1928-29. SCOTTISH CUP: 1994. LEAGUE CUP (2): 1979-80,
1980-81.

## LEAGUE RESULTS 2001-2002

| | |
|---|---|
| Dundee Utd 2 Dundee 2 | Dundee Utd 0 Hearts 2 |
| Motherwell 0 Dundee Utd 0 | Dundee Utd 0 Celtic 4 |
| St Johnstone 0 Dundee Utd 1 | Hibernian 0 Dundee Utd 1 |
| Dundee Utd 3 Dunfermline 2 | Motherwell 2 Dundee Utd 0 |
| Dundee Utd 0 Kilmarnock 2 | Dundee Utd 1 Dundee 0 |
| Livingston 2 Dundee Utd 0 | St Johnstone 1 Dundee Utd 4 |
| Aberdeen 2 Dundee Utd 1 | Dundee Utd 0 Dunfermline 2 |
| Dundee Utd 1 Rangers 6 | Dundee Utd 0 Kilmarnock 2 |
| Hearts 1 Dundee Utd 2 | Livingston 1 Dundee Utd 1 |
| Dundee Utd 3 Hibernian 1 | Aberdeen 4 Dundee Utd 0 |
| Celtic 5 Dundee Utd 1 | Dundee Utd 0 Rangers 1 |
| Dundee Utd 1 Motherwell 1 | Hearts 1 Dundee Utd 2 |
| Dundee 1 Dundee Utd 1 | Celtic 1 Dundee Utd 0 |
| Dundee Utd 2 St Johnstone 1 | Dundee Utd 1 Hibernian 2 |
| Dunfermline 1 Dundee Utd 1 | Dundee Utd 2 Hibernian 1 |
| Kilmarnock 2 Dundee Utd 0 | Dundee Utd 1 Motherwell 0 |
| Dundee Utd 0 Livingston 0 | Dundee 0 Dundee Utd 1 |
| Dundee Utd 1 Aberdeen 1 | Dundee Utd 0 St Johnstone 0 |
| Rangers 3 Dundee Utd 2 | Kilmarnock 2 Dundee Utd 2 |

# DUNFERMLINE

| | |
|---|---|
| **NICKNAME:** | The Pars |
| **COLOURS:** | Black and white |
| **GROUND:** | East End Park |
| **TELEPHONE No:** | 01383 724295 |
| **FAX No:** | 01383 723468 |
| **WEBSITE:** | dunfermline-athletic.com |
| **CAPACITY:** | 12,509 |
| **RECORD ATT:** | 27,816 (v Celtic, 1968) |
| **RECORD VICTORY:** | 11-2 (v Stenhousemuir, 1930) |
| **RECORD DEFEAT:** | 0-10 (v Dundee, 1947) |
| **MANAGER:** | Jimmy Calderwood |
| **CHAIRMAN:** | John Yorkston |
| **CHIEF EXECUTIVE:** | Elaine Cromwell |
| **MOST LEAGUE GOALS (1 SEASON):** | 53, Bobby Skinner, 1925-26 |

### HONOURS

**LEAGUE CHAMPIONS:** Division II – 1925-26. Second Division – 1985-86. First Division (2) – 1988-89, 1995-96. **SCOTTISH CUP (2):** 1961, 1968.

### LEAGUE RESULTS 2001-2002

| | |
|---|---|
| Dunfermline 1 Rangers 1 | Livingston 0 Dunfermline 0 |
| Dunfermline 5 Motherwell 2 | Kilmarnock 0 Dunfermline 0 |
| St Johnstone 0 Dunfermline 2 | Dunfermline 1 Aberdeen 0 |
| Dunfermline 1 Rangers 4 | Dundee 2 Dunfermline 2 |
| Dundee Utd 3 Dunfermline 2 | St Johnstone 0 Dunfermline 1 |
| Dunfermline 0 Hearts 1 | Dunfermline 3 Motherwell 1 |
| Celtic 3 Dunfermline 1 | Dunfermline 2 Rangers 4 |
| Hibernian 5 Dunfermline 1 | Dundee Utd 0 Dunfermline 2 |
| Dunfermline 1 Livingston 2 | Dunfermline 1 Hearts 1 |
| Dunfermline 0 Kilmarnock 2 | Celtic 5 Dunfermline 0 |
| Dunfermline 1 Dundee 0 | Hibernian 1 Dunfermline 1 |
| Aberdeen 3 Dunfermline 2 | Dunfermline 1 Livingston 0 |
| Dunfermline 2 St Johnstone 1 | Dunfermline 2 Kilmarnock 0 |
| Motherwell 1 Dunfermline 0 | Aberdeen 1 Dunfermline 0 |
| Rangers 4 Dunfermline 0 | Dunfermline 2 Dundee 0 |
| Dunfermline 1 Dundee Utd 1 | Dunfermline 0 Aberdeen 0 |
| Hearts 1 Dunfermline 1 | Celtic 5 Dunfermline 0 |
| Dunfermline 0 Celtic 4 | Hearts 2 Dunfermline 0 |
| Dunfermline 1 Hibernian 0 | Livingston 4 Dunfermline 1 |

# EAST FIFE

| | |
|---|---|
| **NICKNAME:** | The Fifers |
| **COLOURS:** | Amber and black |
| **GROUND:** | New Bayview Stadium |
| **TELEPHONE No:** | 01333 426323 |
| **FAX No:** | 01333 426376 |
| **WEBSITE:** | eastfife.org |
| **CAPACITY:** | 2,000 |
| **RECORD ATT:** | 22,515 (v Raith Rovers,1950) |
| **RECORD VICTORY:** | 13-2 (v Edinburgh City, 1937) |
| **RECORD DEFEAT:** | 0-9 (v Hearts, 1957) |
| **MANAGER:** | Jim Moffat |
| **CHAIRMAN:** | Bruce Black |
| **MOST LEAGUE GOALS (1 SEASON):** | 41, Jock Wood, 1926-27, and Henry Morris 1947-48 |

## HONOURS

LEAGUE CHAMPIONSHIP: Division II – 1947-48. SCOTTISH CUP: 1938. LEAGUE CUP (3): 1947-48, 1949-50, 1953-54.

## LEAGUE RESULTS 2001-2002

| | |
|---|---|
| East Fife 0 Albion 0 | East Fife 2 Albion 3 |
| Brechin 6 East Fife 0 | Stirling 0 East Fife 1 |
| East Fife 0 East Stirling 4 | East Fife 2 Peterhead 3 |
| East Fife 0 Peterhead 1 | East Fife 2 Montrose 0 |
| Stirling 2 East Fife 1 | Elgin 2 East Fife 0 |
| Elgin 1 East Fife 1 | East Fife 1 Dumbarton 0 |
| East Fife 1 Montrose 2 | Queen's Park 2 East Fife 0 |
| Queen's Park 1 East Fife 2 | Brechin 1 East Fife 1 |
| East Fife 4 Dumbarton 1 | East Fife 1 East Stirling 0 |
| | |
| Albion 3 East Fife 0 | Peterhead 1 East Fife 1 |
| East Fife 3 Brechin 1 | East Fife 1 Stirling 1 |
| East Fife 1 Stirling 1 | East Fife 0 Elgin 1 |
| Peterhead 1 East Fife 3 | Montrose 0 East Fife 1 |
| East Fife 3 Elgin 0 | East Fife 0 Queen's Park 3 |
| Montrose 2 East Fife 1 | Dumbarton 2 East Fife 0 |
| East Fife 1 Queen's Park 4 | Albion 2 East Fife 1 |
| Dumbarton 1 East Fife 0 | East Fife 1 Brechin 1 |
| East Stirling 2 East Fife 1 | East Stirling 1 East Fife 2 |

# EAST STIRLINGSHIRE

| | |
|---|---|
| **NICKNAME:** | The Shire |
| **COLOURS:** | Black and white |
| **GROUND:** | Firs Park |
| **TELEPHONE No:** | 01324 623583 |
| **FAX No:** | 01324 637862 |
| **CAPACITY:** | 816 |
| **RECORD ATT:** | 12,000 |
| | (v Partick Thistle, 1921) |
| **RECORD VICTORY:** | 11-2 (v Vale of Bannock, 1888) |
| **RECORD DEFEAT:** | 1-12 (v Dundee United, 1936) |
| **HEAD COACH:** | Danny Divers |
| **CHIEF EXECUTIVE:** | Les Thompson |
| **CHAIRMAN:** | Alan Mackin |
| **MOST LEAGUE** | |
| **GOALS (1 SEASON):** | 36, Malcolm Morrison, 1938-39, and Henry Morris 1947-48 |

## HONOURS
LEAGUE CHAMPIONSHIP: Division II – 1931-32. C Division

## LEAGUE RESULTS 2001-2002

Elgin 2 East Stirling 1
East Stirling 0 Montrose 1
East Fife 0 East Stirling 4
Queen's Park 2 East Stirling 3
East Stirling 2 Dumbarton 4
East Stirling 2 Peterhead 3
Albion 0 East Stirling 4
East Stirling 1 Stirling 1
Brechin 1 East Stirling 2

East Stirling 2 Elgin 1
Montrose 2 East Stirling 0
Dumbarton 2 East Stirling 2
East Stirling 0 Queen's Park 1
Peterhead 3 East Stirling 2
East Stirling 1 Albion 2
Stirling 1 East Stirling 1
East Stirling 3 Brechin 4
East Stirling 2 East Fife 1

Elgin 2 East Stirling 2
East Stirling 1 Dumbarton 0
Queen's Park 1 East Stirling 0
Albion 5 East Stirling 1
East Stirling 1 Peterhead 0
Brechin 2 East Stirling 0
East Stirling 3 Stirling 0
East Stirling 2 Montrose 1
East Fife 1 East Stirling 0

East Stirling 3 Queen's Park 1
Dumbarton 2 East Stirling 1
Peterhead 2 East Stirling 1
East Stirling 1 Albion 2
Stirling 1 East Stirling 0
East Stirling 2 Brechin 0
East Stirling 0 Elgin 3
Montrose 2 East Stirling 1
East Stirling 1 East Fife 2

# ELGIN CITY

| | |
|---|---|
| NICKNAME: | The City |
| COLOURS: | Black and white |
| GROUND: | Borough Briggs |
| TELEPHONE No: | 01343 551114 |
| FAX No: | 01343 547921 |
| WEBSITE: | Elgincity.com |
| CAPACITY: | 6,500 |
| RECORD ATT: | 12,608 |
| | (v Arbroath,1968) |
| RECORD VICTORY: | 18-1 (v Brora Rangers, 1960) |
| RECORD DEFEAT: | 1-14 (v Hearts, 1939) |
| MANAGER: | Alex Caldwell |
| CHAIRMAN: | Denis Miller |
| MOST LEAGUE | |
| GOALS (1 SEASON): | 66, Willie Grant, 1960-61 |

## LEAGUE RESULTS 2001-2002

Elgin 2 East Stirling 1
Queen's Park 0 Elgin 0
Elgin 2 Albion 0
Elgin 2 Stirling 3
Peterhead 1 Elgin 1
Elgin 1 East Fife 1
Brechin 1 Elgin 0
Dumbarton 2 Elgin 2
Elgin 1 Montrose 2

East Stirling 2 Elgin 1
Elgin 2 Queen's Park 0
Elgin 4 Peterhead 1
Stirling 0 Elgin 1
East Fife 3 Elgin 0
Elgin 0 Brechin 1
Elgin 0 Dumbarton 3
Montrose 0 Elgin 2
Albion 4 Elgin 4

Elgin 2 East Stirling 2
Peterhead 1 Elgin 0
Elgin 2 Stirling 1
Brechin 1 Elgin 0
Elgin 2 East Fife 0
Elgin 1 Montrose 0
Dumbarton 3 Elgin 1
Queen's Park 3 Elgin 0
Elgin 0 Albion 0

Stirling 3 Elgin 1
Elgin 0 Peterhead 3
East Fife 0 Elgin 1
Elgin 3 Brechin 1
Elgin 2 Dumbarton 0
Montrose 1 Elgin 0
East Stirling 0 Elgin 3
Elgin 0 Queen's Park 1
Albion 2 Elgin 2

# FALKIRK

| | |
|---|---|
| NICKNAME: | The Bairns |
| COLOURS: | Navy Blue and white |
| GROUND: | Brockville Park |
| TELEPHONE No: | 01324 624121 |
| FAX No: | 01324 612418 |
| WEBSITE: | post@falkirkfc.co.uk |
| CAPACITY: | 7,608 |
| RECORD ATT: | 23,100 (v Celtic, 1953) |
| RECORD VICTORY: | 12-1 (v Laurieston, 1893) |
| RECORD DEFEAT: | 1-11 (v Airdrie, 1951) |
| HEAD COACH: | Ian McCall |
| DIRECTOR OF FOOTBALL: | Alex Totten |
| CHAIRMAN: | W. Martin Ritchie |
| MOST LEAGUE GOALS (1 SEASON): | 43, Evelyn Morrison, 1928-29 |
| GOALS (OVERALL): | 86, Dougie Moran, 1957-61, 1964-67 |

Est. 1876

## HONOURS

LEAGUE CHAMPIONS: Division II (3) – 1935-36, 1969-70, 1974-75. First Division (2) – 1990-91, 1993-94. Second Division – 1979-80. SCOTTISH CUP (2): 1913, 1957. LEAGUE CHALLENGE CUP: 1997-98. B&Q CUP: 1993-94.

## LEAGUE RESULTS 2001-2002

| | |
|---|---|
| Falkirk 1 Ayr 2 | Falkirk 0 Ayr 2 |
| Inverness CT 1 Falkirk 2 | Raith 5 Falkirk 1 |
| Falkirk 3 St Mirren 2 | Falkirk 1 Clyde 6 |
| Falkirk 1 Clyde 1 | Airdrie 1 Falkirk 0 |
| Raith 5 Falkirk 1 | Falkirk 1 Partick 4 |
| Airdrie 2 Falkirk 1 | Arbroath 0 Falkirk 1 |
| Falkirk 1 Partick 1 | Falkirk 1 Ross Co 4 |
| Arbroath 1 Falkirk 0 | Falkirk 0 St Mirren 2 |
| Falkirk 4 Ross Co 2 | Inverness CT 3 Falkirk 2 |
| Ayr 2 Falkirk 2 | Clyde 2 Falkirk 3 |
| Falkirk 1 Inverness CT 2 | Falkirk 2 Raith 1 |
| Falkirk 1 Raith 0 | Partick 3 Falkirk 0 |
| Clyde 1 Falkirk 1 | Falkirk 2 Airdrie 2 |
| Partick 5 Falkirk 1 | Falkirk 1 Arbroath 3 |
| Falkirk 1 Airdrie 2 | Ross Co 4 Falkirk 2 |
| Ross Co 1 Falkirk 2 | Ayr 0 Falkirk 0 |
| Falkirk 3 Arbroath 2 | Falkirk 0 Inveress CT 0 |
| St Mirren 1 Falkirk 5 | St Mirren 0 Falkirk 0 |

# Bank of Scotland giving extra to youth football

Throughout this season in the Bank of Scotland Premierleague Scotland's young talent has been recognised in our monthly awards from Aberdeen to Kilmarnock. We might not be in Japan this time around but it's looking good for Munich 2006. This year over 20,000 young people will take part in sporting events made possible by Bank of Scotland. To find out more visit **www.hbosplc.com**

RANGERS players celebrate their Tennent's Scottish Cup Final victory over Celtic

# DRUGS
## Know how to tackle them

For information or advice call
**0800 587 587 9**

**KNOW THE SCORE**

www.knowthescore.info

 SCOTTISH EXECUTIVE

# FORFAR ATHLETIC

| | |
|---|---|
| **NICKNAME:** | The Loons |
| **COLOURS:** | Sky blue and navy |
| **GROUND:** | Station Park |
| **TELEPHONE:** | 01307 463576 |
| **FAX:** | 01307 466956 |
| **WEBSITE:** | forfarathletic.co.uk |
| **CAPACITY:** | 4,640 |
| **RECORD ATT:** | 10,780 |
| | (v Rangers, 1970) |
| **RECORD VICTORY:** | 14-1 (v Lindertis, 1888) |
| **RECORD DEFEAT:** | 2-12 (v King's Park, 1930) |
| **MANAGER:** | Neil Cooper |
| **CHAIRMAN:** | David McGregor |
| **MOST LEAGUE** | |
| **GOALS (1 SEASON):** | 45, Dave Kilgour, 1929-30 |

### HONOURS

LEAGUE CHAMPIONSHIP: Second Division – 1983-84. Third Division – 1994-95.

## LEAGUE RESULTS 2001-2002

Forfar 1 Clydebank 2
QoS 1 Forfar 2
Forfar 1 Stenhousemuir 2
Hamilton 1 Forfar 1
Forfar 2 Cowdenbeath 1
Morton 1 Forfar 3
Forfar 0 Alloa 1
Stranraer 2 Forfar 0
Forfar 2 Berwick 1

Clydebank 1 Forfar 1
Forfar 0 QoS 3
Cowdenbeath 3 Forfar 2
Forfar 3 Hamilton 0
Forfar 2 Morton 1
Alloa 1 Forfar 2
Forfar 1 Stranraer 1
Berwick 1 Forfar 1
Stenhousemuir 1 Forfar 1

Forfar 1 Clydebank 2
Forfar 0 Cowdenbeath 0
Hamilton 2 Forfar 0
Forfar 4 Alloa 1
Morton 1 Forfar 4
Forfar 0 Berwick 0
Stranraer 0 Forfar 3
QoS 3 Forfar 1
Forfar 2 Stenhousemuir 0

Forfar 1 Hamilton 4
Cowdenbeath 1 Forfar 2
Forfar 2 Morton 1
Alloa 2 Forfar 1
Forfar 3 Stranraer 2
Berwick 0 Forfar 2
Clydebank 1 Forfar 0
Forfar 0 QoS 3
Stenhousemuir 0 Forfar 0

# GRETNA

| | |
|---|---|
| NICKNAME: | The Black and Whites |
| COLOURS: | Black and white |
| GROUND: | Raydale Park |
| TELEPHONE No: | 01461 337602 |
| FAX No: | 01461 338047 |
| CAPACITY: | 2200 |
| RECORD ATT: | 2307 (v Rochdale, FA Cup 1991) |
| RECORD VICTORY: | 20-0 (v Siloth, Cumberland League 1962-63) |
| RECORD DEFEAT: | 2-9 (v Ashton Utd, Unibond League Div 1, 2000-01) |
| MANAGER: | Rowan Alexander |
| CHAIRMAN: | Brian Fulton |
| MOST LEAGUE GOALS IN CAREER: | Denis Smith |

**GRETNA FOOTBALL CLUB**

## HONOURS

NORTHERN LEAGUE CHAMPIONS: First Division: 1990-91, 1991-92. CARLISLE DISTRICT LEAGUE CHAMPIONS: 28 times

**ROWAN ALEXANDER**

Gretna have become the newest members of the Scottish Football League after winning the vote to fill the vacancy created by the demise of Airdrie.

Formed in 1946, it was third time lucky for the Borders club who had applied for membership of the SFL in 1993 and 1999.

They have most recently been playing in the Unibond League First Division in the North of England under the management of former Morton and St Mirren striker, Rowan Alexander.

# HAMILTON ACCIES

| | |
|---|---|
| *NICKNAME:* | The Accies |
| *COLOURS:* | Red and white |
| *GROUND:* | New Douglas Park |
| *TELEPHONE No:* | 01698 286103 |
| *FAX No:* | 01698 285422 |
| *CAPACITY:* | 5,330 |
| *RECORD ATT:* | 28,690 (v Hearts, 1937) |
| *RECORD VICTORY:* | 11-1 (v Chryston, 1885) |
| *RECORD DEFEAT:* | 1-11 (v Hibs, 1965) |
| *MANAGER:* | Ally Dawson |
| *CHAIRMAN:* | Jan Stepek |
| *MOST LEAGUE* | |
| *GOALS (1 SEASON):* | 35, David Wilson, 1936-37 |

### HONOURS
LEAGUE CHAMPIONS: First Division: 1985-86. B&Q Cup (2); 1991-92, 1992-93. Third Division: 2000-01.

### LEAGUE RESULTS 2001-2002

| | |
|---|---|
| Hamilton 1 QoS 1 | Hamilton 3 QoS 1 |
| Clydebank 3 Hamilton 2 | Berwick 2 Hamilton 0 |
| Hamilton 1 Cowdenbeath 0 | Hamilton 2 Forfar 0 |
| Hamilton 1 Forfar 1 | Hamilton 2 Stranraer 0 |
| Berwick 0 Hamilton 2 | Stenhousemuir 0 Hamilton 3 |
| Stenhousemuir 2 Hamilton 0 | Hamilton 2 Morton 1 |
| Hamilton 0 Stranraer 1 | Alloa 2 Hamilton 2 |
| Alloa 2 Hamilton 1 | Clydebank 1 Hamilton 1 |
| Hamilton 2 Morton 2 | Hamilton 0 Cowdenbeath 2 |
| | |
| QoS 0 Hamilton 1 | Forfar 1 Hamilton 4 |
| Hamilton 3 Clydebank 0 | Hamilton 3 Berwick 1 |
| Hamilton 0 Berwick 1 | Hamilton 0 Stenhousemuir 0 |
| Forfar 1 Hamilton 0 | Stranraer 3 Hamilton 2 |
| Hamilton 2 Stenhousemuir 3 | Hamilton 1 Alloa 1 |
| Stranraer 2 Hamilton 1 | Morton 0 Hamilton 0 |
| Hamilton 1 Alloa 0 | QoS 3 Hamilton 1 |
| Morton 1 Hamilton 1 | Hamilton 2 Clydebank 0 |
| Cowdenbeath 2 Hamilton 1 | Cowdenbeath 2 Hamilton 1 |

# HEART OF MIDLOTHIAN

| | |
|---|---|
| **NICKNAME:** | The Jam Tarts |
| **COLOURS:** | Maroon and white |
| **GROUND:** | Tynecastle Park |
| **TELEPHONE No:** | 0131 200 7200 |
| **FAX No:** | 0131 200 7222 |
| **WEBSITE:** | heartsfc.co.uk |
| **CAPACITY:** | 18,001 |
| **RECORD ATT:** | 53,396 (v Rangers, 1932) |
| **RECORD VICTORY:** | 21-0 (v Anchor, 1880) |
| **RECORD DEFEAT:** | 1-8 (v Vale of Leven, 1888) |
| **MANAGER:** | Craig Levein |
| **CHAIRMAN:** | Douglas Smith |
| **MOST LEAGUE GOALS (1 SEASON):** | 44, Barney Battles |
| **GOALS (OVERALL):** | 214, John Robertson |

## HONOURS

LEAGUE CHAMPIONS: Division I (4) – 1894-95, 1896-97, 1957-58, 1959-60. First Division – 1979-80. SCOTTISH CUP (6): 1891, 1896, 1901, 1906, 1956, 1998. LEAGUE CUP (4): 1954-55, 1958-59, 1959-60, 1962-63.

## LEAGUE RESULTS 2001-2002

| | |
|---|---|
| Livingston 2 Hearts 1 | Dundee Utd 0 Hearts 2 |
| Hearts 1 Aberdeen 0 | Hearts 1 Hibernian 1 |
| Celtic 2 Hearts 0 | St Johnstone 0 Hearts 2 |
| Hearts 3 Dundee 1 | Hearts 3 Aberdeen 1 |
| Dunfermline 0 Hearts 1 | Livingston 2 Hearts 0 |
| Hearts 2 Rangers 2 | Celtic 1 Hearts 0 |
| Kilmarnock 1 Hearts 0 | Hearts 2 Dundee 0 |
| Motherwell 2 Hearts 0 | Dunfermline 1 Hearts 1 |
| Hearts 1 Dundee Utd 2 | Hearts 0 Rangers 1 |
| Hearts 3 St Johnstone 0 | Kilmarnock 3 Hearts 3 |
| Hibernian 2 Hearts 1 | Motherwell 1 Hearts 2 |
| Aberdeen 3 Hearts 2 | Hearts 1 Dundee Utd 2 |
| Hearts 1 Livingston 3 | Hibernian 1 Hearts 2 |
| Hearts 0 Celtic 1 | Hearts 1 St Johnstone 3 |
| Dundee 1 Hearts 1 | Rangers 2 Hearts 0 |
| Hearts 1 Dunfermline 1 | Aberdeen 2 Hearts 3 |
| Rangers 3 Hearts 1 | Hearts 2 Dunfermline 0 |
| Hearts 1 Kilmarnock 0 | Hearts 1 Celtic 4 |
| Hearts 3 Motherwell 1 | Hearts 2 Livingston 3 |

# HIBERNIAN

| | |
|---|---|
| *NICKNAME:* | The Hibees |
| *COLOURS:* | Green and white |
| *GROUND:* | Easter Road |
| *TELEPHONE No:* | 0131 661 2159 |
| *FAX No:* | 0131 652 2202 |
| *WEBSITE:* | hibs.co.uk |
| *CAPACITY:* | 16,039 |
| *RECORD ATT:* | 65,860 (v Hearts, 1950) |
| *RECORD VICTORY:* | 22-1 (v 42nd Highlanders, 1881) |
| *RECORD DEFEAT:* | 0-10 (v Rangers, 1898) |
| *MANAGER:* | Bobby Williamson |
| *CHAIRMAN:* | Malcolm McPherson |
| *MOST LEAGUE GOALS (1 SEASON):* | 42, Joe Baker |
| *GOALS (OVERALL):* | 364, Gordon Smith |

## HONOURS

**LEAGUE CHAMPIONS: Division I (4) – 1902-03, 1947-48, 1950-51,1951-52. Division II (3) – 1893-94, 1894-94, 1932-33. First Division (2) – 1980-81, 1998-99. SCOTTISH CUP (2): 1887, 1902. LEAGUE CUP (2): 1972-73, 1991-92.**

## LEAGUE RESULTS 2001-2002

| | |
|---|---|
| Hibernian 2 Kilmarnock 2 | Hibernian 0 Rangers 3 |
| Dundee 2 Hibernian 1 | Hearts 1 Hibernian 1 |
| Hibernian 2 Aberdeen 0 | Hibernian 0 Dundee Utd 1 |
| Rangers 2 Hibernian 2 | Dundee 1 Hibernian 0 |
| Hibernian 1 Celtic 4 | Hibernian 2 Kilmarnock 2 |
| Motherwell 1 Hibernian 3 | Hibernian 3 Aberdeen 4 |
| Hibernian 5 Dunfermline 1 | Rangers 1 Hibernian 1 |
| Hibernian 4 St Johnstone 0 | Hibernian 1 Celtic 1 |
| Livingston 1 Hibernian 0 | Motherwell 4 Hibernian 0 |
| Dundee Utd 3 Hibernian 1 | Hibernian 1 Dunfermline 0 |
| Hibernian 2 Hearts 1 | Hibernian 3 St Johnstone 0 |
| Hibernian 1 Dundee 2 | Livingston 0 Hibernian 3 |
| Kilmarnock 0 Hibernian 0 | Hibernian 1 Hearts 2 |
| Aberdeen 1 Hibernian 0 | Dundee Utd 1 Hibernian 2 |
| Hibernian 0 Livingston 3 | Dundee Utd 2 Hibernian 1 |
| Celtic 3 Hibernian 0 | Kilmarnock 1 Hibernian 0 |
| Hibernian 1 Motherwell 1 | Hibernian 4 Motherwell 0 |
| Dunfermline 1 Hibernian 0 | Hibernian 2 Dundee 2 |
| St Johnstone 0 Hibernian 0 | St Johnstone 0 Hibernian 1 |

# INVERNESS CT

| | |
|---|---|
| *NICKNAME:* | Caley Thistle |
| *COLOURS:* | Blue and white |
| *GROUND:* | Caledonian Stadiun |
| *TELEPHONE No:* | 01463 222880 |
| *FAX No:* | 01463 715816 |
| *WEBSITE:* | caley-thistle.co.uk |
| *CAPACITY:* | 6,200 |
| *RECORD ATT:* | 5,821 (v Dundee United, 1998) |
| *RECORD VICTORY:* | 8-1 (v Annan Athletic, 1998) |
| *RECORD DEFEAT:* | 0-4 (v Queen's Park, 1937; v Montrose, 1995) |
| *MANAGER:* | Steve Paterson |
| *CHAIRMAN:* | Ken Mackie |
| *MOST LEAGUE GOALS (1 SEASON):* | 27, Ian Stewart, 1996-97 |

**HONOURS**
LEAGUE CHAMPIONS: Third Division – 1996-97.

## LEAGUE RESULTS 2001-2002

Clyde 1 Inverness CT 1
Inverness CT 1 Falkirk 2
Partick 1 Inverness CT 0
St Mirren 1 Inverness CT 1
Inverness CT 5 Arbroath 1
Ross Co 2 Inverness CT 1
Inverness CT 5 Raith 2
Airdrie 6 Inverness CT 0
Inverness CT 3 Ayr 1

Inverness CT 5 Clyde 1
Falkirk 1 Inverness CT 2
Arbroath 3 Inverness CT 2
Inverness CT 1 St Mirren 2
Raith 1 Inverness CT 5
Inverness CT 3 Ross Co 0
Ayr 3 Inverness CT 0
Inverness CT 1 Airdrie 2
Inverness CT 1 Partick 2

Clyde 1 Inverness CT 0
Inverness CT 3 Arbroath 2
St Mirren 0 Inverness CT 0
Ross Co 0 Inverness CT 0
Inverness CT 5 Raith 0
Airdrie 3 Inverness CT 0
Inverness CT 1 Ayr 1
Partick 4 Inverness CT 1
Inverness CT 3 Falkirk 2

Inverness CT 4 St Mirren 2
Arbroath 1 Inverness CT 0
Raith 0 Inverness CT 0
Inverness CT 1 Ross Co 1
Inverness CT 1 Airdrie 0
Ayr 1 Inverness CT 0
Inverness CT 1 Clyde 1
Falkirk 0 Inverness CT 0
Inverness CT 3 Partick 0

# KILMARNOCK

| | |
|---|---|
| *NICKNAME:* | Killie |
| *COLOURS:* | Blue and white |
| *GROUND:* | Rugby Park |
| *TELEPHONE No:* | 01563 545300 |
| *FAX No:* | 01563 522181 |
| *WEBSITE:* | kilmarnockfc.co.uk |
| *CAPACITY:* | 18,128 |
| *RECORD ATT:* | 35,995 (v Rangers, 1962) |
| *RECORD VICTORY:* | 11-1 (v Paisley Academical, 1930) |
| *RECORD DEFEAT:* | 1-9 (v Celtic, 1938) |
| *MANAGER:* | Jim Jefferies |
| *CHAIRMAN:* | Sir John Orr |
| *MOST LEAGUE* | |
| *GOALS (1 SEASON):* | 34, Harry Cunningham, 1927-28 |
| *GOALS (OVERALL):* | 148, W Culley, 1912-23 |

## HONOURS

LEAGUE CHAMPIONS: Division I – 1964-65. Division II (2) – 1897-98, 1898-99. SCOTTISH CUP (3): 1920, 1929, 1997.

## LEAGUE RESULTS 2001-2002

| | |
|---|---|
| Hibernian 2 Kilmarnock 2 | Kilmarnock 0 Dunfermline 0 |
| Kilmarnock 0 Celtic 1 | Livingston 0 Kilmarnock 1 |
| Motherwell 2 Kilmarnock 2 | Kilmarnock 2 Rangers 2 |
| Kilmarnock 2 St Johnstone 1 | Kilmarnock 0 Celtic 2 |
| Dundee Utd 0 Kilmarnock 2 | Hibernian 2 Kilmarnock 2 |
| Aberdeen 2 Kilmarnock 0 | Motherwell 2 Kilmarnock 0 |
| Kilmarnock 1 Hearts 0 | Kilmarnock 0 St Johnstone 1 |
| Kilmarnock 0 Dundee 1 | Dundee Utd 0 Kilmarnock 2 |
| Dunfermline 0 Kilmarnock 2 | Aberdeen 1 Kilmarnock 1 |
| Rangers 3 Kilmarnock 1 | Kilmarnock 3 Hearts 3 |
| Kilmarnock 1 Livingston 5 | Kilmarnock 3 Dundee 2 |
| Celtic 1 Kilmarnock 0 | Dunfermline 2 Kilmarnock 0 |
| Kilmarnock 0 Hibernian 0 | Kilmarnock 1 Livingston 1 |
| Kilmarnock 2 Motherwell 0 | Rangers 5 Kilmarnock 0 |
| St Johnstone 1 Kilmarnock 0 | Dundee 2 Kilmarnock 0 |
| Kilmarnock 2 Dundee Utd 0 | Kilmarnock 1 Hibernian 0 |
| Kilmarnock 3 Aberdeen 1 | St Johnstone 3 Kilmarnock 3 |
| Hearts 2 Kilmarnock 0 | Kilmarnock 1 Motherwell 4 |
| Dundee 1 Kilmarnock 2 | Kilmarnock 2 Dundee Utd 2 |

# LIVINGSTON

| | |
|---|---|
| **NICKNAME:** | Livi Lions |
| **COLOURS:** | Black and gold |
| **GROUND:** | Almondvale Stadium |
| **TELEPHONE No:** | 01506 417000 |
| **FAX No:** | 01506 418888 |
| **WEBSITE:** | livingstonfc.co.uk |
| **CAPACITY:** | 10,006 |
| **RECORD ATT:** | 10,112 |
| | (v Rangers, 2001) |
| **RECORD VICTORY:** | 6-0 (v Raith Rovers, 1985) |
| **RECORD DEFEAT:** | 0-8 (v Hamilton Accies, 1974) |
| **COACH:** | David Hay |
| **MANAGER/DIRECTOR:** | Jim Leishman |
| **CHAIRMAN:** | Dominic Keane |
| **MOST LEAGUE** | |
| **GOALS (1 SEASON):** | 21, John McGachie, 1986-87 |

## HONOURS

**LEAGUE CHAMPIONS:** Third Division – 1995-96. Second Division (2) – 1986-87, 1998-99. First Division – 2000-01.

## LEAGUE RESULTS 2001-2002

Livingston 2 Hearts 1
Rangers 0 Livingston 0
Dundee 1 Livingston 0
Livingston 0 Celtic 0
Motherwell 0 Livingston 0
Livingston 2 Dundee Utd 0
St Johnstone 2 Livingston 1
Dunfermline 1 Livingston 2
Livingston 1 Hibernian 0
Livingston 2 Aberdeen 2
Kilmarnock 1 Livingston 5
Livingston 0 Rangers 2
Hearts 1 Livingston 3
Livingston 1 Dundee 0
Hibernian 0 Livingston 3
Livingston 3 Motherwell 1
Dundee Utd 0 Livingston 0
Livingston 2 St Johnstone 1
Livingston 0 Dunfermline 0
Celtic 3 Livingston 2

Livingston 0 Kilmarnock 1
Aberdeen 0 Livingston 3
Rangers 3 Livingston 0
Livingston 2 Hearts 0
Dundee 2 Livingston 0
Livingston 1 Celtic 3
Motherwell 1 Livingston 2
Livingston 1 Dundee Utd 1
St Johnstone 3 Livingston 0
Dunfermline 1 Livingston 0
Livingston 0 Hibernian 3
Kilmarnock 1 Livingston 1
Livingston 0 Aberdeen 0
Celtic 5 Livingston 1
Livingston 2 Rangers 1
Aberdeen 3 Livingston 0
Livingston 4 Dunfermline 1
Hearts 2 Livingston 3

# MONTROSE

| | |
|---|---|
| *NICKNAME:* | The Gable Endies |
| *COLOURS:* | Blue and white |
| *GROUND:* | Links Park |
| *TELEPHONE No:* | 01674 673200 |
| *FAX No:* | 01674 677311 |
| *WEBSITE:* | montrosefc.co.uk |
| *CAPACITY:* | 4,338 |
| *RECORD ATT:* | 8,983 (v Dundee, 1973) |
| *RECORD VICTORY:* | 12-0 (v Vale of Leithen, 1975) |
| *RECORD DEFEAT:* | 0-13 (v Aberdeen, 1951) |
| *MANAGER:* | John Sheran |
| *CHAIRMAN:* | John Paton |
| *MOST LEAGUE GOALS (1 SEASON)* | 28, Brian Third, 1972-73 |

## HONOURS

LEAGUE CHAMPIONSHIP: Second Division – 1984-85

## LEAGUE RESULTS 2001-2002

Montrose 3 Queen's Park 1
East Stirling 0 Montrose 1
Montrose 0 Peterhead 3
Dumbarton 0 Montrose 1
Montrose 0 Brechin 1
Montrose 4 Stirling 0
East Fife 1 Montrose 2
Montrose 1 Albion 2
Elgin 1 Montrose 2

Queen's Park 2 Montrose 2
Montrose 2 East Stirling 0
Brechin 0 Montrose 0
Montrose 1 Dumbarton 3
Stirling 1 Montrose 1
Montrose 2 East Fife 1
Albion 0 Montrose 0
Montrose 0 Elgin 2
Peterhead 4 Montrose 0

Montrose 3 Queen's Park 1
Montrose 0 Brechin 0
Dumbarton 0 Montrose 5
East Fife 2 Montrose 0
Montrose 1 Stirling 3
Elgin 1 Montrose 0
Montrose 2 Albion 0
East Stirling 2 Montrose 1
Montrose 2 Peterhead 1

Montrose 1 Dumbarton 1
Brechin 2 Montrose 0
Stirling 0 Montrose 1
Montrose 0 East Fife 1
Albion 0 Montrose 0
Montrose 1 Elgin 0
Queen's Park 0 Montrose 1
Montrose 2 East Stirling 0
Peterhead 3 Montrose 1

# MORTON

| | |
|---|---|
| *NICKNAME:* | The Ton |
| *COLOURS:* | Blue and white |
| *GROUND:* | Cappielow Park |
| *TELEPHONE No:* | 01475 723571 |
| *FAX No:* | 01475 781084 |
| *CAPACITY:* | 8,100 |
| *RECORD ATT:* | 23,500 (v Celtic, 1922) |
| *RECORD VICTORY:* | 11-0 (v Carfin Shamrock, 1886) |
| *RECORD DEFEAT:* | 1-10 (v Port Glasgow Athletic, 1894; v St Bernard's, 1933) |
| *MANAGER:* | Dave McPherson |
| *CHAIRMAN:* | Douglas Rae |
| *MOST LEAGUE GOALS (1 SEASON):* | 58, Allan McGraw, 1963-64 |

## HONOURS

LEAGUE CHAMPIONS: First Division (3) – 1977-78, 1983-84, 1986-87. Division II (3) – 1949-50, 1963-64, 1966-67. Second Division – 1994-95. SCOTTISH CUP: 1922.

## LEAGUE RESULTS 2001-2002

| | |
|---|---|
| Morton 4 Stenhousemuir 1 | Morton 0 Stenhousemuir 1 |
| Alloa 1 Morton 1 | Clydebank 1 Morton 2 |
| Morton 2 QoS 2 | Morton 2 Stranraer 2 |
| Morton 1 Stranraer 1 | Berwick 0 Morton 0 |
| Clydebank 3 Morton 2 | Morton 1 Forfar 4 |
| Morton 1 Forfar 3 | Hamilton 2 Morton 1 |
| Berwick 2 Morton 0 | Morton 0 Cowdenbeath 0 |
| Morton 0 Cowdenbeath 2 | Alloa 4 Morton 0 |
| Hamilton 2 Morton 2 | Morton 0 QoS 3 |
| | |
| Stenhousemuir 0 Morton 3 | Stranraer 0 Morton 0 |
| Morton 1 Alloa 1 | Morton 3 Clydebank 1 |
| Morton 0 Clydebank 2 | Forfar 2 Morton 1 |
| Stranraer 1 Morton 4 | Morton 3 Berwick 0 |
| Forfar 2 Morton 1 | Cowdenbeath 2 Morton 2 |
| Morton 1 Berwick 2 | Morton 0 Hamilton 0 |
| Cowdenbeath 1 Morton 1 | Stenhousemuir 2 Morton 3 |
| Morton 1 Hamilton 1 | Morton 0 Alloa 0 |
| QoS 6 Morton 5 | QoS 4 Morton 0 |

# MOTHERWELL

| | |
|---|---|
| **NICKNAME:** | The Well |
| **COLOURS:** | Claret and amber |
| **GROUND:** | Fir Park |
| **TELEPHONE No:** | 01698 333333 |
| **FAX No:** | 01698 338001 |
| **WEBSITE:** | motherwellfc.co.uk |
| **CAPACITY:** | 13,742 |
| **RECORD ATT:** | 35,632 (v Rangers, 1952) |
| **RECORD VICTORY:** | 12-1 (v Dundee United, 1954) |
| **RECORD DEFEAT:** | 0-8 (v Aberdeen, 1979) |
| **MANAGER:** | Terry Butcher |
| **CHAIRMAN:** | Vacant |
| **MOST LEAGUE GOALS (1 SEASON):** | 52, William McFadyen, 1931-32 |
| **GOALS (OVERALL):** | 283, Hugh Ferguson, 1916-25 |

### HONOURS

LEAGUE CHAMPIONSHIP: Division I – 1931-32. Division II (2) – 1953-54, 1968-69. First Division (2) – 1981-82, 1984-85. SCOTTISH CUP: (2) 1952, 1991. LEAGUE CUP: 1950-51.

### LEAGUE RESULTS 2001-2002

| | |
|---|---|
| Dunfermline 5 Motherwell 2 | Motherwell 1 St Johnstone 2 |
| Motherwell 0 Dundee Utd 0 | Motherwell 4 Dundee 2 |
| Motherwell 2 Kilmarnock 2 | Celtic 2 Motherwell 0 |
| Aberdeen 4 Motherwell 2 | Motherwell 2 Dundee Utd 0 |
| Motherwell 0 Livingston 0 | Dunfermline 3 Motherwell 1 |
| Motherwell 1 Hibernian 3 | Motherwell 2 Kilmarnock 0 |
| Rangers 3 Motherwell 0 | Aberdeen 1 Motherwell 0 |
| Motherwell 2 Hearts 0 | Motherwell 1 Livingston 2 |
| St Johnstone 2 Motherwell 3 | Motherwell 4 Hibernian 0 |
| Motherwell 1 Celtic 2 | Rangers 3 Motherwell 0 |
| Dundee 3 Motherwell 1 | Motherwell 1 Hearts 2 |
| Dundee Utd 1 Motherwell 1 | St Johnstone 0 Motherwell 2 |
| Motherwell 1 Dunfermline 0 | Dundee 2 Motherwell 0 |
| Kilmarnock 2 Motherwell 0 | Motherwell 0 Celtic 4 |
| Motherwell 3 Aberdeen 2 | Motherwell 1 St Johnstone 1 |
| Livingston 3 Motherwell 1 | Dundee Utd 1 Motherwell 0 |
| Hibernian 1 Motherwell 1 | Hibernian 4 Motherwell 0 |
| Motherwell 2 Rangers 2 | Kilmarnock 1 Motherwell 4 |
| Hearts 3 Motherwell 1 | Motherwell 2 Dundee 1 |

# PARTICK THISTLE

| | |
|---|---|
| **NICKNAME:** | The Jags |
| **COLOURS:** | Red and yellow |
| **GROUND:** | Firhill Park |
| **TELEPHONE No:** | 0141 579 1971 |
| **FAX No:** | 0141 945 1525 |
| **WEBSITE:** | ptfc.co.uk |
| **CAPACITY:** | 13,300 |
| **RECORD ATT:** | 49,838 |
| | (v Rangers, 1922) |
| **RECORD VICTORY:** | 16-0 (v Royal Albert, 1931) |
| **RECORD DEFEAT:** | 0-10 (v Queen's Park, 1881) |
| **MANAGER:** | John Lambie |
| **CHAIRMAN:** | T Brown McMaster |
| **MOST LEAGUE** | |
| **GOALS (1 SEASON):** | 41, Alex Hair, 1926-27 |

## HONOURS

LEAGUE CHAMPIONS: Division II (3) – 1896-97, 1899-1900, 1970-71. First Division (2) – 1975-76, 2001-2002. Second Division – 2000-01. SCOTTISH CUP: 1921. LEAGUE CUP: 1971-72.

## LEAGUE RESULTS 2001-2002

| | |
|---|---|
| Partick 3 St Mirren 3 | Partick 1 St Mirren 0 |
| Raith 1 Partick 2 | Partick 2 Ayr 1 |
| Partick 1 Inverness CT 0 | Arbroath 1 Partick 0 |
| Arbroath 1 Partick 3 | Partick 2 Clyde 1 |
| Partick 2 Ayr 1 | Falkirk 1 Partick 4 |
| Partick 3 Clyde 0 | Ross Co 0 Partick 1 |
| Falkirk 1 Partick 1 | Partick 1 Airdrie 1 |
| Ross Co 3 Partick 2 | Partick 4 Inverness CT 1 |
| Partick 1 Airdrie 1 | Raith 2 Partick 0 |
| | |
| St Mirren 1 Partick 1 | Partick 2 Arbroath 2 |
| Partick 2 Raith 1 | Ayr 1 Partick 1 |
| Ayr 0 Partick 2 | Partick 3 Falkirk 0 |
| Partick 4 Arbroath 1 | Clyde 2 Partick 1 |
| Partick 5 Falkirk 1 | Partick 1 Ross Co 1 |
| Clyde 3 Partick 1 | Airdrie 1 Partick 1 |
| Airdrie 1 Partick 0 | St Mirren 2 Partick 2 |
| Partick 0 Ross Co 0 | Partick 1 Raith 0 |
| Inverness CT 1 Partick 2 | Inverness CT 3 Partick 0 |

# PETERHEAD

| | |
|---|---|
| **NICKNAME:** | The Blue Toon |
| **COLOURS:** | Blue and white |
| **GROUND:** | Balmore Stadium |
| **TELEPHONE:** | 01779 478256 |
| **FAX:** | 01779 490682 |
| **WEBSITE:** | peterheadfc.co.uk |
| **CAPACITY:** | 2,500 |
| **RECORD ATT:** | 1,500 (v Fraserburgh, 1999) |
| **RECORD VICTORY:** | 17-1 (v Fort William, 1998) |
| **MANAGER:** | Ian Wilson |
| **CHAIRMAN:** | Roger Taylor |
| **MOST LEAGUE GOALS (1 SEASON):** | 12, Craig Yates, 2000-01 |

## LEAGUE RESULTS 2001-2002

Stirling 2 Peterhead 1
Peterhead 0 Dumbarton 3
Montrose 0 Peterhead 3
East Fife 0 Peterhead 1
Peterhead 1 Elgin 1
East Stirling 2 Peterhead 3
Peterhead 2 Queen's Park 1
Peterhead 4 Brechin 2
Albion 1 Peterhead 0

Peterhead 3 Stirling 3
Dumbarton 0 Peterhead 3
Elgin 4 Peterhead 1
Peterhead 1 East Fife 3
Peterhead 3 East Stirling 2
Queen's Park 0 Peterhead 1
Brechin 4 Peterhead 3
Peterhead 0 Albion 0
Peterhead 4 Montrose 0

Stirling 0 Peterhead 2
Peterhead 1 Elgin 0
East Fife 2 Peterhead 3
Peterhead 1 Queen's Park 2
East Stirling 1 Peterhead 0
Albion 2 Peterhead 1
Peterhead 1 Brechin 3
Peterhead 4 Dumbarton 0
Montrose 2 Peterhead 1

Peterhead 1 East Fife 1
Elgin 0 Peterhead 3
Peterhead 2 East Stirling 1
Queen's Park 2 Peterhead 0
Brechin 1 Peterhead 1
Peterhead 0 Albion 2
Peterhead 5 Stirling 1
Dumbarton 3 Peterhead 0
Peterhead 3 Montrose 1

# QUEEN OF THE SOUTH

| | |
|---|---|
| **NICKNAME:** | The Doonhamers |
| **COLOURS:** | Royal blue |
| **GROUND:** | Palmerston Park |
| **TELEPHONE No:** | 01387 254853 |
| **FAX No:** | 01387 254853 |
| **WEBSITE:** | qosfc.co.uk |
| **CAPACITY:** | 6,412 |
| **RECORD ATT:** | 24,500 (v Hearts, 1952) |
| **RECORD VICTORY:** | 11-1 (v Stranraer, 1932) |
| **RECORD DEFEAT:** | 2-10 (v Dundee, 1962) |
| **MANAGER:** | John Connolly |
| **CHAIRMAN:** | Ronald Bradford |
| **MOST LEAGUE GOALS (1 SEASON):** | 41, Jimmy Rutherford, 1931-32 |

## HONOURS

LEAGUE CHAMPIONS: Division II – 1950-51. Second Division – 2001-02.

## LEAGUE RESULTS 2001-2002

| | |
|---|---|
| Hamilton 1 QoS 1 | Hamilton 3 QoS 1 |
| QoS 1 Forfar 2 | Stranraer 1 QoS 2 |
| Morton 2 QoS 2 | QoS 1 Clydebank 0 |
| QoS 1 Clydebank 0 | QoS 1 Stenhousemuir 0 |
| Stranraer 2 QoS 2 | Cowdenbeath 1 QoS 2 |
| Cowdenbeath 1 QoS 1 | QoS 0 Alloa 1 |
| QoS 2 Stenhousemuir 0 | Berwick 1 QoS 0 |
| Berwick 0 QoS 4 | QoS 3 Forfar 1 |
| QoS 2 Alloa 1 | Morton 0 QoS 3 |
| | |
| QoS 0 Hamilton 1 | Clydebank 0 QoS 1 |
| Forfar 0 QoS 3 | QoS 3 Stranraer 1 |
| QoS 1 Stranraer 0 | QoS 2 Cowdenbeath 1 |
| Clydebank 3 QoS 0 | Stenhousemuir 1 QoS 4 |
| QoS 1 Cowdenbeath 3 | QoS 0 Berwick 0 |
| Stenhousemuir 1 QoS 1 | Alloa 4 QoS 1 |
| QoS 2 Berwick 2 | QoS 3 Hamilton 1 |
| Alloa 2 QoS 0 | Forfar 0 QoS 3 |
| QoS 6 Morton 5 | QoS 4 Morton 0 |

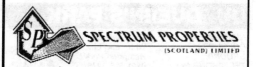

# QUEEN'S PARK

| | |
|---|---|
| *NICKNAME:* | The Spiders |
| *COLOURS:* | White and black |
| *GROUND:* | Hampden Park |
| *TELEPHONE No:* | 0141 632 1275 |
| *FAX No:* | 0141 636 1612 |
| *WEBSITE:* | queensparkfc.co.uk |
| *CAPACITY:* | 52,046 |
| *RECORD ATT:* | 95,772 |
| | (v Rangers, 1930). |
| | 149,547 (for ground |
| | Scotland v England, 1937) |
| *RECORD VICTORY:* | 16-0 (v St Peter's, 1885) |
| *RECORD DEFEAT:* | 0-9 (v Motherwell, 1930) |
| *MANAGER:* | John McCormack |
| *PRESIDENT:* | Kenny Harvey |
| *MOST LEAGUE* | |
| *GOALS (1 SEASON):* | 30, William Martin, 1937-38 |

## HONOURS

LEAGUE CHAMPIONSHIP: Division II – 1922-23. B Division – 1955-56. Second Division – 1980-81. Third Division – 1999-00.
SCOTTISH CUP (10): 1874, 1875, 1876, 1880, 1881, 1882, 1884, 1886, 1890, 1893.

## LEAGUE RESULTS 2001-2002

| | |
|---|---|
| Montrose 3 Queen's Park 1 | Montrose 3 Queen's Park 1 |
| Queen's Park 0 Elgin 0 | Albion 2 Queen's Park 0 |
| Dumbarton 2 Queen's Park 1 | Queen's Park 1 East Stirling 0 |
| Queen's Park 2 East Stirling 3 | Peterhead 1 Queen's Park 2 |
| Albion 2 Queen's Park 1 | Queen's Park 0 Brechin 0 |
| Queen's Park 1 Brechin 3 | Stirling 3 Queen's Park 2 |
| Peterhead 2 Queen's Park 1 | Queen's Park 2 East Fife 0 |
| Queen's Park 1 East Fife 2 | Queen's Park 3 Elgin 0 |
| Stirling 0 Queen's Park 0 | Dumbarton 1 Queen's Park 1 |
| | |
| Queen's Park 2 Montrose 2 | East Stirling 3 Queen's Park 1 |
| Elgin 2 Queen's Park 0 | Queen's Park 0 Albion 3 |
| Queen's Park 1 Albion 2 | Brechin 5 Queen's Park 0 |
| East Stirling 0 Queen's Park 1 | Queen's Park 2 Peterhead 0 |
| Brechin 2 Queen's Park 1 | East Fife 0 Queen's Park 3 |
| Queen's Park 0 Peterhead 1 | Queen's Park 0 Stirling 0 |
| East Fife 1 Queen's Park 4 | Queen's Park 0 Montrose 1 |
| Queen's Park 2 Stirling 2 | Elgin 0 Queen's Park 1 |
| Queen's Park 0 Dumbarton 0 | Queen's Park 0 Dumbarton 2 |

# RAITH ROVERS

| | |
|---|---|
| *NICKNAME:* | The Rovers |
| *COLOURS:* | Navy blue and white |
| *GROUND:* | Stark's Park |
| *TELEPHONE No:* | 01592 263514 |
| *FAX No:* | 01592 642833 |
| *CAPACITY:* | 10,104 |
| *RECORD ATT:* | 31,306 (v Hearts, 1953) |
| *RECORD VICTORY:* | 10-1 (v Coldstream, 1954) |
| *RECORD DEFEAT:* | 2-11 (v Morton, 1936) |
| *MANAGER:* | Vacant |
| *CHAIRMAN:* | William Gray |
| *MOST LEAGUE* | |
| *GOALS (1 SEASON):* | 38, Norman Haywood, 1937-38 |

## HONOURS

**LEAGUE CHAMPIONS:** First Division (2) – 1992-93, 1994-95.
Division II (4) – 1907-08, 1909-10 (shared), 1937-38, 1948-49.
**LEAGUE CUP** – 1994-95.

## LEAGUE RESULTS 2001-2002

| | |
|---|---|
| Airdrie 2 Raith 2 | Airdrie 1 Raith 1 |
| Raith 1 Partick 2 | Raith 5 Falkirk 1 |
| Ross Co 1 Raith 0 | Ayr 3 Raith 1 |
| Ayr 1 Raith 1 | Raith 0 Arbroath 0 |
| Raith 5 Falkirk 2 | Inverness CT 5 Raith 0 |
| Raith 3 Arbroath 1 | Raith 1 St Mirren 0 |
| Inverness CT 5 Raith 2 | Clyde 1 Raith 2 |
| Raith 3 St Mirren 0 | Ross Co 4 Raith 2 |
| Clyde 3 Raith 2 | Raith 2 Partick 0 |
| | |
| Raith 2 Airdrie 2 | Raith 3 Ayr 3 |
| Partick 2 Raith 1 | Falkirk 2 Raith 1 |
| Falkirk 1 Raith 0 | Raith 0 Inverness CT 0 |
| Raith 1 Ayr 1 | Arbroath 2 Raith 2 |
| Raith 1 Inverness CT 5 | St Mirren 1 Raith 0 |
| Arbroath 1 Raith 1 | Raith 0 Clyde 1 |
| Raith 1 Clyde 2 | Raith 2 Airdrie 1 |
| St Mirren 1 Raith 1 | Partick 1 Raith 0 |
| Raith 1 Ross Co 3 | Raith 0 Ross Co 1 |

# RANGERS

| | |
|---|---|
| *NICKNAME:* | The Gers |
| *COLOURS:* | Blue, red and white |
| *GROUND:* | Ibrox Stadium |
| *TELEPHONE No:* | 0141 580 8500 |
| *FAX No:* | 0141 580 8580 |
| *WEBSITE:* | rangers.co.uk |
| *CAPACITY:* | 50,467 |
| *RECORD ATT:* | 118,567 (v Celtic, 1939) |
| *RECORD VICTORY:* | 14-2 (v Blairgowrie, 1934) |
| *RECORD DEFEAT:* | 2-10 (v Airdrie, 1886) |
| *MANAGER:* | Alex McLeish |
| *CHAIRMAN:* | David Murray |
| *MOST LEAGUE GOALS (1 SEASON):* | 44, Sam English, 1931-32 |
| *GOALS (OVERALL):* | 250, Ally McCoist |

## HONOURS

**LEAGUE CHAMPIONSHIP (49):** 1890-91 (shared), 1898-99, 1899-1900, 1900-01, 1901-02, 1910-11, 1911-12, 1912-13, 1917-18, 1919-20, 1920-21, 1922-23, 1923-24, 1924-25, 1926-27, 1927-28, 1928-29, 1929-30, 1930-31, 1932-33, 1933-34, 1934-35, 1936-37, 1938-39, 1946-47, 1948-49, 1949-50, 1952-53, 1955-56, 1956-57, 1958-59, 1960-61, 1962-63, 1963-64, 1974-75, 1975-76, 1977-78, 1986-87, 1988-89, 1989-90, 1990-91, 1991-92, 1992-93, 1993-94, 1994-95, 1995-96, 1996-97, 1998-99, 1999-00.

**SCOTTISH CUP (30):** 1894, 1897, 1898, 1903, 1928, 1930, 1932, 1934, 1935, 1936, 1948, 1949, 1950, 1953, 1960, 1962, 1963, 1964, 1966, 1973, 1976, 1978, 1979, 1981, 1992, 1993, 1996, 1999, 2000, 2002.

**LEAGUE CUP (22):** 1946-47, 1948-49, 1960-61, 1961-62, 1963-64, 1964-65, 1970-71, 1975-76, 1977-78, 1978-79, 1981-82, 1983-84, 1984-85, 1986-87, 1987-88, 1988-89, 1990-91, 1992-93, 1993-94, 1996-97, 1998-99, 2001-02.

**EUROPEAN CUP-WINNERS' CUP:** 1971-72.

**STEPHEN HUGHES**     **LORENZO AMORUSO**

## LEAGUE RESULTS 2001-2002

| | |
|---|---|
| Aberdeen 0 Rangers 3 | Hibernian 0 Rangers 3 |
| Rangers 0 Livingston 0 | Rangers 1 St Johnstone 0 |
| Dunfermline 1 Rangers 4 | Kilmarnock 2 Rangers 2 |
| Rangers 2 Hibernian 2 | Rangers 3 Livingston 0 |
| Rangers 2 Dundee 0 | Aberdeen 0 Rangers 1 |
| Hearts 2 Rangers 2 | Dunfermline 2 Rangers 4 |
| Rangers 3 Motherwell 0 | Rangers 1 Hibernian 1 |
| Dundee Utd 1 Rangers 6 | Rangers 2 Dundee 1 |
| Rangers 0 Celtic 2 | Hearts 0 Rangers 2 |
| Rangers 3 Kilmarnock 1 | Rangers 3 Motherwell 0 |
| St Johnstone 0 Rangers 2 | Dundee Utd 0 Rangers 1 |
| Livingston 0 Rangers 2 | Rangers 1 Celtic 1 |
| Rangers 2 Aberdeen 0 | St Johnstone 0 Rangers 2 |
| Rangers 4 Dunfermline 0 | Rangers 5 Kilmarnock 0 |
| Celtic 2 Rangers 1 | Rangers 2 Hearts 0 |
| Dundee 0 Rangers 0 | Livingston 2 Rangers 1 |
| Rangers 3 Hearts 1 | Celtic 1 Rangers 1 |
| Motherwell 2 Rangers 2 | Rangers 2 Aberdeen 0 |
| Rangers 3 Dundee Utd 2 | Dunfermline 1 Rangers 1 |

# ROSS COUNTY

| | |
|---|---|
| *NICKNAME:* | The County |
| *COLOURS:* | Dark blue, white and red |
| *GROUND:* | Victoria Park |
| *TELEPHONE No:* | 01349 860860 |
| *FAX No:* | 01349 866277 |
| *WEBSITE:* | rosscountyfootball club.co.uk |
| *CAPACITY:* | 6,700 |
| *RECORD ATT:* | 8,000 (v Rangers, 1966) |
| *RECORD VICTORY:* | 11-0 (v St Cuthbert's Wanderers, 1993) |
| *RECORD DEFEAT:* | 1-10 (v Inverness Thistle) |
| *MANAGER:* | Neale Cooper |
| *CHAIRMAN:* | Roy McGregor |
| *MOST LEAGUE GOALS (1 SEASON):* | 22, Derek Adams, 1997-98 |

## LEAGUE RESULTS 2001-2002

| | |
|---|---|
| Ross Co 0 Arbroath 2 | Ross Co 0 Arbroath 1 |
| Ayr 2 Ross Co 0 | Clyde 0 Ross Co 0 |
| Ross Co 1 Raith 0 | Ross Co 4 Airdrie 1 |
| Ross Co 0 Airdrie 1 | Ross Co 0 Inverness CT 0 |
| Clyde 3 Ross Co 0 | St Mirren 1 Ross Co 1 |
| Ross Co 2 Inverness CT 1 | Ross Co 0 Partick 1 |
| St Mirren 1 Ross Co 0 | Falkirk 1 Ross Co 4 |
| Ross Co 3 Partick 2 | Ross Co 4 Raith 2 |
| Falkirk 4 Ross Co 2 | Ayr 0 Ross Co 0 |
| | |
| Arbroath 2 Ross Co 1 | Airdrie 0 Ross Co 2 |
| Ross Co 3 Ayr 2 | Ross Co 2 Clyde 1 |
| Ross Co 4 Clyde 0 | Ross Co 4 St Mirren 1 |
| Airdrie 1 Ross Co 1 | Inverness CT 1 Ross Co 1 |
| Ross Co 0 St Mirren 1 | Partick 1 Ross Co 1 |
| Inverness CT 3 Ross Co 0 | Ross Co 4 Falkirk 2 |
| Ross Co 1 Falkirk 2 | Arbroath 1 Ross Co 1 |
| Partick 0 Ross Co 0 | Ross Co 1 Ayr 1 |
| Raith 1 Ross Co 3 | Raith 0 Ross Co 1 |

# ST JOHNSTONE

| | |
|---|---|
| **NICKNAME:** | The Saints |
| **COLOURS:** | Blue and white |
| **GROUND:** | McDiarmid Park |
| **TELEPHONE No:** | 01738 459090 |
| **FAX No:** | 01738 625771 |
| **WEBSITE:** | stjohnstonefc.co.uk |
| **CAPACITY:** | 10,673 |
| **RECORD ATT:** | 10,504 |
| | (v Rangers, 1990) |
| **RECORD VICTORY:** | 9-0 (v Albion Rovers, 1946) |
| **RECORD DEFEAT:** | 1-10 (v Third Lanark, 1903) |
| **MANAGER:** | Billy Stark |
| **CHAIRMAN:** | Geoffrey S Brown |
| **MOST LEAGUE** | |
| **GOALS (1 SEASON):** | 36, Jimmy Benson, 1931-32 |
| **GOALS (OVERALL):** | 140, John Brogan, 1977-83 |

## HONOURS

LEAGUE CHAMPIONSHIP: First Division (3) – 1982-83, 1989-90, 1996-97. Division II (3) – 1923-24, 1959-60, 1962-63.

## LEAGUE RESULTS 2001-2002

| | |
|---|---|
| Celtic 3 St Johnstone 0 | Motherwell 1 St Johnstone 2 |
| St Johnstone 0 Dunfermline 2 | Rangers 1 St Johnstone 0 |
| St Johnstone 0 Dundee Utd 1 | St Johnstone 0 Hearts 2 |
| Kilmarnock 2 St Johnstone 1 | St Johnstone 0 Dunfermline 1 |
| St Johnstone 1 Aberdeen 1 | Celtic 2 St Johnstone 1 |
| Dundee 1 St Johnstone 1 | St Johnstone 1 Dundee Utd 4 |
| St Johnstone 2 Livingston 2 | Kilmarnock 0 St Johnstone 1 |
| Hibernian 4 St Johnstone 0 | St Johnstone 0 Aberdeen 1 |
| St Johnstone 2 Motherwell 3 | Dundee 1 St Johnstone 0 |
| Hearts 3 St Johnstone 0 | St Johnstone 3 Livingston 0 |
| St Johnstone 0 Rangers 2 | Hibernian 3 St Johnstone 0 |
| Dunfermline 2 St Johnstone 1 | St Johnstone 0 Motherwell 2 |
| St Johnstone 1 Celtic 2 | St Johnstone 0 Rangers 2 |
| Dundee Utd 2 St Johnstone 1 | Hearts 1 St Johnstone 3 |
| St Johnstone 1 Kilmarnock 0 | Motherwell 1 St Johnstone 3 |
| Aberdeen v St Johnstone | St Johnstone 0 Dundee 1 |
| St Johnstone 0 Dundee 2 | St Johnstone 0 Kilmarnock 3 |
| Livingston 2 St Johnstone 1 | Dundee Utd 0 St Johnstone 0 |
| St Johnstone 0 Hibernian 0 | St Johnstone 0 Hibernian 1 |

# ST MIRREN

| | |
|---|---|
| **NICKNAME:** | The Buddies |
| **COLOURS:** | Black and white |
| **GROUND:** | St Mirren Park |
| **TELEPHONE No:** | 0141 889 2558 |
| **FAX No:** | 0141 848 6444 |
| **WEBSITE:** | saintmirren.net |
| **CAPACITY:** | 10,800 |
| **RECORD ATT:** | 47,438 (v Celtic, 1925) |
| **RECORD VICTORY:** | 15-0 (v Glasgow University, 1960) |
| **RECORD DEFEAT** | 0-9 (v Rangers, 1897) |
| **MANAGER:** | Tom Hendrie |
| **CHAIRMAN:** | Stewart Gilmour |
| **MOST LEAGUE** | |
| **GOALS (1 SEASON):** | 45, Dunky Walker, 1921-22 |
| **GOALS (OVERALL):** | 221, David McCrae |

## HONOURS

LEAGUE CHAMPIONS: First Division (2) – 1976-77, 1999-00.
Division II – 1967-68. SCOTTISH CUP (3): 1926, 1959, 1987.

## LEAGUE RESULTS 2001-2002

| | |
|---|---|
| Partick 3 St Mirren 3 | Partick 1 St Mirren 0 |
| St Mirren 4 Clyde 1 | Airdrie 2 St Mirren 3 |
| Falkirk 3 St Mirren 2 | St Mirren 0 Inverness CT 0 |
| St Mirren 1 Inverness CT 1 | Ayr 4 St Mirren 0 |
| Airdrie 0 St Mirren 0 | St Mirren 1 Ross Co 1 |
| Ayr 4 St Mirren 2 | Raith 1 St Mirren 0 |
| St Mirren 1 Ross Co 0 | St Mirren 2 Arbroath 3 |
| Raith 3 St Mirren 0 | Falkirk 0 St Mirren 0 |
| St Mirren 1 Arbroath 0 | St Mirren 2 Clyde 2 |
| | |
| St Mirren 1 Partick 1 | Inverness CT 4 St Mirren 2 |
| Clyde 1 St Mirren 1 | St Mirren 2 Airdrie 1 |
| St Mirren 0 Airdrie 0 | Ross Co 4 St Mirren 1 |
| Inverness CT 1 St Mirren 2 | St Mirren 1 Ayr 1 |
| Ross Co 0 St Mirren 1 | St Mirren 1 Raith 0 |
| Arbroath 0 St Mirren 2 | Arbroath 0 St Mirren 3 |
| St Mirren 1 Raith 1 | St Mirren 0 Partick 2 |
| St Mirren 1 Falkirk 5 | Clyde 3 St Mirren 1 |
| | St Mirren 0 Falkirk 0 |

# STENHOUSEMUIR

| | |
|---|---|
| *NICKNAME:* | The Warriors |
| *COLOURS:* | Maroon and white |
| *GROUND:* | Ochilview Park |
| *TELEPHONE No:* | 01324 562992 |
| *FAX No:* | 01324 562980 |
| *E-MAIL ADDRESS:* | stenhousemuirfc@ talk21.com |
| *CAPACITY:* | 2,354 |
| *RECORD ATT:* | 12,500 (v East Fife, 1950) |
| *RECORD VICTORY:* | 9-2 (v Dundee United, 1937) |
| *RECORD DEFEAT:* | 2-11 (v Dunfermline, 1930) |
| *MANAGER:* | John McVeigh |
| *CHAIRMAN:* | Mike Laing |
| *MOST LEAGUE GOALS (1 SEASON):* | 32, Robert Taylor, 1995-96 |

## HONOURS

LEAGUE CHALLENGE CUP: 1995-96.

## LEAGUE RESULTS 2001-2002

Morton 4 Stenhousemuir 1
Stenhousemuir 0 Stranraer 0
Forfar 1 Stenhousemuir 1
Stenhousemuir 3 Berwick 0
Alloa 0 Stenhousemuir 1
Stenhousemuir 2 Hamilton 0
QoS 2 Stenhousemuir 0
Stenh'semuir 2 Clydebank 2
Cowdenb'th 1 Stenh'semuir 1

Morton 0 Stenhousemuir 1
Alloa 4 Stenhousemuir 0
Stenhousemuir 1 Berwick 3
QoS 1 Stenhousemuir 0
Stenhousemuir 0 Hamilton 3
Cowdenb'th 2 Stenh'semuir 4
Stenh'semuir 0 Clydebank 0
Stenhousemuir 0 Stranraer 0
Forfar 2 Stenhousemuir 0

Stenhousemuir 0 Morton 3
Stranraer 6 Stenhousemuir 1
Stenhousemuir 1 Alloa 1
Berwick 1 Stenhousemuir 1
Hamilton 2 Stenhousemuir 3
Stenhousemuir 1 QoS 1
Clydebank 3 Stenh'semuir 2
Stenh'semuir 0 Cowdenb'th 3
Stenhousemuir 1 Forfar 1

Berwick 2 Stenhousemuir 1
Stenhousemuir 1 Alloa 0
Hamilton 0 Stenhousemuir 0
Stenhousemuir 1 QoS 4
Clydebank 0 Stenh'semuir 0
Stenh'semuir 0 Cowdenb'th 1
Stenhousemuir 2 Morton 3
Stranraer 1 Stenhousemuir 0
Stenhousemuir 0 Forfar 0

# STIRLING ALBION

| | |
|---|---|
| *NICKNAME:* | The Binos |
| *COLOURS:* | Red and white |
| *GROUND:* | Forthbank Stadium |
| *TELEPHONE No:* | 01786 450399 |
| *FAX No:* | 01786 448400 |
| *CAPACITY:* | 3,808 |
| *RECORD ATT:* | 26,400 (v Celtic, 1959, at Annfield) |
| *RECORD VICTORY:* | 20-0 (v Selkirk, 1984) |
| *RECORD DEFEAT:* | 0-9 (v Dundee United, 1967) |
| *MANAGER:* | Vacant |
| *CHAIRMAN:* | Peter McKenzie |
| *MOST LEAGUE GOALS (1 SEASON:)* | 27, Joe Hughes, 1969-70 |

## HONOURS

**LEAGUE CHAMPIONS:** Division II (4) – 1952-53, 1957-58, 1960-61, 1964-65. Second Division (3) – 1976-77, 1990-91, 1995-96.

## LEAGUE RESULTS 2001-2002

| | |
|---|---|
| Stirling 2 Peterhead 1 | Stirling 0 Peterhead 2 |
| Albion 1 Stirling 3 | Stirling 0 East Fife 1 |
| Stirling 1 Brechin 3 | Elgin 2 Stirling 1 |
| Elgin 2 Stirling 3 | Stirling 2 Dumbarton 1 |
| Stirling 2 East Fife 1 | Montrose 1 Stirling 3 |
| Montrose 4 Stirling 0 | Stirling 3 Queen's Park 2 |
| Stirling 4 Dumbarton 5 | East Stirling 3 Stirling 0 |
| East Stirling 1 Stirling 1 | Albion 2 Stirling 0 |
| Stirling 0 Queen's Park 0 | Stirling 1 Brechin 3 |
| | |
| Peterhead 3 Stirling 3 | Stirling 3 Elgin 1 |
| Stirling 2 Albion 2 | East Fife 1 Stirling 1 |
| East Fife 1 Stirling 1 | Stirling 0 Montrose 1 |
| Stirling 0 Elgin 1 | Dumbarton 2 Stirling 0 |
| Stirling 1 Montrose 1 | Stirling 1 East Stirling 0 |
| Dumbarton 4 Stirling 1 | Queen's Park 0 Stirling 0 |
| Stirling 1 East Stirling 1 | Peterhead 5 Stirling 1 |
| Queen's Park 2 Stirling 2 | Stirling 0 Albion 3 |
| Brechin 3 Stirling 1 | Brechin 2 Stirling 1 |

# STRANRAER

| | |
|---|---|
| *NICKNAME:* | The Blues |
| *COLOURS:* | Blue and white |
| *GROUND:* | Stair Park |
| *TELEPHONE No:* | 01776 703271 |
| *FAX No:* | 01776 702194 |
| *WEBSITE:* | stranraerfc.co.uk |
| *CAPACITY:* | 5,600 |
| *RECORD ATT:* | 6,500 |
| | (v Rangers, 1948) |
| *RECORD VICTORY:* | 7-0 (v Brechin, 1965) |
| *RECORD DEFEAT:* | 1-11 (v Queen of the South, 1932) |
| *MANAGER:* | Billy McLaren |
| *CHIEF EXECUTIVE:* | James Hannah |
| *MOST LEAGUE GOALS (1 SEASON):* | 27, Derek Frye, 1997-98 |

## HONOURS

LEAGUE CHAMPIONS: Second Division (2) – 1993-94, 1997-98. LEAGUE CHALLENGE CUP: 1996-97.

## LEAGUE RESULTS 2001-2002

| | |
|---|---|
| Stranraer 3 Cowdenbeath 0 | Stranraer 2 Cowdenbeath 1 |
| Stenhousemuir 0 Stranraer 0 | Stranraer 1 QoS 2 |
| Stranraer 1 Alloa 1 | Morton 2 Stranraer 2 |
| Morton 1 Stranraer 1 | Hamilton 2 Stranraer 0 |
| Stranraer 2 QoS 2 | Stranraer 2 Berwick 2 |
| Stranraer 0 Berwick 2 | Clydebank 1 Stranraer 2 |
| Hamilton 0 Stranraer 1 | Stranraer 0 Forfar 3 |
| Stranraer 2 Forfar 0 | Stenhousemuir 0 Stranraer 0 |
| Clydebank 1 Stranraer 3 | Stranraer 0 Alloa 2 |
| | |
| Cowdenbeath 2 Stranraer 2 | Stranraer 0 Morton 0 |
| Stranraer 6 Stenhousemuir 1 | QoS 3 Stranraer 1 |
| QoS 1 Stranraer 0 | Berwick 4 Stranraer 1 |
| Stranraer 1 Morton 4 | Stranraer 3 Hamilton 2 |
| Berwick 2 Stranraer 2 | Forfar 3 Stranraer 2 |
| Stranraer 2 Hamilton 1 | Stranraer 1 Clydebank 1 |
| Forfar 1 Stranraer 1 | Cowdenbeath 1 Stranraer 1 |
| Stranraer 0 Clydebank 1 | Stranraer 1 Stenhousemuir 0 |
| Alloa 2 Stranraer 2 | Alloa 0 Stranraer 0 |

## "Mum says all the best clubs are investing in youth. Are you listening Dad?"

For information on Savings Plans and a wide range of other Financial Products call

### 08457 46 46 46*

**You watch your team, CIS will watch your money.**

making dreams
come true at macs
with guitars from £59
and Fender USA series
Strats from £629
Lindsay Reid
singer/songwriter
Jim Deacon acoustic
£249
McCormack's
Serious about music!
Visit us online at
www.mccormacks-music.com
info@mccormacks-music.com
29-35 Bath Street, Glasgow G2 1HT
Tel: 0141 332 6644 Fax: 0141 353 3095

CHRIS SUTTON heads in Celtic's second goal in the Champions League clash with Juventus

IT'S that champion feeling for Celtic stars Didier Agathe and Lubo Moravcik

# THE FUTURE OF MOTOR AUCTIONS IS HERE now

| DAY | OPENING HOURS | DETAILS |
|-----|---------------|---------|
| Tuesdays | 9.00am-10.00pm | **Sale Day** - General Sale from 6.30pm 1st & 3rd Tuesday of each month. Fleet Sale from 12 noon. |
| Fridays | 9.00am-9.00pm | **Sale Day** - From 4.30pm. Dealer Direct & Part Ex From 11.00am. LCV, HGV & Plant Sale 2nd Friday of each month. |

**MANHEIM SCOTTISH AUCTIONS**
199 Siemens Street, Blochairn Glasgow G21 2BU
Tel: 0870 444 0419    Fax: 0870 444 0469

SCOTT BOOTH stretches for the ball during our World Cup qualifying defeat in Belgium

RANGERS lift their first trophy under Alex McLeish by beating Ayr in the CIS Cup Final

IT'S the real deal as Real Madrid fans take over Glasgow for the Champions League Final

# M∆KE R⊘AD SAFETY Y⊘UR

GOAL

Glasgow

GLASGOW CITY COUNCIL LAND SERVICES
ROAD SAFETY UNIT

**OUCH:** Celtic's Henrik Larsson and Johan Mjallby challenge Rangers' Stefan Klos for the ball in the final Old Firm league game of the season as Lorenzo Amoruso arrives to help his goalkeeper.

PARTICK THISTLE celebrate clinching the Bell's First Division championship

**Everybody gets depressed**
It helps to get some breathing space

0800 83 85 87

# LEAGUE CHAMPIONS

| YEAR | WINNERS |
|------|---------|
| 1890-91 | RANGERS/DUMBARTON |
| 1891-92 | DUMBARTON |
| 1892-93 | CELTIC |
| 1893-94 | CELTIC |
| 1894-95 | HEARTS |
| 1895-96 | CELTIC |
| 1896-97 | HEARTS |
| 1897-98 | CELTIC |
| 1898-99 | RANGERS |
| 1899-1900 | RANGERS |
| 1900-01 | RANGERS |
| 1901-02 | RANGERS |
| 1902-03 | HIBERNIAN |
| 1903-04 | THIRD LANARK |
| 1904-05 | CELTIC |
| 1905-06 | CELTIC |
| 1906-07 | CELTIC |
| 1907-08 | CELTIC |
| 1908-09 | CELTIC |
| 1909-10 | CELTIC |
| 1910-11 | RANGERS |
| 1911-12 | RANGERS |
| 1912-13 | RANGERS |
| 1913-14 | CELTIC |
| 1914-15 | CELTIC |
| 1915-16 | CELTIC |
| 1916-17 | CELTIC |
| 1917-18 | RANGERS |
| 1918-19 | CELTIC |
| 1919-20 | RANGERS |
| 1920-21 | RANGERS |
| 1921-22 | CELTIC |
| 1922-23 | RANGERS |
| 1923-24 | RANGERS |
| 1924-25 | RANGERS |
| 1925-26 | CELTIC |
| 1926-27 | RANGERS |
| 1927-28 | RANGERS |
| 1928-29 | RANGERS |

| YEAR | WINNERS |
|------|---------|
| 1929-30 | RANGERS |
| 1930-31 | RANGERS |
| 1931-32 | MOTHERWELL |
| 1932-33 | RANGERS |
| 1933-34 | RANGERS |
| 1934-35 | RANGERS |
| 1935-36 | CELTIC |
| 1936-37 | RANGERS |
| 1937-38 | CELTIC |
| 1938-39 | RANGERS |

## NO CHAMPIONSHIP

| YEAR | WINNERS |
|------|---------|
| 1946-47 | RANGERS |
| 1947-48 | HIBERNIAN |
| 1948-49 | RANGERS |
| 1949-50 | RANGERS |
| 1950-51 | HIBERNIAN |
| 1951-52 | HIBERNIAN |
| 1952-53 | RANGERS |
| 1953-54 | CELTIC |
| 1954-55 | ABERDEEN |
| 1955-56 | RANGERS |
| 1956-57 | RANGERS |
| 1957-58 | HEARTS |
| 1958-59 | RANGERS |
| 1959-60 | HEARTS |
| 1960-61 | RANGERS |
| 1961-62 | DUNDEE |
| 1962-63 | RANGERS |
| 1963-64 | RANGERS |
| 1964-65 | KILMARNOCK |
| 1965-66 | CELTIC |
| 1966-67 | CELTIC |
| 1967-68 | CELTIC |
| 1968-69 | CELTIC |
| 1969-70 | CELTIC |
| 1970-71 | CELTIC |
| 1971-72 | CELTIC |
| 1972-73 | CELTIC |
| 1973-74 | CELTIC |
| 1974-75 | RANGERS |

## PREMIER DIVISION

| YEAR | WINNERS |
|------|---------|
| 1975-76 | RANGERS |
| 1976-77 | CELTIC |
| 1977-78 | RANGERS |
| 1978-79 | CELTIC |
| 1979-80 | ABERDEEN |
| 1980-81 | CELTIC |
| 1981-82 | CELTIC |
| 1982-83 | DUNDEE UNITED |
| 1983-84 | ABERDEEN |
| 1984-85 | ABERDEEN |
| 1985-86 | CELTIC |
| 1986-87 | RANGERS |
| 1987-88 | CELTIC |
| 1988-89 | RANGERS |
| 1989-90 | RANGERS |
| 1990-91 | RANGERS |
| 1991-92 | RANGERS |
| 1992-93 | RANGERS |
| 1993-94 | RANGERS |
| 1994-95 | RANGERS |
| 1995-96 | RANGERS |
| 1996-97 | RANGERS |
| 1997-98 | CELTIC |
| 1998-99 | RANGERS |
| 1999-00 | RANGERS |
| 2000-01 | CELTIC |
| 2001-02 | CELTIC |

**JOHAN MJALLBY:** played 35 games to help Celtic successfully defend their SPL title

# PROMOTION/RELEGATION

| 1921-1922 | Promoted | Alloa |
| | Relegated | Dumbarton, Queen's Park, Clydebank |
| 1922-23 | Promoted | Queen's Park, Clydebank |
| | Relegated | Albion Rovers, Alloa |
| 1923-24 | Promoted | St Johnstone, Cowdenbeath |
| | Relegated | Clyde, Clydebank |
| 1924-25 | Promoted | Dundee Utd, Clydebank |
| | Relegated | Ayr United, Third Lanark |
| 1925-26 | Promoted | Dunfermline, Clyde |
| | Relegated | Raith Rovers, Clydebank |
| 1926-27 | Promoted | Bo'ness, Raith Rovers |
| | Relegated | Morton, Dundee United |
| 1927-28 | Promoted | Ayr United, Third Lanark |
| | Relegated | Bo'ness, Dunfermline |
| 1928-29 | Promoted | Dundee United, Morton |
| | Relegated | Third Lanark, Raith Rovers |
| 1929-30 | Promoted | Leith Ath, East Fife |
| | Relegated | Dundee United, St Johnstone |
| 1930-31 | Promoted | Third Lanark, Dundee United |
| | Relegated | Hibernian, East Fife |
| 1931-32 | Promoted | East Stirling, St Johnstone |
| | Relegated | Dundee United, Leith Ath |
| 1932-33 | Promoted | Hibernian, Queen of the South |
| | Relegated | Morton, East Stirling |
| 1933-34 | Promoted | Albion Rovers, Dunfermline |
| | Relegated | Third Lanark, Cowdenbeath |
| 1934-35 | Promoted | Third Lanark, Arbroath |
| | Relegated | St Mirren, Falkirk |
| 1935-36 | Promoted | Falkirk, St Mirren |
| | Relegated | Airdrie, Ayr United |
| 1936-37 | Promoted | Ayr United, Morton |
| | Relegated | Dunfermline, Albion Rovers |
| 1937-38 | Promoted | Raith Rovers, Albion Rovers |
| | Relegated | Dundee, Morton |
| 1938-39 | Promoted | Cowdenbeath, Alloa |
| | Relegated | Queen's Park, Raith Rovers |
| 1946-47 | Promoted | Dundee, Airdrie |
| | Relegated | Kilmarnock, Hamilton |
| 1947-48 | Promoted | East Fife, Albion Rovers |
| | Relegated | Airdrie, Queen's Park |
| 1948-49 | Promoted | Raith Rovers, Stirling Albion |
| | Relegated | Morton, Albion Rovers |

| | | |
|---|---|---|
| 1949-50 | **Promoted** | Morton, Airdrie |
| | **Relegated** | Queen of the South, Stirling Alb |
| 1950-51 | **Promoted** | Queen of the South, Stirling Alb |
| | **Relegated** | Clyde, Falkirk |
| 1951-52 | **Promoted** | Clyde, Falkirk |
| | **Relegated** | Morton, Stirling Albion |
| 1952-53 | **Promoted** | Stirling Albion, Hamilton Accies |
| | **Relegated** | Motherwell, Third Lanark |
| 1953-54 | **Promoted** | Motherwell, Kilmarnock |
| | **Relegated** | Airdrie, Hamilton Accies |
| 1954-55 | **Promoted** | Airdrie, Dunfermline |
| | **Relegated** | Motherwell, Stirling Albion |
| 1955-56 | **Promoted** | Queen's Park, Ayr United |
| | **Relegated** | Clyde, Stirling Albion |
| 1956-57 | **Promoted** | Clyde, Third Lanark |
| | **Relegated** | Dunfermline, Ayr United |
| 1957-58 | **Promoted** | Stirling Albion, Dunfermline |
| | **Relegated** | East Fife, Queen's Park |
| 1958-59 | **Promoted** | Ayr United, Arbroath |
| | **Relegated** | Falkirk, Queen of the South |
| 1959-60 | **Promoted** | St Johnstone, Dundee United |
| | **Relegated** | Stirling Albion, Arbroath |
| 1960-61 | **Promoted** | Stirling Albion, Falkirk |
| | **Relegated** | Clyde, Ayr United |
| 1961-62 | **Promoted** | Clyde, Queen of the South |
| | **Relegated** | St Johnstone, Stirling Albion |
| 1962-63 | **Promoted** | St Johnstone, East Stirling |
| | **Relegated** | Clyde, Raith Rovers |
| 1963-64 | **Promoted** | Morton, Clyde |
| | **Relegated** | Queen of the South, East Stirling |
| 1964-65 | **Promoted** | Stirling Albion, Hamilton Accies |
| | **Relegated** | Airdrie, Third Lanark |
| 1965-66 | **Promoted** | Ayr United, Airdrie |
| | **Relegated** | Morton, Hamilton Accies |
| 1966-67 | **Promoted** | Morton, Raith Rovers |
| | **Relegated** | St Mirren, Ayr United |
| 1967-68 | **Promoted** | St Mirren, Arbroath |
| | **Relegated** | Motherwell, Stirling Albion |
| 1968-69 | **Promoted** | Motherwell, Ayr United |
| | **Relegated** | Falkirk, Arbroath |
| 1969-70 | **Promoted** | Falkirk, Cowdenbeath |
| | **Relegated** | Raith Rovers, Partick Thistle |
| 1970-71 | **Promoted** | Partick Thistle, East Fife |
| | **Relegated** | St Mirren, Cowdenbeath |
| 1971-72 | **Promoted** | Dumbarton, Arbroath |
| | **Relegated** | Clyde, Dunfermline |

| 1972-73 | **Promoted** | Clyde, Dunfermline |
| | **Relegated** | Kilmarnock, Airdrie |
| 1973-74 | **Promoted** | Airdrie, Kilmarnock |
| | **Relegated** | East Fife, Falkirk |

*1974-75 Leagues reformed into Premier, First and Second Divisions*

| 1975-76 | **Promoted to Premier** – Kilmarnock, Partick Th |
| | **Relegated to First** – Dundee, St Johnstone |
| | **Promoted to First** – Clydebank, Raith Rovers |
| | **Relegated to Second** – Clyde, Dunfermline |
| 1976-77 | **Promoted to Premier** – St Mirren, Clydebank |
| | **Relegated to First** – Hearts, Kilmarnock |
| | **Promoted to First** – Alloa, Stirling Albion |
| | **Relegated to Second** – Falkirk, Raith Rovers |
| 1977-78 | **Promoted to Premier** – Morton, Hearts |
| | **Relegated to First** – Ayr United, Clydebank |
| | **Promoted to First** – Clyde, Raith Rovers |
| | **Relegated to Second** – Alloa Athletic, East Fife |
| 1978-79 | **Promoted to Premier** – Dundee, Kilmarnock |
| | **Relegated to First** – Hearts, Motherwell |
| | **Promoted to First** – Berwick Ran, Dunfermline |
| | **Relegated to Second** – Montrose, QOS |
| 1979-80 | **Promoted to Premier** – Hearts, Airdrie |
| | **Relegated to First** – Dundee, Hibernian |
| | **Promoted to First** – East Stirling, Falkirk |
| | **Relegated to Second** – Arbroath, Clyde |
| 1980-81 | **Promoted to Premier** – Dundee, Hibernian |
| | **Relegated to First** – Hearts, Kilmarnock |
| | **Promoted to First** – Queen's Park, QOS |
| | **Relegated to Second** – Berwick R, Stirling Alb |
| 1981-82 | **Promoted to Premier** – Motherwell, Kilmarnock |
| | **Relegated to First** – Airdrie, Partick Thistle |
| | **Promoted to First** – Clyde, Alloa Athletic |
| | **Relegated to Second** – QOS, East Stirling |
| 1982-83 | **Promoted to Premier** – St Johnstone, Hearts |
| | **Relegated to First** – Kilmarnock, Morton |
| | **Promoted to First** – Brechin, Meadowbank |
| | **Relegated to Second** – Queen's Pk, Dunf'line |
| 1983-84 | **Promoted to Premier** — Dumbarton, Morton |
| | **Relegated to First** — Motherwell, St Johnstone |
| | **Promoted to First** — East Fife, Forfar |
| | **Relegated to Second** — Alloa, Raith Rovers |
| 1984-85 | **Promoted to Premier** — Motherwell, Clydebank |
| | **Relegated to First** — Dumbarton, Morton |
| | **Promoted to First** — Montrose, Alloa Athletic |
| | **Relegated to Second** — M'dowbank, St Johnstone |

| | |
|---|---|
| 1985-86 | **Promoted to Premier** – Hamilton Accies, Falkirk |
| | **No relegation to First** – league reorganisation |
| | **Promoted to First** – Dunfermline, QOS |
| | **Relegated to Second** – Ayr United, Alloa |
| 1986-87 | **Promoted to Premier** – Morton, Dunfermline Ath |
| | **Relegated to First** – Clydebank, Hamilton Accies |
| | **Promoted to First** – Meadowbank Th, Raith Rovers |
| | **Relegated to Second** – Brechin, Montrose |
| 1987-88 | **Promoted to Premier** – Hamilton Accies |
| | **Relegated to First** – Falkirk, Dunfermline, Morton |
| | **Promoted to First** – Ayr United, St Johnstone |
| | **Relegated to Second** – East Fife, Dumbarton |
| 1988-89 | **Promoted to Premier** – Dunfermline Ath |
| | **Relegated to First** – Hamilton Accies |
| | **Promoted to First** – Albion Rovers, Alloa Ath |
| | **Relegated to Second** – QOS, Kilmarnock |
| 1989-90 | **Promoted to Premier** – St Johnstone |
| | **Relegated to First** – Dundee |
| | **Promoted to First** – Brechin, Kilmarnock |
| | **Relegated to Second** – Alloa Ath, Albion Rovers |
| 1990-91 | **Promoted to Premier** – Falkirk, Airdrie |
| | *No relegation to First* |
| | **Promoted to First** – Stirling Albion, Montrose |
| | **Relegated to Second** – Brechin, Clyde |
| 1991-92 | **Promoted to Premier** – Dundee, Partick Thistle |
| | **Relegated to First** – Dunfermline Ath, St Mirren |
| | **Promoted to First** – Dumbarton, Cowdenbeath |
| | **Relegated to Second** – Montrose, Forfar |
| 1992-93 | **Promoted to Premier** – Raith Rov, Kilmarnock |
| | **Relegated to First** – Airdrie, Falkirk |
| | **Promoted to First** – Clyde, Brechin |
| | **Relegated to Second** – Cowdenbeath, Meadowb'k |
| 1993-94 | **Promoted to Premier** – Falkirk |
| | **Relegated to First** – St Johnstone, Raith Rovers, Dundee |
| | **Promoted to First** – Stranraer |
| | **Relegated to Second** – Dumbarton, Stirling Alb, Clyde, Morton, Brechin |
| | **Relegated to Third** – Alloa, Forfar |
| | East Stirling, Montrose, Queen's Park, Arbroath |
| | Albion Rovers, Cowdenbeath |
| | *Leagues reformed into* |
| | *Premier, First, Second and Third Divisions* |

| 1994-95 | **Promoted to Premier** — Raith Rovers |
| | **Relegated to First** — Dundee United |
| | **Promoted to First** — Morton, Dumbarton |
| | **Relegated to Second** — Ayr United, Stranraer |
| | **Relegated to Third** — Meadowbank, Brechin City |
| 1995-96 | **Promoted to Premier** — Dunfermline Ath, Dundee U |
| | **Relegated to First** — Falkirk, Partick Thistle |
| | **Promoted to First** — Stirling Albion, East Fife |
| | **Relegated to Second** — Dumbarton, Hamilton |
| | **Promoted to Second** — Livingston, Brechin C |
| | **Relegated to Third** — Forfar, Montrose |
| 1996-97 | **Promoted to Premier** – St Johnstone |
| | **Relegated to First** – Raith Rovers |
| | **Promoted to First** – Ayr United, Hamilton Accies |
| | **Relegated to Second** –Clydebank, East Fife |
| | **Promoted to Second** – Inverness CT, Forfar |
| | **Relegated to Third** – Dumbarton, Berwick Rangers |
| 1997-98 | **Promoted to Premier** – Dundee |
| | **Relegated to First** – Hibs |
| | **Promoted to First** – Stranraer, Clydebank |
| | **Relegated to Second** –Partick Thistle, Stirling Alb |
| | **Promoted to Second** – Alloa, Arbroath |
| | **Relegated to Third** – Stenhousemuir, Brechin |
| 1998-99 | **Promoted to Premier** – Hibs |
| | **Relegated to First** – Dunfermline |
| | **Promoted to First** – Livingston, Inverness CT |
| | **Relegated to Second** – Hamilton, Stranraer |
| | **Promoted to Second** – Ross Co, Stenhousemuir |
| | **Relegated to Third** – East Fife, Forfar Athletic |
| 1999-00 | **Promoted to Premier** – St Mirren, Dunfermline |
| | **Relegated to First** – No relegation |
| | **Promoted to First** – Clyde, Alloa, Ross County |
| | **Relegated to Second** – Clydebank |
| | **Promoted to Second** – Queen's Pk, Berwick Forfar |
| | **Relegated to Third** – Hamilton Accies |
| | **New league entrants** – Elgin City, Peterhead |
| 2000-01 | **Promoted to Premier** – Livingston |
| | **Relegated to First** – St Mirren |
| | **Promoted to First** – Partick Thistle, Arbroath |
| | **Relegated to Second** – Morton, Alloa |
| | **Promoted to Second** – Hamilton, Cowdenbeath |
| | **Relegated to Third** – Queen's Park, Stirling Albion |
| 2001-02 | **Promoted to Premier** – Partick Thistle |
| | **Relegated to First** – St Johnstone |
| | **Promoted to First** – Queen of the South, Alloa |
| | **Relegated to Second** – Raith Rovers |
| | **Promoted to Second** – Brechin, Dumbarton |
| | **Relegated to Third** – Morton |

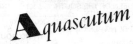

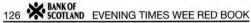

# CIS INSURANCE LEAGUE CUP 2001-2002

## FIRST ROUND

| | | | |
|---|---|---|---|
| AIRDRIE | 3 | MORTON | 0 |
| ALBION ROVERS | 0 | INVERNESS CT | 2 |
| ALLOA | 4 | PETERHEAD | 0 |
| BERWICK RANGERS | 0 | PARTICK THISTLE | 3 |
| CLYDE | 2 | STENHOUSEMUIR | 2 |

(aet, Clyde won 4-2 on pens, 90mins 1-1 )

| | | | |
|---|---|---|---|
| DUMBARTON | 2 | CLYDEBANK | 0 |
| EAST FIFE | 1 | ARBROATH | 0 |
| EAST STIRLING | 0 | QUEEN OF THE SOUTH | 3 |
| ELGIN | 2 | STRANRAER | 3 |
| FORFAR | 1 | FALKIRK | 2 |
| QUEEN'S PARK | 0 | HAMILTON | 1 |
| RAITH ROVERS | 1 | MONTROSE | 0 |
| ROSS COUNTY | 3 | BRECHIN CITY | 0 |
| STIRLING ALBION | 3 | COWDENBEATH | 2 |

## SECOND ROUND

| | | | |
|---|---|---|---|
| AIRDRIE | 2 | MOTHERWELL | 1 |
| AYR UNITED | 4 | STRANRAER | 2 |
| CLYDE | 1 | ST JOHNSTONE | 0 |
| DUNDEE UNITED | 3 | DUMBARTON | 0 |
| DUNFERMLINE | 3 | ALLOA | 0 |
| FALKIRK | 0 | RAITH ROVERS | 2 |
| HAMILTON | 0 | DUNDEE | 2 |
| INVERNESS CT | 3 | PARTICK THISTLE | 3 |

(aet, Inverness CT won 4-3 on penalties, 90mins, 2-2)

| | | | |
|---|---|---|---|
| LIVINGSTON | 3 | EAST FIFE | 0 |
| QUEEN OF THE SOUTH | 1 | ABERDEEN | 2 |
| ROSS COUNTY | 0 | HEARTS | 0 |

(aet, Ross County won 5-4 on penalties)

| | | | |
|---|---|---|---|
| STIRLING ALBION | 2 | ST MIRREN | 1 |

## THIRD ROUND

| | | | |
|---|---|---|---|
| ABERDEEN | 1 | LIVINGSTON | 6 |
| AYR UNITED | 0 | KILMARNOCK | 0 |

(aet, Ayr won 5-4 on penalties)

| | | | |
|---|---|---|---|
| CELTIC | 8 | STIRLING ALBION | 0 |
| DUNDEE UNITED | 3 | ST JOHNSTONE | 2 |

(aet, 90mins 2-2)

| | | | |
|---|---|---|---|
| DUNFERMLINE | 1 | INVERNESS CT | 1 |

(aet, Inverness CT won 4-1 on penalties, 90mins 1-1)

| | | | |
|---|---|---|---|
| RAITH | 0 | HIBERNIAN | 2 |
| RANGERS | 3 | AIRDRIE | 0 |
| ROSS COUNTY | 2 | DUNDEE | 1 |

## QUARTER-FINALS

| | | | |
|---|---|---|---|
| AYR UNITED | 5 | INVERNESS CT | 1 |
| HIBERNIAN | 2 | DUNDEE UNITED | 0 |
| LIVINGSTON | 0 | CELTIC | 2 |
| ROSS COUNTY | 1 | RANGERS | 2 |

## SEMI-FINALS

| | | | |
|---|---|---|---|
| HIBERNIAN | 0 | AYR UNITED | 1 |

(aet, 90mins 0-0)

| | | | |
|---|---|---|---|
| RANGERS | 2 | CELTIC | 1 |

(aet, 90mins 1-1)

## FINAL

| | | | |
|---|---|---|---|
| AYR UNITED | 0 | RANGERS | 4 |

## LEAGUE CUP WINNERS

| | | | | |
|---|---|---|---|---|
| 1946-47 | Rangers | 4 | Aberdeen | 0 |
| 1947-48 | East Fife | 4 | Falkirk | 1 |

*(after 0-0 draw)*

| | | | | |
|---|---|---|---|---|
| 1948-49 | Rangers | 2 | Raith Rovers | 0 |
| 1949-50 | East Fife | 3 | Dunfermline | 0 |
| 1950-51 | Motherwell | 3 | Hibernian | 0 |
| 1951-52 | Dundee | 3 | Rangers | 2 |
| 1952-53 | Dundee | 2 | Kilmarnock | 0 |
| 1953-54 | East Fife | 3 | Partick Thistle | 2 |
| 1954-55 | Hearts | 4 | Motherwell | 2 |
| 1955-56 | Aberdeen | 2 | St Mirren | 1 |
| 1956-57 | Celtic | 3 | Partick Thistle | 0 |
| 1957-58 | Celtic | 7 | Rangers | 1 |
| 1958-59 | Hearts | 5 | Partick Thistle | 1 |
| 1959-60 | Hearts | 2 | Third Lanark | 1 |
| 1960-61 | Rangers | 2 | Kilmarnock | 0 |
| 1961-62 | Rangers | 3 | Hearts | 1 |

*(after 1-1 draw)*

| | | | | |
|---|---|---|---|---|
| 1962-63 | Hearts | 1 | Kilmarnock | 0 |
| 1963-64 | Rangers | 5 | Morton | 0 |
| 1964-65 | Rangers | 2 | Celtic | 1 |
| 1965-66 | Celtic | 2 | Rangers | 1 |
| 1966-67 | Celtic | 1 | Rangers | 0 |
| 1967-68 | Celtic | 5 | Dundee | 3 |
| 1968-69 | Celtic | 6 | Hibs | 2 |
| 1969-70 | Celtic | 1 | St Johnstone | 0 |
| 1970-71 | Rangers | 1 | Celtic | 0 |
| 1971-72 | Partick Thistle | 4 | Celtic | 1 |
| 1972-73 | Hibs | 2 | Celtic | 1 |
| 1973-74 | Dundee | 1 | Celtic | 0 |
| 1974-75 | Celtic | 6 | Hibs | 3 |
| 1975-76 | Rangers | 1 | Celtic | 0 |
| 1976-77 | Aberdeen | 2 | Celtic | 1 |

*(after extra time)*

| | | | | |
|---|---|---|---|---|
| 1977-78 | Celtic | 1 | Rangers | 2 |

*(after extra time)*

| | | | | |
|---|---|---|---|---|
| 1978-79 | Rangers | 2 | Aberdeen | 1 |
| 1979-80 | Aberdeen | 0 | Dundee United | 3 |

*(after 0-0 draw)*

| | | | | |
|---|---|---|---|---|
| 1980-81 | Dundee | 0 | Dundee United | 3 |
| 1981-82 | Rangers | 2 | Dundee United | 1 |
| 1982-83 | Celtic | 2 | Rangers | 1 |
| 1983-84 | Rangers | 3 | Celtic | 2 |

*(after extra time)*

| | | | | |
|---|---|---|---|---|
| 1984-85 | Dundee United | 0 | Rangers | 1 |
| 1985-86 | Aberdeen | 3 | Hibernian | 0 |
| 1986-87 | Celtic | 1 | Rangers | 2 |
| 1987-88 | Rangers | 3 | Aberdeen | 3 |
| (after extra time, Rangers won 5-3 on penalties) | | | | |
| 1988-89 | Aberdeen | 2 | Rangers | 3 |
| 1989-90 | Aberdeen | 2 | Rangers | 1 |
| (after extra time) | | | | |
| 1990-91 | Rangers | 2 | Celtic | 1 |
| (after extra time) | | | | |
| 1991-92 | Hibernian | 2 | Dunfermline | 0 |
| 1992-93 | Rangers | 2 | Aberdeen | 1 |
| (after extra time) | | | | |
| 1993-94 | Rangers | 2 | Hibernian | 1 |
| 1994-95 | Celtic | 2 | Raith Rovers | 2 |
| (after extra time, Raith Rovers won 6-5 on penalties) | | | | |
| 1995-96 | Aberdeen | 2 | Dundee | 0 |
| 1996-97 | Rangers | 4 | Hearts | 3 |
| 1997-98 | Celtic | 3 | Dundee United | 0 |
| 1998-99 | Rangers | 2 | St Johnstone | 1 |
| 1999-2000 | Celtic | 2 | Aberdeen | 0 |
| 2000-2001 | Celtic | 3 | Kilmarnock | 0 |
| 2001-2002 | Ayr United | 0 | Rangers | 4 |

**CIS CUP FINAL KEEPERS . . . Craig Nelson and Stefan Klos**

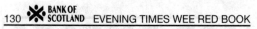
# BELL'S CHALLENGE CUP 2001-2002

## FIRST ROUND

| | | | |
|---|---|---|---|
| AIRDRIE | 2 | QUEEN OF THE SOUTH | 0 |
| ALBION ROVERS | 2 | MONTROSE | 0 |

(aet)

| | | | |
|---|---|---|---|
| BERWICK | 3 | ELGIN CITY | 0 |
| BRECHIN CITY | 4 | STIRLING ALBION | 1 |
| COWDENBEATH | 0 | ROSS COUNTY | 2 |

(aet)

| | | | |
|---|---|---|---|
| EAST FIFE | 2 | RAITH ROVERS | 3 |
| EAST STIRLING | 0 | ALLOA | 1 |
| FALKIRK | 4 | ARBROATH | 1 |
| INVERNESS CT | 3 | FORFAR | 2 |

(aet, 90 minutes 2-2)

| | | | |
|---|---|---|---|
| MORTON | 1 | CLYDE | 3 |
| PARTICK THISTLE | 5 | QUEEN'S PARK | 0 |
| PETERHEAD | 2 | HAMILTON | 0 |
| ST MIRREN | 1 | AYR UNITED | 3 |
| STENHOUSEMUIR | 1 | STRANRAER | 4 |

## SECOND ROUND

| | | | |
|---|---|---|---|
| ALBION ROVERS | 1 | AIRDRIE | 4 |
| ALLOA | 3 | INVERNESS CT | 2 |

(aet, 90 minutes 1-1)

| | | | |
|---|---|---|---|
| BRECHIN | 4 | PETERHEAD | 0 |
| CLYDE | 5 | BERWICK | 0 |
| DUMBARTON | 0 | ROSS COUNTY | 2 |
| FALKIRK | 0 | CLYDEBANK | 0 |

(aet, Clydebank won 5-4 on penalties)

| | | | |
|---|---|---|---|
| RAITH ROVERS | 3 | PARTICK THISTLE | 5 |

(aet, 90 minutes 2-2)

| | | | |
|---|---|---|---|
| STRANRAER | 3 | AYR UNITED | 2 |

## QUARTER-FINALS

| | | | |
|---|---|---|---|
| ALLOA | 4 | STRANRAER | 3 |

(aet, 90 minutes 3-3)

| | | | |
|---|---|---|---|
| CLYDE | 1 | PARTICK THISTLE | 0 |
| CLYDEBANK | 1 | AIRDRIE | 2 |
| ROSS COUNTY | 0 | BRECHIN | 2 |

## SEMI-FINALS

| | | | |
|---|---|---|---|
| AIRDRIE | 1 | BRECHIN | 1 |

(aet, 90 minutes 1-1, Airdrie won 4-3 on penalties)

| | | | |
|---|---|---|---|
| CLYDE | 0 | ALLOA | 1 |

## FINAL

| | | | |
|---|---|---|---|
| AIRDRIE | 2 | ALLOA | 1 |

## TENNENT'S SCOTTISH CUP 2001-2002

**FIRST ROUND:** Albion Rovers 1 Elgin City 0 (after 0-0 draw), Alloa Athletic 3 Dumbarton 1, Brechin City 4 Stenhousemuir 0, Clydebank 1 Peterhead 0, Morton 1 Queen of the South 2, Stirling Albion 2 Buckie Thistle 1, Tarff Rovers 1 Montrose 4, Wick Academy 2 Threave Rovers 3.

**SECOND ROUND:** Alloa Athletic 1 Queen of the South 0, Berwick Rangers 1 Cowdenbeath 0, Brechin City 0 Albion Rovers 1, Clydebank 0 Stranraer 1, Spartans 1 Deveronvale 2 (after 0-0 draw), Forres Mechanics 3 East Stirling 1 (after 1-1 draw), Forfar Athletic 2 Threave Rovers 0, Gala Fairydean 1 Stirling Albion 0, Hamilton Academical 4 Montrose 0, Queen's Park 2 East Fife 2 (aet, 90 mins 2-2, East Fife won 4-2 on pens; after 0-0 draw).

### THIRD ROUND

| | | | |
|---|---|---|---|
| Albion Rovers | 1 | Livingston | 4 |
| Alloa Athletic | 0 | Celtic | 5 |
| Arbroath | 0 | Inverness Caledonian Thistle | 2 |
| Clyde | 1 | St Mirren | 0 |
| Deveronvale | 0 | Ayr United | 6 |
| Dundee United | 3 | Forres Mechanics | 0 |
| Dunfermline | 3 | Motherwell | 1 |
| East Fife | 1 | Partick Thistle | 4 |
| Falkirk | 0 | Dundee | 1 |
| | (after 1-1 draw) | | |
| Gala Fairydean | 0 | Forfar | 5 |
| Hamilton Academical | 1 | Raith Rovers | 0 |
| Hearts | 2 | Ross County | 1 |
| Hibernian | 4 | Stranraer | 0 |
| | (after 0-0 draw) | | |
| Kilmarnock | 3 | Airdrie | 0 |
| Rangers | 3 | Berwick Rangers | 0 |
| | (after 0-0 draw) | | |
| St Johnstone | 0 | Aberdeen | 2 |

### FOURTH ROUND

| | | | |
|---|---|---|---|
| Aberdeen | 2 | Livingston | 0 |
| Ayr United | 3 | Dunfermline | 1 |
| Clyde | 1 | Forfar Athletic | 2 |
| Dundee United | 4 | Hamilton Academical | 0 |
| Hearts | 1 | Inverness CT | 3 |
| Kilmarnock | 0 | Celtic | 2 |
| Dundee | 1 | Partick Thistle | 2 |
| | (after 1-1 draw) | | |
| Rangers | 4 | Hibernian | 1 |

### QUARTER-FINALS

| | | | |
|---|---|---|---|
| Aberdeen | 0 | Celtic | 2 |
| Ayr United | 2 | Dundee United | 0 |
| | (after 2-2 draw) | | |
| Forfar Athletic | 0 | Rangers | 6 |
| Inverness Caledonian Thistle | 0 | Partick Thistle | 1 |
| | (after 2-2 draw) | | |

### SEMI-FINALS

| | | | |
|---|---|---|---|
| Celtic | 3 | Ayr United | 0 |
| Rangers | 3 | Partick Thistle | 0 |

### FINAL

| | | | |
|---|---|---|---|
| Celtic | 2 | Rangers | 3 |

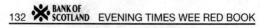
# PREVIOUS WINNERS

| | | | | |
|---|---|---|---|---|
| 1873-74 | QUEEN'S PARK | 2 | CLYDESDALE | 0 |
| 1874-75 | QUEEN'S PARK | 3 | RENTON | 0 |
| 1875-76 | QUEEN'S PARK | 2 | 3RD LANARK RIFLES | 0 |

(After 1-1 draw)

| | | | | |
|---|---|---|---|---|
| 1876-77 | VALE OF LEVEN | 3 | RANGERS | 2 |

After two replays 0-0, 1-1

| | | | | |
|---|---|---|---|---|
| 1877-78 | VALE OF LEVEN | 1 | 3RD LANARK RIFLES | 0 |
| 1878-79 | VALE OF LEVEN | 1 | RANGERS | 1 |

(Vale of Leven awarded cup.
Rangers failed to appear)

| | | | | |
|---|---|---|---|---|
| 1879-80 | QUEEN'S PARK | 3 | THORNLIEBANK | 0 |
| 1880-81 | QUEEN'S PARK | 3 | DUMBARTON | 1 |

(After Dumbarton protested first game)

| | | | | |
|---|---|---|---|---|
| 1881-82 | QUEEN'S PARK | 4 | DUMBARTON | 1 |

(After 2-2 draw)

| | | | | |
|---|---|---|---|---|
| 1882-83 | DUMBARTON | 2 | VALE OF LEVEN | 1 |

After 2-2 draw

| | | | | |
|---|---|---|---|---|
| 1883-84 | QUEEN'S PARK | wo | VALE OF LEVEN | |

(Queen's Park awarded cup.
Vale of Leven failed to appear.)

| | | | | |
|---|---|---|---|---|
| 884-85 | RENTON | 3 | VALE OF LEVEN | 1 |

(After 0-0 draw)

| | | | | |
|---|---|---|---|---|
| 1885-86 | QUEEN'S PARK | 3 | RENTON | 1 |
| 1886-87 | HIBERNIAN | 2 | DUMBARTON | 1 |
| 1887-88 | RENTON | 6 | CAMBUSLANG | 1 |
| 1888-89 | THIRD LANARK | 2 | CELTIC | 1 |

(After replay by order of Scottish FA
because of playing conditions in first match)

| | | | | |
|---|---|---|---|---|
| 1889-90 | QUEEN'S PARK | 2 | VALE OF LEVEN | 1 |

(After 1-1 draw)

| | | | | |
|---|---|---|---|---|
| 1890-91 | HEARTS | 1 | DUMBARTON | 0 |
| 1891-92 | CELTIC | 5 | QUEEN'S PARK | 1 |

(After mutually protested first game)

| | | | | |
|---|---|---|---|---|
| 1892-93 | QUEEN'S PARK | 2 | CELTIC | 1 |

(After 0-0 draw)

| | | | | |
|---|---|---|---|---|
| 1893-94 | RANGERS | 3 | CELTIC | 1 |
| 1894-95 | ST BERNARD'S | 2 | RENTON | 1 |
| 1895-96 | HEARTS | 3 | HIBS | 1 |
| 1896-97 | RANGERS | 5 | DUMBARTON | 1 |
| 1897-98 | RANGERS | 2 | KILMARNOCK | 0 |
| 1898-99 | CELTIC | 2 | RANGERS | 0 |
| 1899-00 | CELTIC | 4 | QUEEN'S PARK | 3 |
| 1900-01 | HEARTS | 4 | CELTIC | 3 |
| 1901-02 | HIBS | 1 | CELTIC | 0 |

| | | | |
|---|---|---|---|
| 1902-03 | RANGERS ..............2 | HEARTS ...........................0 | |

(After two replays, 1-1, 0-0)

| 1903-04 | CELTIC .....................3 | RANGERS ........................2 |
| 1904-05 | THIRD LANARK ......3 | RANGERS ........................1 |

(After 0-0 draw)

| 1905-06 | HEARTS ..................1 | THIRD LANARK .................0 |
| 1906-07 | CELTIC .....................3 | HEARTS ...........................0 |
| 1907-08 | CELTIC .....................5 | ST MIRREN ......................1 |
| 1908-09 | CELTIC .....................— | RANGERS.........................— |

(Owing to riot, cup was withheld after two drawn games)

| 1909-10 | DUNDEE ..................2 | CLYDE .............................1 |

(After two draws, 2-2, 0-0)

| 1910-11 | CELTIC .....................2 | HAMILTON ACCIES ..........0 |

(After 0-0 draw)

| 1911-12 | CELTIC .....................2 | CLYDE .............................0 |
| 1912-13 | FALKIRK...................2 | RAITH ROVERS ...............0 |
| 1913-14 | CELTIC .....................4 | HIBS ................................1 |

(After 0-0 draw)

| 1919-20 | KILMARNOCK ........3 | ALBION ROVERS ..............2 |
| 1920-21 | PARTICK THISTLE...1 | RANGERS ........................0 |
| 1921-22 | MORTON ..................1 | RANGERS ........................0 |
| 1922-23 | CELTIC .....................1 | HIBS ................................0 |
| 1923-24 | AIRDRIE ..................2 | HIBS ................................0 |
| 1924-25 | CELTIC .....................2 | DUNDEE ..........................1 |
| 1925-26 | ST MIRREN .............2 | CELTIC .............................0 |
| 1926-27 | CELTIC .....................3 | EAST FIFE .......................1 |
| 1927-28 | RANGERS ...............4 | CELTIC .............................0 |
| 1928-29 | KILMARNOCK ........2 | RANGERS ........................0 |
| 1929-30 | RANGERS ...............2 | PARTICK THISTLE ...........1 |

(After 0-0 draw)

| 1930-31 | CELTIC .....................4 | MOTHERWELL...................2 |

(After 2-2 draw)

| 1931-32 | RANGERS ...............3 | KILMARNOCK ...................0 |

(After 1-1 draw)

| 1932-33 | CELTIC .....................1 | MOTHERWELL...................0 |
| 1933-34 | RANGERS ...............5 | ST MIRREN ......................0 |
| 1934-35 | RANGERS ...............2 | HAMILTON ACCIES ..........1 |
| 1935-36 | RANGERS ...............1 | THIRD LANARK .................0 |
| 1936-37 | CELTIC .....................2 | ABERDEEN.......................1 |
| 1937-38 | EAST FIFE ..............4 | KILMARNOCK ...................2 |

(After 1-1 draw)

| 1938-39 | CLYDE .....................4 | MOTHERWELL...................0 |
| 1946-47 | ABERDEEN .............2 | HIBS ................................1 |
| 1947-48 | RANGERS ...............1 | MORTON ..........................0 |

(After extra time. After 1-1 draw)

| 1948-49 | RANGERS | 4 | CLYDE | 1 |
|---|---|---|---|---|
| 1949-50 | RANGERS | 3 | EAST FIFE | 0 |
| 1950-51 | CELTIC | 1 | MOTHERWELL | 0 |
| 1951-52 | MOTHERWELL | 4 | DUNDEE | 0 |
| 1952-53 | RANGERS | 1 | ABERDEEN | 0 |

(After 1-1 draw)

| 1953-54 | CELTIC | 2 | ABERDEEN | 1 |
| 1954-55 | CLYDE | 1 | CELTIC | 0 |

(After 1-1 draw)

| 1955-56 | HEARTS | 3 | CELTIC | 1 |
| 1956-57 | FALKIRK | 2 | KILMARNOCK | 1 |

(After extra time. After 1-1 draw)

| 1957-58 | CLYDE | 1 | HIBS | 0 |
| 1958-59 | ST MIRREN | 3 | ABERDEEN | 1 |
| 1959-60 | RANGERS | 2 | KILMARNOCK | 0 |
| 1960-61 | DUNFERMLINE | 2 | CELTIC | 0 |

(After 0-0 draw)

| 1961-62 | RANGERS | 2 | ST MIRREN | 0 |
| 1962-63 | RANGERS | 3 | CELTIC | 0 |

(After 1-1 draw)

| 1963-64 | RANGERS | 3 | DUNDEE | 1 |
| 1964-65 | CELTIC | 3 | DUNFERMLINE ATH. | 2 |
| 1965-66 | RANGERS | 1 | CELTIC | 0 |

(After 0-0 draw)

| 1966-67 | CELTIC | 2 | ABERDEEN | 0 |
| 1967-68 | DUNFERMLINE | 3 | HEARTS | 1 |
| 1968-69 | CELTIC | 4 | RANGERS | 0 |
| 1969-70 | ABERDEEN | 3 | CELTIC | 1 |
| 1970-71 | CELTIC | 2 | RANGERS | 1 |

(After 1-1 draw)

| 1971-72 | CELTIC | 6 | HIBS | 1 |
| 1972-73 | RANGERS | 3 | CELTIC | 2 |
| 1973-74 | CELTIC | 3 | DUNDEE UNITED | 0 |
| 1974-75 | CELTIC | 3 | AIRDRIE | 1 |
| 1975-76 | RANGERS | 3 | HEARTS | 1 |
| 1976-77 | CELTIC | 1 | RANGERS | 0 |
| 1977-78 | RANGERS | 2 | ABERDEEN | 1 |
| 1978-79 | RANGERS | 3 | HIBS | 2 |

(After two 0-0 draws, and extra time)

| 1979-80 | CELTIC | 1 | RANGERS | 0 |

(After extra time)

| 1980-81 | RANGERS | 4 | DUNDEE UNITED | 1 |

(After 0-0 draw)

| 1981-82 | ABERDEEN | 4 | RANGERS | 1 |

(After extra time)

| | | | |
|---|---|---|---|
| 1982-83 | ABERDEEN ............1 | RANGERS ........................0 | |
| | (After extra time) | | |
| 1983-84 | ABERDEEN ............2 | CELTIC ..............................1 | |
| | (After extra time) | | |
| 1984-85 | CELTIC....................2 | DUNDEE UNITED................1 | |
| 1985-86 | ABERDEEN ............3 | HEARTS ............................0 | |
| 1986-87 | ST MIRREN ............1 | DUNDEE UNITED................0 | |
| | (After extra time) | | |
| 1987-88 | CELTIC....................2 | DUNDEE UNITED................1 | |
| 1988-89 | CELTIC....................1 | RANGERS ........................0 | |
| 1989-90 | ABERDEEN ............0 | CELTIC ..............................0 | |
| | (After extra time. Aberdeen won 9-8 on penalties) | | |
| 1990-91 | MOTHERWELL ......4 | DUNDEE UNITED................3 | |
| | (After extra time) | | |
| 1991-92 | RANGERS ............2 | AIRDRIE ............................1 | |
| 1992-93 | RANGERS ............2 | ABERDEEN........................1 | |
| 1993-94 | DUNDEE UTD ........1 | RANGERS ........................0 | |
| 1994-95 | CELTIC....................1 | AIRDRIE ............................0 | |
| 1995-96 | RANGERS ............5 | HEARTS ............................1 | |
| 1996-97 | KILMARNOCK ........1 | FALKIRK ............................0 | |
| 1997-98 | HEARTS..................2 | RANGERS ........................1 | |
| 1998-99 | RANGERS ............1 | CELTIC ..............................0 | |
| 1999-00 | RANGERS ............4 | ABERDEEN........................0 | |
| 2000-01 | CELTIC....................3 | HIBS ..................................0 | |
| 2001-02 | RANGERS ............3 | CELTIC ..............................2 | |

**PAUL LAMBERT and BARRY FERGUSON led Celtic and Rangers out on cup final day at Hampden**

## SCOTTISH CUP-WINNING TEAMS

**1976-77 – CELTIC:** Latchford, McGrain, Lynch, Stanton, McDonald, Aitken, Dalglish, Edvaldsson, Craig, Conn, Wilson.

**1977-78 – RANGERS:** McCloy, Jardine, Greig, Forsyth, Jackson, MacDonald, McLean, Russell, Johnstone, Smith, Cooper.

**1978-79 – RANGERS:** McCloy, Jardine, Dawson, Johnstone, Jackson, Watson, McLean, Russell, Parlane, McDonald, Cooper.

**1979-80 – CELTIC:** Latchford, Sneddon, McGrain, Aitken, Conroy, MacLeod, Provan, Doyle, McCluskey, Burns, McGarvey.

**1980-81 – RANGERS:** Stewart, Jardine, Dawson, Stevens, Forsyth, Bett, Cooper, Russell, D. Johnstone, Redford, MacDonald.

**1981-82 – ABERDEEN:** Leighton, Kennedy, Rougvie, McMaster, McLeish, Miller, Strachan, Cooper, McGhee, Simpson, Hewitt.

**1982-83 – ABERDEEN:** Leighton, Rougvie, McMaster, Cooper, McLeish, Miller, Strachan, Simpson, McGhee, Black, Weir.

**1983-84 – ABERDEEN:** Leighton, McKimmie, Rougvie, Cooper, McLeish, Miller, Strachan, Simpson, McGhee, Black, Weir.

**1984-85 – CELTIC:** Bonner, W. McStay, McGrain, Aitken, McAdam, MacLeod, Provan, P. McStay, Johnston, Burns, McGarvey.

**1985-86 – ABERDEEN:** Leighton, McKimmie, McQueen, McMaster, McLeish, Miller, Hewitt, Cooper, McDougall, Bett, Weir.

**1986-87 – ST MIRREN:** Money, Wilson, D. Hamilton, Abercromby, Winnie, Cooper, Ferguson, McGarvey, McDowall, B. Hamilton, Lambert.

**1987-88 – CELTIC:** McKnight, Morris, Rogan, Aitken, McCarthy, Whyte, Miller, McStay, McAvennie, Walker, Burns.

**1988-89 – CELTIC:** Bonner, Morris, Rogan, Aitken, McCarthy, Whyte, Grant, McStay, Miller, McGhee, Burns.

**1989-90 – ABERDEEN:** Snelders, McKimmie, Robertson, Grant, McLeish, Irvine, Nicholas, Bett, Mason, Connor, Gillhaus.

**1990-91 – MOTHERWELL:** Maxwell, Nijholt, Boyd, Griffin, Paterson, McCart, Arnott, Angus, Ferguson (Kirk), O'Donnell, Cooper (O'Neill).

**1991-92 – RANGERS:** Goram, Stevens, Robertson, Gough, Spackman, Brown, McCall, McCoist, Hateley, Mikhailitchenko, Durrant. Subs: Gordon, Rideout.

**1992-93 – RANGERS:** Goram, McPherson, Gough, Brown, Robertson, Murray, Ferguson, McCall, Durrant, Hateley, Huistra. Subs: Pressley, McSwegan.

**1993-94 – DUNDEE UNITED:** Van De Kamp, Cleland, Malpas, McInally, Petric, Welsh, Bowman, Hannah, McLaren, Brewster, Dailly. Subs: Nixon, Bollan.

**1994-95 – CELTIC:** Bonner, Boyd, McKinlay, Vata, McNally, Grant, McLaughlin, McStay, Van Hooijdonk (Falconer), Donnelly (O'Donnell), Collins.,

**1995-96 – RANGERS:** Goram, Cleland, Robertson, Gough, McLaren, Brown, Durie, Gascoigne, Ferguson (Durrant), McCall, Laudrup. Subs (not used): Petric, Andersen.

**1996-97 – KILMARNOCK:** Lekovic, MacPherson, Kerr, Montgomerie, McGowne, Reilly, Bagan (Mitchell 88), Holt, Wright (Henry 77), McIntyre (Brown 83), Burke.

**1997-98 – HEARTS:** Rousett, McPherson, Naysmith, Weir, Salvatore, Ritchie, McCann, Fulton, Adam (Hamilton), Cameron, Flogel.

**1998-99 – RANGERS:** Klos, Porrini (Kanchelskis), Vidmar, Amoruso, Hendry, McCann (I Ferguson), McInnes, Wallace, van Bronckhorst, Amato (Wilson), Albertz.

**1999-00 – RANGERS:** Klos, Reyna, Moore (Porrini), Vidmar, Numan, Kanchelskis, Ferguson, Albertz, van Bronckhorst (Tugay), Wallace (McCann), Dodds

**2000-01 – CELTIC:** Douglas, Mjallby, Vega, Valgaeren, Agathe, Lennon, Lambert (Boyd) Moravcik (McNamara) Thompson (Johnson), Larsson, Sutton.

**2001-02 – RANGERS:** Klos, Ross, Moore, Amoruso, Numan, Ricksen, de Boer, Ferguson, Lovenkrands, McCann, Caniggia (Arveladze).

**HUGH DALLAS took charge of the 2002 Tennent's Scottish Cup Final**

## PLAYER OF THE YEAR

*AWARDED BY THE SCOTTISH FOOTBALL WRITERS' ASSOCIATION.*

| | |
|---|---|
| 1965 | BILLY McNEILL (Celtic) |
| 1966 | JOHN GREIG (Rangers) |
| 1967 | RONNIE SIMPSON (Celtic) |
| 1968 | GORDON WALLACE (Raith Rovers) |
| 1969 | BOBBY MURDOCH (Celtic) |
| 1970 | PAT STANTON (Hibernian) |
| 1971 | MARTIN BUCHAN (Aberdeen) |
| 1972 | DAVE SMITH (Rangers) |
| 1973 | GEORGE CONNELLY (Celtic) |
| 1974 | WORLD CUP SQUAD |
| 1975 | SANDY JARDINE (Rangers) |
| 1976 | JOHN GREIG (Rangers) |
| 1977 | DANNY McGRAIN (Celtic) |
| 1978 | DEREK JOHNSTONE (Rangers) |
| 1979 | ANDY RITCHIE (Morton) |
| 1980 | GORDON STRACHAN (Aberdeen) |
| 1981 | ALAN ROUGH (Partick Thistle) |
| 1982 | PAUL STURROCK (Dundee United) |
| 1983 | CHARLIE NICHOLAS (Celtic) |
| 1984 | WILLIE MILLER (Aberdeen) |
| 1985 | HAMISH McALPINE (Dundee United) |
| 1986 | SANDY JARDINE (Hearts) |
| 1987 | BRIAN McCLAIR (Celtic) |
| 1988 | PAUL McSTAY (Celtic) |
| 1989 | RICHARD GOUGH (Rangers) |
| 1990 | ALEX McLEISH (Aberdeen) |
| 1991 | MAURICE MALPAS (Dundee United) |
| 1992 | ALLY McCOIST (Rangers) |
| 1993 | ANDY GORAM (Rangers) |
| 1994 | MARK HATELEY (Rangers) |
| 1995 | BRIAN LAUDRUP (Rangers) |
| 1996 | PAUL GASCOIGNE (Rangers) |
| 1997 | BRIAN LAUDRUP (Rangers) |
| 1998 | CRAIG BURLEY (Celtic) |
| 1999 | HENRIK LARSSON (Celtic) |
| 2000 | BARRY FERGUSON (Rangers) |
| 2001 | HENRIK LARSSON (Celtic) |
| 2002 | PAUL LAMBERT (Celtic) |

# PLAYER OF THE YEAR

*AWARDED BY THE SCOTTISH PROFESSIONAL FOOTBALLERS' ASSOCIATION*

## 1977-78

Premier Division .................................Derek Johnstone (Rangers)
First Division ....................................Billy Pirie (Dundee)
Second Division ...........................Dave Smith (Berwick Rangers)

**Young Player of the Year**
Graeme Payne (Dundee United)

## 1978-79

Premier Division ...............................Paul Hegarty (Dundee United)
First Division....................................Brian McLaughlin (Ayr United)
Second Division.......................Michael Leonard (Dunfermline Ath)

**Young Player of the Year**
Raymond Stewart (Dundee United)

## 1979-80

Premier Division.................................Davie Provan (Celtic)
First Division.....................................Sandy Clark (Airdrie)
Second Division.................................Paul Leetion (Falkirk)

**Young Player of the Year**
John MacDonald (Rangers)

## 1980-81

Premier Division.......................................Mark McGhee (Aberdeen)
First Division ....................................Eric Sinclair (Dundee)
Second Division ...............Jimmy Robertson (Queen of the South)

**Young Player of the Year**
Charlie Nicholas (Celtic)

## 1981-82

Premier Division...............................Sandy Clark (Airdrie)
First Division....................................Brian McLaughlin (Motherwell)
Second Division ...........................................Pat Nevin (Clyde)

**Young Player of the Year**
Frank McAvennie (St Mirren)

## 1982-83

Premier Division .........................................Charlie Nicholas (Celtic)
First Division.......................................Gerry McCabe (Clydebank)
Second Division ...........................John Colquhoun (Stirling Albion)

**Young Player of the Year**
Paul McStay (Celtic)

## 1983-84

Premier Division .........................................Willie Miller (Aberdeen)
First Division......................................Gerry McCabe (Clydebank)
Second Division ................................Jim Liddle (Forfar Athletic)

**Young Player of the Year**
John Robertson (Hearts)

## 1984-85

Premier Division ..................................................Jim Duffy (Morton)
First Division.........................................Gerry McCabe (Clydebank)
Second Division ...............................Bernie Slaven (Albion Rovers)

**Young Player of the Year**
Craig Levein (Hearts)

**1985-86**

Premier Division............................Richard Gough (Dundee United)
First Division.................................................John Brogan (Hamilton)
Second Division .....................................Mark Smith (Queen's Park)

**Young Player of the Year**
Craig Levein (Hearts)

**1986-87**

Premier Division .........................................Brian McClair (Celtic)
First Division .................................................Jim Holmes (Morton)
Second Division .....................................John Sludden (Ayr United)

**Young Player of the Year**
Robert Fleck (Rangers)

**1987-88**

Premier Division.........................................Paul McStay (Celtic)
First Division.................................................Alex Taylor (Hamilton)
Second Division ...............................Henry Templeton (Ayr United)

**Young Player of the Year**
John Collins (Hibernian)

**1988-89**

Premier Division .................................Theo Snelders (Aberdeen)
First Division ..............................................Ross Jack (Dunfermline)
Second Division .....................................Paul Hunter (East Fife)

**Young Player of the Year**
Billy McKinlay (Dundee United)

**1989-90**

Premier Division.............................................Jim Bett (Aberdeen)
First Division.................................................Ken Eadie (Clydebank)
Second Division ...................................Willie Watters (Kilmarnock)

**Young Player of the Year**
Scott Crabbe (Hearts)

**1990-91**

Premier Division..........................................Paul Elliott (Celtic)
First Division .............................................Simon Stainrod (Falkirk)
Second Division...............................Kevin Todd (Berwick Rangers)

**Young Player of the Year – Eoin Jess (Aberdeen)**

**1991-92**

Premier Division...........................................Ally McCoist (Rangers)
First Division .....................................Gordon Dalziel (Raith Rovers)
Second Division ...................Andy Thomson (Queen of the South)

**Young Player of the Year – Phil O'Donnell (Motherwell)**

**1992-93**

Premier Division..........................................Andy Goram (Rangers)
First Division .....................................Gordon Dalziel (Raith Rovers)
Second Division .....................................Sandy Ross (Brechin City)

**Young Player of the Year – Eoin Jess (Aberdeen)**

**1993-94**

Premier Division .........................................Mark Hateley (Rangers)
First Division...........................................Richard Cadette (Falkirk)
Second Division ...................Andy Thomson (Queen of the South)

**Young Player of the Year – Phil O'Donnell (Motherwell)**

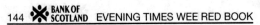

**1994-95**

| | |
|---|---|
| Premier Division | Brian Laudrup (Rangers) |
| First Division | Stephen Crawford (Raith Rovers) |
| Second Division | Derek McInnes (Morton) |
| Third Division | David Bingham (Forfar Ath.) |

**Young Player of the Year –** Charlie Miller (Rangers)

**1995-96**

| | |
|---|---|
| Premier Division | Paul Gascoigne (Rangers) |
| First Division | George O'Boyle (St Johnstone) |
| Second Division | Steven McCormick (Stirling A.) |
| Third Division | Jason Young (Livingston) |

**Young Player of the Year –** Jackie McNamara (Celtic)

**1996-97**

| | |
|---|---|
| Premier Division | Paolo di Canio (Celtic) |
| First Division | Roddy Grant (St Johnstone) |
| Second Division | Paul Ritchie (Hamilton) |
| Third Division | Ian Stewart (Inverness CT) |

**Young Player of the Year –** Robbie Winters (Dundee United)

**1997-98**

| | |
|---|---|
| Premier Division | Jackie McNamara (Celtic) |
| First Division | James Grady (Dundee) |
| Second Division | Paul Lovering (Clydebank) |
| Third Division | Willie Irvine (Alloa) |

**Young Player of the Year –** Gary Naysmith (Hearts)

**1998-99**

| | |
|---|---|
| Premier Division | Henrik Larsson (Celtic) |
| First Division | Russell Latapy (Hibs) |
| Second Division | David Bingham (Livingston) |
| Third Division | Neil Tarrant (Ross County) |

**Young Player of the Year –** Barry Ferguson (Rangers)

**1999-2000**

| | |
|---|---|
| Premier Division | Mark Viduka (Celtic) |
| First Division | Stevie Crawford (Dunfermline) |
| Second Division | Brian Carrigan (Clyde) |
| Third Division | Stevie Milne (Forfar) |

**Young Player of the Year –** Kenny Miller (Hibs)

**2000-2001**

| | |
|---|---|
| Premier Division | Henrik Larsson (Celtic) |
| First Division | David Bingham (Livingston) |
| Second Division | Scott McLean (Partick Thistle) |
| Third Division | Steve Hislop (East Stirling) |

**Young Player of the Year –** Stilian Petrov (Celtic)

**2001-2002**

| | |
|---|---|
| Premier Division | Lorenzo Amoruso (Rangers) |
| First Division | Owen Coyle (Airdrie) |
| Second Division | John O'Neil (Queen of the South) |
| Third Division | Paul McManus (East Fife) |

**Young Player of the Year –** Kevin McNaughton (Aberdeen)

## ENGLISH PLAYER OF THE YEAR

*AWARDED BY THE ENGLISH FOOTBALL WRITERS' ASSOCIATION*

1948 **Stanley Matthews** (Blackpool)
1949 **Johnny Carey** (Man U)
1950 **Joe Mercer** (Arsenal)
1951 **Harry Johnston** (Blackpool)
1952 **Billy Wright** (Wolves)
1953 **Nat Lofthouse** (Bolton W.)
1954 **Tom Finney** (Preston NE)
1955 **Don Revie** (Man City)
1956 **Bert Trautmann** (Man City)
1957 **Tom Finney** (Preston NE)
1958 **Danny Blanchflower** (Spurs)
1959 **Syd Owen** (Luton Town)
1960 **Bill Slater** (Wolves)
1961 **Danny Blanchflower** (Spurs)
1962 **Jimmy Adamson** (Burnley)
1963 **Stanley Matthews** (Stoke C)
1964 **Bobby Moore** (West Ham)
1965 **Bobby Collins** (Leeds U)
1966 **Bobby Charlton** (Man U)
1967 **Jackie Charlton** (Leeds U)
1968 **George Best** (Man U)
1969 **Dave Mackay** (Derby)/ **Tony Book** (Man City)
1970 **Billy Bremner** (Leeds U)
1971 **Frank McLintock** (Arsenal)
1972 **Gordon Banks** (Stoke City)
1973 **Pat Jennings** (Spurs)
1974 **Ian Callaghan** (Liverpool)
1975 **Alan Mullery** (Fulham)

1976 **Kevin Keegan** (Liverpool)
1977 **Emlyn Hughes** (Liverpool)
1978 **Kenny Burns** (Notts Forest)
1979 **Kenny Dalglish** (Liverpool)
1980 **Terry McDermott** (Liverpool)
1981 **Frans Thijssen** (Ipswich T)
1982 **Steve Perryman** (Spurs)
1983 **Kenny Dalglish** (Liverpool)
1984 **Ian Rush** (Liverpool)
1985 **Neville Southall** (Everton)
1986 **Gary Lineker** (Everton)
1987 **Clive Allen** (Tottenham H.)
1988 **John Barnes** (Liverpool)
1989 **Steve Nicol** (Liverpool)
1990 **John Barnes** (Liverpool)
1991 **Gordon Strachan** (Leeds U)
1992 **Gary Lineker** (Spurs)
1993 **Chris Waddle** (Sheffield W)
1994 **Alan Shearer** (Blackburn R)
1995 **Jurgen Klinsmann** (Spurs)
1996 **Eric Cantona** (Man U)
1997 **Gianfranco Zola** (Chelsea)
1998 **Dennis Bergkamp** (Arsenal)
1999 **David Ginola** (Spurs)
2000 **Roy Keane** (Man U)
2001 **Teddy Sheringham** (Man U)
2002 **Robert Pires** (Arsenal)

**ROBERT PIRES**

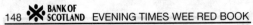
# EUROPEAN FOOTBALLER OF THE YEAR

|  |  |
|---|---|
| 1956 | STANLEY MATTHEWS (Blackpool) |
| 1957 | ALFREDO DI STEFANO (Real Madrid) |
| 1958 | RAYMOND KOPA (Real Madrid) |
| 1959 | ALFREDO DI STEFANO (Real Madrid) |
| 1960 | LUIS SUAREZ (Barcelona) |
| 1961 | OMAR SIVORI (Juventus) |
| 1962 | JOSEF MASOPUST (Dukla Prague) |
| 1963 | LEV YASHIN (Moscow Dynamo) |
| 1964 | DENIS LAW (Manchester United) |
| 1965 | EUSEBIO (Benfica) |
| 1966 | BOBBY CHARLTON (Manchester United) |
| 1967 | FLORIAN ALBERT (Ferencvaros) |
| 1968 | GEORGE BEST (Manchester United) |
| 1969 | GIANNI RIVERA (AC Milan) |
| 1970 | GERD MULLER (Bayern Munich) |
| 1971 | JOHAN CRUYFF (Ajax Amsterdam) |
| 1972 | FRANZ BECKENBAUER (Bayern Munich) |
| 1973 | JOHAN CRUYFF (Barcelona) |
| 1974 | JOHAN CRUYFF (Barcelona) |
| 1975 | OLEG BLOKHIN (Dynamo Kiev) |
| 1976 | FRANZ BECKENBAUER (Bayern Munich) |
| 1977 | ALLAN SIMONSEN (Borussia Moenchengladbach) |
| 1978 | KEVIN KEEGAN (SV Hamburg) |
| 1979 | KEVIN KEEGAN (SV Hamburg) |
| 1980 | KARL-HEINZ RUMMENIGGE (Bayern Munich) |
| 1981 | KARL-HEINZ RUMMENIGGE (Bayern Munich) |
| 1982 | PAOLO ROSSI (Juventus) |
| 1983 | MICHEL PLATINI (Juventus) |
| 1984 | MICHEL PLATINI (Juventus) |
| 1985 | MICHEL PLATINI (Juventus) |
| 1986 | IGOR BELANOV (Dynamo Kiev) |
| 1987 | RUUD GULLIT (AC Milan) |
| 1988 | MARCO VAN BASTEN (AC Milan) |
| 1989 | MARCO VAN BASTEN (AC Milan) |
| 1990 | LOTHAR MATTHAUS (West Germany World Cup winning captain) |
| 1991 | JEAN-PIERRE PAPIN (Marseilles) |
| 1992 | MARCO VAN BASTEN (AC Milan) |
| 1993 | ROBERTO BAGGIO (Juventus) |
| 1994 | HIRSTO STOICHKOV (Barcelona) |
| 1995 | GEORGE WEAH (AC Milan) |
| 1996 | MATTHIAS SAMMER (Borussia Dortmund) |
| 1997 | RONALDO (Inter Milan) |
| 1998 | ZINEDINE ZIDANE (Juventus) |
| 1999 | RIVALDO (Barcelona) |
| 2000 | LUIS FIGO (Real Madrid) |
| 2001 | MICHAEL OWEN (Liverpool) |

# SCOTLAND'S INTERNATIONAL RECORD
## v ENGLAND (Scotland scores first)
### The year refers to the season, i.e. 1873 is season 1872-73

| | | | | | |
|---|---|---|---|---|---|
| 1873 | 0-0 | Partick | 1913 | 0-1 | Chelsea |
| 1873 | 2-4 | The Oval | 1914 | 3-1 | Hampden |
| 1874 | 2-1 | Partick | 1920 | 4-5 | Sheffield |
| 1875 | 2-2 | The Oval | 1921 | 3-0 | Hampden |
| 1876 | 3-0 | Partick | 1922 | 1-0 | Aston Villa |
| 1877 | 3-1 | The Oval | 1923 | 2-2 | Hampden |
| 1878 | 7-2 | Hampden | 1924 | 1-1 | Wembley |
| 1879 | 4-5 | The Oval | 1925 | 2-0 | Hampden |
| 1880 | 5-4 | Hampden | 1926 | 1-0 | Manchester |
| 1881 | 6-1 | The Oval | 1927 | 1-2 | Hampden |
| 1882 | 5-1 | Hampden | 1928 | 5-1 | Wembley |
| 1883 | 3-2 | Sheffield | 1929 | 1-0 | Hampden |
| 1884 | 1-0 | Cathkin | 1930 | 2-5 | Wembley |
| 1885 | 1-1 | The Oval | 1931 | 2-0 | Hampden |
| 1886 | 1-1 | Hampden | 1932 | 0-3 | Wembley |
| 1887 | 3-2 | Blackburn | 1933 | 2-1 | Hampden |
| 1888 | 0-5 | Hampden | 1934 | 0-3 | Wembley |
| 1889 | 3-2 | The Oval | 1935 | 2-0 | Hampden |
| 1890 | 1-1 | Hampden | 1936 | 1-1 | Wembley |
| 1891 | 1-2 | Blackburn | 1937 | 3-1 | Hampden |
| 1892 | 1-4 | Ibrox | 1938 | 1-0 | Wembley |
| 1893 | 2-5 | Richmond | 1939 | 1-2 | Hampden |
| 1894 | 2-2 | Celtic Park | 1947 | 1-1 | Wembley |
| 1895 | 0-3 | Everton | 1948 | 0-2 | Hampden |
| 1896 | 2-1 | Celtic Park | 1949 | 3-1 | Wembley |
| 1897 | 2-1 | Crystal Pal | 1950 | 0-1 | Hampden |
| 1898 | 1-3 | Celtic Park | 1951 | 3-2 | Wembley |
| 1899 | 1-2 | Birmingham | 1952 | 1-2 | Hampden |
| 1900 | 4-1 | Celtic Park | 1953 | 2-2 | Wembley |
| 1901 | 2-2 | Crystal Pal | 1954 | 2-4 | Hampden |
| 1902 | 2-2 | Birmingham | 1955 | 2-7 | Wembley |
| 1903 | 2-1 | Sheffield | 1956 | 1-1 | Hampden |
| 1904 | 0-1 | Celtic Park | 1957 | 1-2 | Wembley |
| 1905 | 0-1 | Crystal Pal | 1958 | 0-4 | Hampden |
| 1906 | 2-1 | Hampden | 1959 | 0-1 | Wembley |
| 1907 | 1-1 | Newcastle | 1960 | 1-1 | Hampden |
| 1908 | 1-1 | Hampden | 1961 | 3-9 | Wembley |
| 1909 | 0-2 | Crystal Pal | 1962 | 2-0 | Hampden |
| 1910 | 2-0 | Hampden | 1963 | 2-1 | Wembley |
| 1911 | 1-1 | Liverpool | 1964 | 1-0 | Hampden |
| 1912 | 1-1 | Hampden | 1965 | 2-2 | Wembley |

| 1966 | 3-4 | Hampden |
| 1967 | 3-2 | Wembley |
| 1968 | 1-1 | Hampden |
| 1969 | 1-4 | Wembley |
| 1970 | 0-0 | Hampden |
| 1971 | 1-3 | Wembley |
| 1972 | 0-1 | Hampden |
| 1973 | 0-5 | Hampden |
| 1973 | 0-1 | Wembley |
| 1974 | 2-0 | Hampden |
| 1975 | 1-5 | Wembley |
| 1976 | 2-1 | Hampden |
| 1977 | 2-1 | Wembley |
| 1978 | 0-1 | Hampden |
| 1979 | 1-3 | Wembley |
| 1980 | 0-2 | Hampden |
| 1981 | 1-0 | Wembley |
| 1982 | 0-1 | Hampden |
| 1983 | 0-2 | Wembley |

| 1984 | 1-1 | Hampden |

**SIR STANLEY ROUS CUP**

| 1985 | 1-0 | Hampden |
| 1986 | 1-2 | Wembley |

**BECAME A THREE-NATION COMPETITION**

| 1987 | 0-0 | Hampden |

*(Scotland 0 Brazil 2. England 1 Brazil 1; Winners – Brazil)*

| 1988 | 0-1 | Wembley |

*(Scotland 0 Colombia 0; England 1 Colombia 1. Winners: England)*

| 1989 | 0-2 | Hampden |

*(Scotland 2 Chile 0; England 0 Chile 0. Winners – England)*

| 1996 | 0-2 | Wembley |
| 1999 | 0-2 | Hampden |
| 1999 | 1-0 | Wembley |

**RICHARD GOUGH** holds the Sir Stanley Rous Cup aloft after scoring the only goal of the game in a Scotland win over England at Hampden in 1985

## v NORTHERN IRELAND
### (Scotland scores first)

| | | | | | | |
|------|------|--------|------|------|--------|
| 1884 | 5-0 | Belfast | 1932 | 3-1 | Glasgow |
| 1885 | 8-2 | Glasgow | 1933 | 4-0 | Belfast |
| 1886 | 7-2 | Belfast | 1934 | 1-2 | Glasgow |
| 1887 | 4-1 | Glasgow | 1935 | 1-2 | Belfast |
| 1888 | 10-2 | Belfast | 1936 | 2-1 | Edinburgh |
| 1889 | 7-0 | Glasgow | 1937 | 3-1 | Belfast |
| 1890 | 4-1 | Belfast | 1938 | 1-1 | Aberdeen |
| 1891 | 2-1 | Glasgow | 1939 | 2-0 | Belfast |
| 1892 | 3-2 | Belfast | 1947 | 0-0 | Glasgow |
| 1893 | 6-1 | Glasgow | 1948 | 0-2 | Belfast |
| 1894 | 2-1 | Belfast | 1949 | 3-2 | Glasgow |
| 1895 | 3-1 | Glasgow | 1950 | 8-2 | Belfast |
| 1896 | 3-3 | Belfast | 1951 | 6-1 | Glasgow |
| 1897 | 5-1 | Glasgow | 1952 | 3-0 | Belfast |
| 1898 | 3-0 | Belfast | 1953 | 1-1 | Glasgow |
| 1899 | 9-1 | Glasgow | 1954 | 3-1 | Belfast |
| 1900 | 3-0 | Belfast | 1955 | 2-2 | Glasgow |
| 1901 | 11-0 | Glasgow | 1956 | 1-2 | Belfast |
| 1902 | 5-1 | Belfast | 1957 | 1-0 | Glasgow |
| 1903 | 0-2 | Glasgow | 1958 | 1-1 | Belfast |
| 1904 | 1-1 | Dublin | 1959 | 2-2 | Glasgow |
| 1905 | 4-0 | Glasgow | 1960 | 4-0 | Belfast |
| 1906 | 1-0 | Dublin | 1961 | 5-2 | Glasgow |
| 1907 | 3-0 | Glasgow | 1962 | 6-1 | Belfast |
| 1908 | 5-0 | Dublin | 1963 | 5-1 | Glasgow |
| 1909 | 5-0 | Glasgow | 1964 | 1-2 | Belfast |
| 1910 | 0-1 | Belfast | 1965 | 3-2 | Glasgow |
| 1911 | 2-0 | Glasgow | 1966 | 2-3 | Belfast |
| 1912 | 4-1 | Belfast | 1967 | 2-1 | Glasgow |
| 1913 | 2-1 | Dublin | 1968 | 0-1 | Belfast |
| 1914 | 1-1 | Belfast | 1969 | 1-1 | Glasgow |
| 1920 | 3-0 | Glasgow | 1970 | 1-0 | Belfast |
| 1921 | 2-0 | Belfast | 1971 | 0-1 | Glasgow |
| 1922 | 2-1 | Glasgow | 1972 | 2-0 | Glasgow |
| 1923 | 1-0 | Belfast | 1973 | 1-2 | Glasgow |
| 1924 | 2-0 | Glasgow | 1974 | 0-1 | Glasgow |
| 1925 | 3-0 | Belfast | 1975 | 3-0 | Glasgow |
| 1926 | 4-0 | Glasgow | 1976 | 3-0 | Glasgow |
| 1927 | 2-0 | Belfast | 1977 | 3-0 | Glasgow |
| 1928 | 0-1 | Glasgow | 1978 | 1-1 | Glasgow |
| 1929 | 7-3 | Belfast | 1979 | 1-0 | Glasgow |
| 1930 | 3-1 | Glasgow | 1980 | 0-1 | Belfast |
| 1931 | 0-0 | Belfast | 1981 | 1-1 | Glasgow |

| 1981 | 2-0 | Glasgow |
| 1982 | 0-0 | Belfast |
| 1982 | 1-1 | Belfast |

| 1983 | 0-0 | Glasgow |
| 1984 | 0-2 | Belfast |
| 1992 | 1-0 | Glasgow |

## v WALES
### (Scotland scores first)

| 1876 | 4-0 | Glasgow |
| 1877 | 2-0 | Wrexham |
| 1878 | 9-0 | Glasgow |
| 1879 | 3-0 | Wrexham |
| 1880 | 5-1 | Glasgow |
| 1881 | 5-1 | Wrexham |
| 1882 | 5-0 | Glasgow |
| 1883 | 4-1 | Wrexham |
| 1884 | 4-1 | Glasgow |
| 1885 | 8-1 | Wrexham |
| 1886 | 4-1 | Glasgow |
| 1887 | 2-0 | Wrexham |
| 1888 | 5-1 | Edinburgh |
| 1889 | 0-0 | Wrexham |
| 1890 | 5-0 | Paisley |
| 1891 | 4-3 | Wrexham |
| 1892 | 6-1 | Edinburgh |
| 1893 | 8-0 | Wrexham |
| 1894 | 5-2 | Kilmarnock |
| 1895 | 2-2 | Wrexham |
| 1896 | 4-0 | Dundee |
| 1897 | 2-2 | Wrexham |
| 1898 | 5-2 | Motherwell |
| 1899 | 6-0 | Wrexham |
| 1900 | 5-2 | Aberdeen |
| 1901 | 1-1 | Wrexham |
| 1902 | 5-1 | Greenock |
| 1903 | 1-0 | Cardiff |
| 1904 | 1-1 | Dundee |
| 1905 | 1-3 | Wrexham |
| 1906 | 0-2 | Edinburgh |
| 1907 | 0-1 | Wrexham |
| 1908 | 2-1 | Dundee |
| 1909 | 2-3 | Wrexham |
| 1910 | 1-0 | Kilmarnock |
| 1911 | 2-2 | Cardiff |
| 1912 | 1-0 | Edinburgh |
| 1913 | 0-0 | Wrexham |

| 1914 | 0-0 | Glasgow |
| 1920 | 1-1 | Cardiff |
| 1921 | 2-1 | Aberdeen |
| 1922 | 1-2 | Wrexham |
| 1923 | 2-0 | Paisley |
| 1924 | 0-2 | Cardiff |
| 1925 | 3-1 | Edinburgh |
| 1926 | 3-0 | Cardiff |
| 1927 | 3-0 | Glasgow |
| 1928 | 2-2 | Wrexham |
| 1929 | 4-2 | Glasgow |
| 1930 | 4-2 | Cardiff |
| 1931 | 1-1 | Glasgow |
| 1932 | 3-2 | Wrexham |
| 1933 | 2-5 | Edinburgh |
| 1934 | 2-3 | Cardiff |
| 1935 | 3-2 | Aberdeen |
| 1936 | 1-1 | Cardiff |
| 1937 | 1-2 | Dundee |
| 1938 | 1-2 | Cardiff |
| 1939 | 3-2 | Edinburgh |
| 1946 | 1-3 | Wrexham |
| 1947 | 1-2 | Glasgow |
| 1948 | 3-1 | Cardiff |
| 1949 | 2-0 | Glasgow |
| 1950 | 3-1 | Cardiff |
| 1951 | 0-1 | Glasgow |
| 1952 | 2-1 | Cardiff |
| 1953 | 3-3 | Glasgow |
| 1954 | 1-0 | Cardiff |
| 1955 | 2-0 | Glasgow |
| 1956 | 2-2 | Cardiff |
| 1957 | 1-1 | Glasgow |
| 1958 | 3-0 | Cardiff |
| 1959 | 1-1 | Glasgow |
| 1960 | 0-2 | Cardiff |
| 1961 | 2-0 | Glasgow |
| 1962 | 3-2 | Cardiff |

| Year | Score | Venue | | Year | Score | Venue |
|------|-------|-------|---|------|-------|-------|
| 1963 | 2-1 | Glasgow | | 1977 | 0-0 | Wrexham |
| 1964 | 2-3 | Cardiff | | 1978 | 2-0 | Liverpool |
| 1965 | 4-1 | Glasgow | | | *(Wales' home game in* | |
| 1966 | 1-1 | Cardiff | | | *World Cup qualifier)* | |
| 1967 | 3-2 | Glasgow | | 1978 | 1-1 | Glasgow |
| 1969 | 5-3 | Wrexham | | 1979 | 0-3 | Cardiff |
| 1970 | 0-0 | Glasgow | | 1980 | 1-0 | Glasgow |
| 1971 | 0-0 | Cardiff | | 1981 | 0-2 | Swansea |
| 1972 | 1-0 | Glasgow | | 1982 | 1-0 | Glasgow |
| 1973 | 2-0 | Wrexham | | 1983 | 2-0 | Cardiff |
| 1974 | 2-0 | Glasgow | | 1984 | 2-1 | Glasgow |
| 1975 | 2-2 | Cardiff | | 1985 | 0-1 | Glasgow |
| 1976 | 3-1 | Glasgow | | 1986 | 1-1 | Cardiff |
| 1977 | 1-0 | Glasgow | | 1997 | 0-1 | Kilmarnock |

**JOHN HARTSON**
leads the line for
Wales

## AMERICA
### (Scotland scores first)

| | | | |
|---|---|---|---|
| 1952 | 6-0 ................Glasgow | 1996 | 1-2....................Hartford |
| 1992 | 1-0.....................Denver | 1998 | 0-0 .............Washington |

## ARGENTINA
### (Scotland scores first)

| | | | |
|---|---|---|---|
| 1977 | 1-1 ............Buenos Aires | 1990 | 1-0 .................Glasgow |
| 1979 | 1-3 .................Glasgow | | |

## AUSTRALIA
### (Scotland scores first)

| | | | |
|---|---|---|---|
| 1986 | 2-0 .................Glasgow | 1996 | 1-0 .................Glasgow |
| 1986 | 0-0...............Melbourne | 2000 | 0-2 .................Glasgow |

## AUSTRIA
### (Scotland scores first)

| | | | |
|---|---|---|---|
| 1931 | 0-5 .....................Vienna | 1963 | 4-1 .................Glasgow |
| 1934 | 2-2 .................Glasgow | | *(Referee abandoned match ....* |
| 1937 | 1-1 .....................Vienna | | *after 79 minutes)* |
| 1951 | 0-1 .................Glasgow | 1969 | 2-1 .................Glasgow |
| 1951 | 0-4 .....................Vienna | 1970 | 0-2 .....................Vienna |
| 1954 | 0-1 .....................Zurich | 1979 | 2-3 .....................Vienna |
| 1955 | 4-1 .....................Vienna | 1980 | 1-1 .................Glasgow |
| 1956 | 1-1 .................Glasgow | 1994 | 2-1 .....................Vienna |
| 1960 | 1-4 .....................Vienna | 1997 | 0-0 .....................Vienna |
| | | 1997 | 2-0 .................Glasgow |

## BELARUS
### (Scotland scores first)

| | | | |
|---|---|---|---|
| 1997 | 1-0 ........................Minsk | 1998 | 4-1 .................Aberdeen |

## BELGIUM
### (Scotland scores first)

| | | | |
|---|---|---|---|
| 1946 | 2-2 .................Glasgow | 1980 | 1-3 ...................Glasgow |
| 1947 | 1-2 .................Brussels | 1983 | 2-3 .................Brussels |
| 1948 | 2-0 .................Glasgow | 1984 | 1-1 ...................Glasgow |
| 1951 | 5-0 .................Brussels | 1987 | 1-4 .................Brussels |
| 1971 | 0-3 ....................Liege | 1988 | 2-0 .................Glasgow |
| 1972 | 1-0 .................Aberdeen | 2001 | 2-2 .................Glasgow |
| 1974 | 1-2 .................Brussels | 2001 | 0-2 .................Brussels |
| 1980 | 0-2 .................Brussels | | |

## BOSNIA
### (Scotland scores first)

| | | | |
|---|---|---|---|
| 1999 | 2-1 .................Sarajevo | 1999 | 1-0 .................Glasgow |

## BRAZIL
### (Scotland scores first)

| | | | |
|---|---|---|---|
| 1966 | 1-1 .................Glasgow | 1982 | 1-4 ...................Seville |
| 1972 | 0-1 .....................Rio | 1987 | 0-2 .................Glasgow |
| 1973 | 0-1 .................Glasgow | 1990 | 0-1 ....................Turin |
| 1974 | 0-0 .................Frankfurt | 1998 | 1-2 .....................Paris |
| 1977 | 0-2 .....................Rio | | |

## BULGARIA
### (Scotland scores first)

| | | | |
|---|---|---|---|
| 1978 | 2-1 .................Glasgow | 1991 | 1-1 .....................Sofia |
| 1987 | 0-0 .................Glasgow | 1991 | 1-1 .................Glasgow |
| 1988 | 1-0 .....................Sofia | | |

## CANADA
### (Scotland scores first)

| | | | |
|---|---|---|---|
| 1983 | 2-0 .............Vancouver | 1983 | 2-0 ...................Toronto |
| 1983 | 3-0 .............Edmonton | 1992 | 3-1 ...................Toronto |

## CHILE
### (Scotland scores first)

| | | | |
|---|---|---|---|
| 1977 | 4-2 .................Santiago | 1989 | 2-0 .................Glasgow |

## C.I.S.
### (Scotland score first)

1992 3-0 ...................Sweden

## COLOMBIA
### (Scotland scores first)

| | | |
|---|---|---|
| 1988 0-0 ................Glasgow | 1998 2-2 ...........New Jersey |
| 1996 0-1 ..................Miami | |

## COSTA RICA
### (Scotland score first)

1990 0-1 .....................Genoa

## CROATIA
### (Scotland score first)

| | |
|---|---|
| 2001 1-1..................Zagreb | 2002 0-0.................Glasgow |

## CYPRUS
### (Scotland scores first)

| | |
|---|---|
| 1969 5-0 ................Nicosia | 1989 3-2 ...............Limassol |
| 1969 8-0 ...............Glasgow | 1989 2-1 ...............Glasgow |

## CZECHOSLOVAKIA
### (Scotland scores first)

| | |
|---|---|
| 1937 3-1 ..................Prague | 1972 0-0 ..........Porto Alegre |
| 1938 5-0 ................Glasgow | 1974 2-1 ...............Glasgow |
| 1961 0-4 ..............Bratislava | 1974 0-1 ..............Bratislava |
| 1962 3-2 ................Glasgow | 1977 0-2 ..................Prague |
| 1962 2-4 ................Brussels | 1978 3-1 ................Glasgow |

## CZECH REPUBLIC
### (Scotland scores first)

| | |
|---|---|
| 1999 1-2 ................Glasgow | 1999 2-3...................Prague |

## DENMARK
### (Scotland scores first)

| | |
|---|---|
| 1951 3-1 ................Glasgow | 1973 2-0 ................Glasgow |
| 1952 2-1 ............Copenhagen | 1976 1-0 ..........Copenhagen |
| 1969 1-0 ............Copenhagen | 1976 3-1 ................Glasgow |
| 1971 1-0 ................Glasgow | 1986 0-1 ...................Neza |
| 1971 0-1 ............Copenhagen | 1996 0-2 ..........Copenhagen |
| 1973 4-1 ............Copenhagen | 1998 0-1 ................Glasgow |

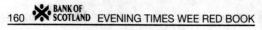
## EAST GERMANY
### (Scotland scores first)

| | |
|---|---|
| 1975 3-0 .................Glasgow | 1984 1-2 ....................Halle |
| 1978 0-1 ................East Berlin | 1986 0-0 .................Glasgow |
| 1983 2-0 .................Glasgow | 1990 0-1 .................Glasgow |

## ECUADOR
### (Scotland score first)

1995 2-1 ...................Toyama

## EGYPT
### (Scotland score first)

1990    1-3 ...........Aberdeen

## EIRE
### (Scotland scores first)

| | |
|---|---|
| 1961 4-1 .................Glasgow | 1987 0-0 ...................Dublin |
| 1961 3-0 ...................Dublin | 1987 0-1 ................Glasgow |
| 1963 0-1 ...................Dublin | 2000 2-1 ...................Dublin |
| 1970 1-1 ...................Dublin | |

## ESTONIA
### (Scotland scores first)

| | |
|---|---|
| 1993 3-0 ...................Tallinn | 1997 0-0 .................Monaco |
| 1993 3-1.................Aberdeen | 1997 2-0 ...........Kilmarnock |
| 1997 0-0 ...................Tallinn | 1998 3-2 ..............Tynecastle |
| (abandoned after 3 seconds, | 1999 0-0 .....................Tallin |
| replay ordered in Monaco) | |

## FAROE ISLANDS
### (Scotland scores first)

| | |
|---|---|
| 1995 5-1 .................Glasgow | 1998 2-1.................Aberdeen |
| 1995 2-0 .................Torshavn | 1999 1-1 .....................Toftir |

## FINLAND
### (Scotland scores first)

| | |
|---|---|
| 1954 2-1 ...................Helsinki | 1992 1-1 .................Glasgow |
| 1965 3-1 .................Glasgow | 1995 2-0 .................Helsinki |
| 1965 2-1 ...................Helsinki | 1996 1-0 .................Glasgow |
| 1977 6-0 .................Glasgow | 1998 1-1 ...............Edinburgh |

## FRANCE
### (Scotland scores first)

| | | |
|---|---|---|
| 1930 | 2-0 | Paris |
| 1932 | 3-1 | Paris |
| 1948 | 0-3 | Paris |
| 1949 | 2-0 | Glasgow |
| 1950 | 1-0 | Paris |
| 1951 | 1-0 | Glasgow |
| 1958 | 1-2 | Obrero |
| 1984 | 0-2 | Marseilles |
| 1989 | 2-0 | Glasgow |
| 1990 | 0-3 | Paris |
| 1998 | 1-2 | St Etienne |
| 2000 | 0-2 | Glasgow |
| 2002 | 0-5 | Paris |

## GERMANY
### (Scotland scores first)

| | | |
|---|---|---|
| 1929 | 1-1 | Berlin |
| 1937 | 2-0 | Glasgow |
| 1992 | 0-2 | Sweden |
| 1993 | 0-1 | Glasgow |
| 1999 | 1-0 | Bremen |

## GREECE
### (Scotland scores first)

| | | |
|---|---|---|
| 1995 | 0-1 | Athens |
| 1996 | 1-0 | Glasgow |

**DAVID TREZEGUET** scored twice v Scotland in March, 2002

## HOLLAND
### (Scotland scores first)

| | | |
|---|---|---|
| 1929 2-0 .............Amsterdam | 1982 2-1 .................Glasgow |
| 1938 3-1 .............Amsterdam | 1986 0-0................Eindhoven |
| 1959 2-1 .............Amsterdam | 1992 0-1 ..................Sweden |
| 1966 0-3 ................Glasgow | 1994 0-1 .................Glasgow |
| 1968 0-0 .............Amsterdam | 1994 1-3 ...................Utrecht |
| 1972 1-2 .............Amsterdam | 1996 0-0...........Birmingham |
| 1978 3-2.................Argentina | 2000 0-0 ...................Arnhem |

## HUNGARY
### (Scotland scores first)

| | | |
|---|---|---|
| 1939 3-1.................Glasgow | 1960 3-3 ...............Budapest |
| 1955 2-4 ................Glasgow | 1980 1-3 ...............Budapest |
| 1955 1-3 ................Budapest | 1988 2-0 ................Glasgow |
| 1958 1-1 ................Glasgow | |

## ICELAND
### (Scotland scores first)

| | |
|---|---|
| 1985 3-0.................Glasgow | 1985 1-0.................Reykjavik |

## IRAN
### (Scotland score first)

| |
|---|
| 1978 1-1 .................Cordoba |

## ISRAEL
### (Scotland scores first)

| | |
|---|---|
| 1981 1-0 .................Tel Aviv | 1986 1-0 ...................Tel Aviv |
| 1981 3-1 ................Glasgow | |

## ITALY
### (Scotland scores first)

| | |
|---|---|
| 1931 0-3......................Rome | 1989 0-2 ...................Perugia |
| 1965 1-0.................Glasgow | 1993 0-0 .......................Ibrox |
| 1965 0-3.....................Naples | 1994 1-3......................Rome |

## JAPAN
### (Scotland score first)

| |
|---|
| 1995 0-0 .............Hiroshima |

## LATVIA
### (Scotland scores first)

| | | |
|---|---|---|
| 1997 2-0................Riga | 2000 1-0................Riga |
| 1998 2-0.........Celtic Park | 2001 2-1.........Glasgow |

## LITHUANIA
### (Scotland scores first)

| | |
|---|---|
| 1998 0-0................Vilnius | 1999 3-0.........Glasgow |

## LUXEMBOURG
### (Scotland scores first)

| | |
|---|---|
| 1947 6-0........Luxembourg | 1988 0-0........Luxembourg |
| 1987 3-0.........Glasgow | |

## MALTA
### (Scotland scores first)

| | |
|---|---|
| 1988 1-1................Valetta | 1994 2-0................Valetta |
| 1990 2-1................Valetta | 1997 3-2................Valetta |
| 1993 3-0.........Glasgow | |

## MOROCCO
### (Scotland score first)

1998 0-3...........St Etienne

## NEW ZEALAND
### (Scotland score first)

1982 5-2...........Malaga

## NIGERIA
### (Scotland score first)

2002 1-2...........Aberdeen

## NORWAY
### (Scotland scores first)

| | |
|---|---|
| 1929 7-3................Bergen | 1979 3-2.........Glasgow |
| 1954 1-0.........Glasgow | 1979 4-0................Oslo |
| 1954 1-1................Oslo | 1989 2-1................Oslo |
| 1963 3-4................Bergen | 1990 1-1.........Glasgow |
| 1964 6-1.........Glasgow | 1992 0-0................Oslo |
| 1974 2-1................Oslo | 1998 1-1.........Bordeaux |

## PARAGUAY
### (Scotland score first)

1958 2-3 ..............Norrkoping

## PERU
### (Scotland scores first)

| | | |
|---|---|---|
| 1972 2-0 ..................Glasgow | 1980 1-1 ..................Glasgow |
| 1978 1-3 ..................Cordoba | |

## POLAND
### (Scotland scores first)

| | |
|---|---|
| 1958 2-1 ..................Warsaw | 1980 0-1 ..................Poznan |
| 1960 2-3 ..................Glasgow | 1990 1-1 ................Glasgow |
| 1965 1-1 ..................Chorzow | 2001 1-1 ............Bydgoszcz |
| 1966 1-2 ..................Glasgow | |

## PORTUGAL
### (Scotland score first)

| | |
|---|---|
| 1950 2-2 ....................Lisbon | 1979 1-0 ....................Lisbon |
| 1955 3-0 ..................Glasgow | 1980 4-1 ................Glasgow |
| 1959 0-1 ....................Lisbon | 1981 0-0 ................Glasgow |
| 1966 0-1 ..................Glasgow | 1982 1-2 ....................Lisbon |
| 1971 0-2 ....................Lisbon | 1993 0-0 ................Glasgow |
| 1972 2-1 ..................Glasgow | 1993 0-5 ....................Lisbon |
| 1975 1-0 ..................Glasgow | |

## ROMANIA
### (Scotland scores first)

| | |
|---|---|
| 1975 1-1..................Bucharest | 1991 2-1 ..................Glasgow |
| 1976 1-1..................Glasgow | 1992 0-1..................Bucharest |
| 1986 3-0..................Glasgow | |

## RUSSIA
### (Scotland scores first)

| | |
|---|---|
| 1995 1-1 ..................Glasgow | 1995 0-0 ..................Moscow |

## SAN MARINO
### (Scotland scores first)

| | | | | | |
|---|---|---|---|---|---|
| 1991 | 2-0 | Serravalle | 1996 | 5-0 | Glasgow |
| 1992 | 4-0 | Glasgow | 2000 | 2-0 | Serravalle |
| 1995 | 2-0 | Serravalle | 2001 | 4-0 | Glasgow |

## SAUDI ARABIA
### (Scotland score first)

1988  2-2 .....................Riyadh

## SOUTH AFRICA
### (Scotland score first)

2002  0-2 .............Hong Kong

## SOUTH KOREA
### (Scotland score first)

2002  1-4 .....................Busan

## SOVIET UNION
### (Scotland scores first)

| | | | | | |
|---|---|---|---|---|---|
| 1967 | 0-2 | Glasgow | 1982 | 2-2 | Malaga |
| 1971 | 0-1 | Moscow | 1991 | 0-1 | Glasgow |

## SPAIN
### (Scotland scores first)

| | | | | | |
|---|---|---|---|---|---|
| 1957 | 4-2 | Glasgow | 1975 | 1-1 | Valencia |
| 1957 | 1-4 | Madrid | 1982 | 0-3 | Valencia |
| 1963 | 6-2 | Madrid | 1985 | 3-1 | Glasgow |
| 1965 | 0-0 | Glasgow | 1985 | 0-1 | Seville |
| 1975 | 1-2 | Glasgow | 1988 | 0-0 | Madrid |

## SWEDEN
### (Scotland scores first)

| | | | | | |
|---|---|---|---|---|---|
| 1952 | 1-3 | Stockholm | 1982 | 2-0 | Glasgow |
| 1953 | 1-2 | Glasgow | 1990 | 2-1 | Genoa |
| 1975 | 1-1 | Gothenburg | 1996 | 0-2 | Stockholm |
| 1977 | 3-1 | Glasgow | 1997 | 1-0 | Glasgow |
| 1981 | 1-0 | Stockholm | 1997 | 1-2 | Gothenburg |

## SWITZERLAND
### (Scotland scores first)

| | | |
|---|---|---|
| 1931 | 3-2 | Geneva |
| 1946 | 3-1 | Glasgow |
| 1948 | 1-2 | Berne |
| 1950 | 3-1 | Glasgow |
| 1957 | 2-1 | Basle |
| 1958 | 3-2 | Glasgow |
| 1973 | 0-1 | Berne |
| 1976 | 1-0 | Glasgow |
| 1983 | 0-2 | Berne |
| 1983 | 2-2 | Glasgow |
| 1991 | 2-1 | Glasgow |
| 1992 | 2-2 | Berne |
| 1993 | 1-3 | Berne |
| 1994 | 1-1 | Aberdeen |
| 1996 | 1-0 | Birmingham |

## TURKEY
### (Scotland score first)

| | | |
|---|---|---|
| 1960 | 2-4 | Ankara |

## URUGUAY
### (Scotland scores first)

| | | |
|---|---|---|
| 1954 | 0-7 | Switzerland |
| 1962 | 2-3 | Glasgow |
| 1984 | 2-0 | Glasgow |
| 1986 | 0-0 | Neza |

## WEST GERMANY
### (Scotland scores first)

| | | |
|---|---|---|
| 1957 | 3-1 | Stuttgart |
| 1959 | 3-2 | Glasgow |
| 1964 | 2-2 | Hanover |
| 1969 | 1-1 | Glasgow |
| 1970 | 2-3 | Hamburg |
| 1974 | 1-1 | Glasgow |
| 1974 | 1-2 | Frankfurt |
| 1986 | 1-2 | Queretaro |

## YUGOSLAVIA
### (Scotland scores first)

| | | |
|---|---|---|
| 1955 | 2-2 | Belgrade |
| 1957 | 2-0 | Glasgow |
| 1958 | 1-1 | Vaasteras |
| 1972 | 2-2 | Belo Horizonte |
| 1974 | 1-1 | Frankfurt |
| 1985 | 6-1 | Glasgow |
| 1989 | 1-1 | Glasgow |
| 1990 | 1-3 | Zagreb |

## ZAIRE
### (Scotland score first)

| | | |
|---|---|---|
| 1974 | 2-0 | Dortmund |

# LIST OF PLAYERS HONOURED

This is a list of full international appearances by Scots in matches against the Home Countries and against foreign nations.

*The code for countries is as follows*

A, Austria; Arg, Argentina; Aus, Australia; Bel, Belgium; Blr, Belarus; Bos, Bosnia; Br, Brazil; Bul, Bulgaria; Ca, Canada; Ch, Chile; CIS Commonwealth of Independent States; Co, Columbia; Cr, Costa Rica; Cro, Croatia; Cy, Cyprus; Cz, Czechoslovakia; CzR, Czech Republic; D, Denmark; E, England; Ec, Ecquador; Ei, Eire; EG, East Germany; Eg, Egypt; Est, Estonia; Fr, France; Fin, Finland; Fi, Faroe Islands; G, Germany; Gr, Greece; H, Hungary; Holl, Holland; I, Italy; Ice, Iceland; Ir, Iran; Is, Israel; J, Japan; L, Luxembourg; La, Latvia; Lth, Lithuania; M, Morocco; Ma, Malta; Nig, Nigeria; N, Norway; Ni, Northern Ireland; Nz, New Zealand; Por, Portugal; Pe, Peru; Pol, Poland; R, Romania; Ru, Russia; S.Ar, Saudi Arabia; Se, Sweden; Sm, San Marino; SA, South Africa; Skor, South Korea; Sp, Spain; Sw, Switzerland; T, Turkey; U, Uruguay; US, United States of America; USSR, Soviet Union; W, Wales; WG, West Germany; Y, Yugoslavia; Z, Zaire.

**The year refers to the season. For example, 1989 is the 1988-89 season**

**ADAMS, J.** (Hearts) (3): 1889 v Ni; 1892 v W; 1893 v Ni.

**AGNEW, W. B.** (Kilmarnock) (3): 1907 v Ni; 1908 v W, Ni.

**AIRD, J.** (Burnley) (4): 1954 v N (2); A, U.

**AITKEN A.** (Newcastle Utd, Middlesbrough, Leicester Fosse) (14): 1901 v E; 1902 v E; 1903 v E, W; 1904 v E; 1905 v E, W; 1906 v E; 1907 v E, W; 1908 v E; 1910 v E; 1911 v E, Ni.

**AITKEN, G, G.** (East Fife, Sunderland) (8): 1949 v E, Fr; 1950 v W, Ni, Sw; 1953 v W, Ni; 1954 v E.

**AITKEN, R.** (Dumbarton) (2): 1886 v E: 1888 v Ni.

**AITKEN, R.** (Celtic, Newcastle Utd, St Mirren) (57): 1980 v Pe, Bel, W, E, Pol; 1983 v Bel, Ca (2); 1984 v Bel, Ni, W; 1985 v E, Ice; 1986 v W, EG, Aus (2), Is, R, E, D, WG, U; 1987 v Bul, Ei (2), L, Bel, E, Br; 1988 v H, Bel, Bul, L, S.Ar., Ma, Sp, Co, E; 1989 v N, Y, I, Cy, (2), Fr, E, Ch; 1990 v Y, Fr, N, Arg, Pol, Ma, Cr, Se, Br; 1992 v R.

**AITKENHEAD, W. A. C.** (Blackburn R.) (1): 1912 v Ni.

**ALBISTON, A.** (Manchester Utd) (14): 1982 v Ni; 1984 v U, Bel, EG, W, E; 1985 v Y, Ice, Sp (2), W; 1986 v Is, Holl, U.

**ALEXANDER, D.** (East Stirlingshire) (2): 1894 v W, Ni.

**ALEXANDER, G.** (Preston) (3): 2002 v Nig, Skor, SA.

**ALLAN, D. S.** (Queen's Park) (3): 1885 v E, W; 1886 v W.

**ALLAN, G.** (Liverpool) (1): 1897 v E.

**ALLAN, H.** (Hearts, b) (1): 1902 v W.

**ALLAN, J.** (Queen's Park) (2): 1887 v E, W.

**ALLAN, T.** (Dundee) (2): 1974 v WG, N.

**ANCELL, R. F. D.** (Newcastle Utd) (2): 1937 v W, Ni.

**ANDERSON, A.** (Hearts) (23): 1933 v E; 1934 v A, E, W, Ni; 1935 v E, W, Ni; 1936 v E, W, Ni; 1937 v G, E, W, Ni, A; 1938 v E, W, Ni, Cz, Holl; 1939 v W, H.

**ANDERSON, F.** (Clydesdale) (1): 1874 v E.

**ANDERSON, G.** (Kilmarnock) (1): 1901 v Ni.

**ANDERSON, H. A.** (Raith Rovers) (1): 1914 v W.

**ANDERSON, J.** (Leicester City) (1): 1954 v Fin.

**ANDERSON, K.** (Queen's Park) (3): 1896 v W; 1898 v E, Ni.

**ANDERSON, W.** (Queen's Park) (6): 1882 v E: 1883 v E, W; 1884 v E; 1885 v E, W.

**ANDREWS, P.** (Eastern) (1): 1875 v E.

**ARCHIBALD, A.** (Rangers) (8): 1921 v W; 1922 v W, E; 1923 v Ni; 1924 v E, W; 1931 v E; 1932 v E.

**ARCHIBALD, S.** (Aberdeen, Tottenham H., Barcelona) (27): 1980 v Por, Ni, Pol, H; 1981 v Se, Is (2), Ni (2), E; 1982 v Ni, Por, Sp, Holl, Nz, Br, USSR; 1983 v EG, Sw, Bel; 1984 v EG, E, Fr; 1985 v Sp, E, Ice; 1986 v WG.

**ARMSTRONG, M. W.** (Aberdeen) (3): 1936 v W, Ni; 1937 v G.

**ARNOTT, W.** (Queen's Park) (14): 1883 v W; 1884 v E, Ni; 1885 v E, W; 1886 v E; 1887 v E, W; 1888 v E; 1889 v E; 1890 v E; 1891 v E; 1892 v E; 1893 v E.

**AULD, J. R.** (Third Lanark) (3): 1887 v E, W; 1889 v W.
**AULD, R.** (Celtic) (3): 1959 v H, Por; 1960 W.
**BAIRD, A.** (Queen's Park) (2): 1892 v Ni; 1894 v W.
**BAIRD, D.** (Hearts) (3): 1890 v Ni; 1891 v E; 1892 v W.
**BAIRD, H.** (Airdrie) (1): 1956 v A.
**BAIRD, J. C.** (Vale of Leven) (3): 1876 v E; 1878 v W; 1880 v E.
**BAIRD, S.** (Rangers) (7): 1957 v Y, Sp (2), Sw, WG; 1958 v Fr, Ni.
**BAIRD, W. U.** (St Bernard) (1): 1897 v Ni.
**BANNON, E.** (Dundee Utd) (11): 1980 v Bel; 1983 v Ni, W, E, Ca; 1984 v EG; 1986 v Is, R, E, D, WG.
**BARBOUR, A.** (Renton) (1): 1885 v Ni.
**BARKER, J. B.** (Rangers) (2): 1893 v W: 1894 v W.
**BARRETT, F.** (Dundee) (2): 1894 v Ni; 1895 v W.
**BATTLES, B.** (Celtic) (3): 1901 v E, W, Ni.
**BATTLES, B.** (Hearts) (1): 1931 v W.
**BAULD, W.** (Hearts) (3): 1950 v E, Sw, Por.
**BAXTER, J. C.** (Rangers, Sunderland) (34): 1961 v Ni, Ei (2), Cz; 1962 v Ni, W, E, Cz (2), U; 1963 v W, Ni, E, A, N, Ei, Sp; 1964 v W, E, N, WG; 1965 v W, Ni, Fin; 1966 v Por, Br, Ni, W, E, I; 1967 v W, E, USSR; 1968 v W.
**BAXTER, R. D.** (Middlesbrough) (3): 1939 v E, W, H.
**BEATTIE, A.** (Preston NE) (7): 1937 v E, A, Cz; 1938 v E; 1939 v W, Ni, H.
**BEATTIE, R.** (Preston NE) (1): 1939 v W.
**BEGBIE, I.** (Hearts) (4): 1890 v Ni; 1891 v E; 1892 v W; 1894 v E.
**BELL, A.** (Manchester Utd) (1): 1912 v Ni.
**BELL, J.** (Dumbarton, Everton, Celtic) (10): 1890 v Ni; 1892 v E; 1896 v E; 1897 v E; 1898 v E; 1899 v E, W, Ni; 1900 v E, W.
**BELL, M.** (Hearts) (1): 1901 v W.
**BELL, W. J.** (Leeds Utd) (2): 1966 v Por, Br.
**BENNETT, A.** (Celtic, Rangers) (11): 1904 v W; 1907 v Ni; 1908 v W: 1909 v W, Ni, E; 1910 v E, W; 1911 E, W; 1913 v Ni.
**BENNIE, R.** (Airdrie) (3): 1925 v W, Ni; 1926 v Ni.
**BERNARD, P.** (Oldham Ath.) (2): 1995 v J, Ec.
**BERRY, D.** (Queen's Park) (3): 1894 v W; 1899 v W, Ni.
**BERRY, W. H.** (Queen's Park) (4): 1888 v E; 1889 v E; 1890 v E; 1891 v E.
**BETT, J.** (Rangers, Lokeren, Aberdeen) (25): 1982 v Holl; 1983 v Bel; 1984 v Bel, W, E, Fr; 1985 v Y, Ice, (2), Sp (2), W, E; 1986 v W, Is, Holl; 1987 v Bel; 1988 v H; 1989 v Y; 1990 v Fr, N, Arg, Eg, Ma, Cr.
**BEVERIDGE, W. W.** (Glasgow University) (3): 1879 v E, W; 1880 v W.
**BLACK, A** (Hearts) (3): 1938 v Cz, Holl; 1939 v H.
**BLACK, D.** (Hurlford) (1): 1889 v W.
**BLACK, E.** (Metz) (2): 1988 v H, L.
**BLACK, I. H.** (Southampton) (1): 1948 v E.
**BLACKBURN, J. E.** (Royal Engineers) (1): 1873 v E.

**BLACKLAW, A. S.** (Burnley) (3): 1963 v N, Sp; 1966 v I.

**BLACKLEY, J.** (Hibernian) (7): 1974 v Cz, E, Bel, Z; 1976 v Sw; 1977 v W, Se.

**BLAIR, D.** (Clyde, Aston Villa) (8): 1929 v W, Ni; 1931 v E, A, I; 1932 v W, Ni; 1933 v W.

**BLAIR, J.** (Sheffield W., Cardiff City) (8): 1920 v E, Ni; 1921 v E; 1922 v E; 1923 v E, W, Ni; 1924 v W.

**BLAIR, J.** (Motherwell) (1): 1934 v W.

**BLAIR, J. A.** (Blackpool) (1): 1947 v W.

**BLAIR, W.** (Third Lanark) (1): 1896 v W.

**BLESSINGTON, J.** (Celtic) (4): 1894 v E, Ni; 1896 v E, Ni.

**BLYTH, J. A.** (Coventry City) (2): 1978 v Bul, W.

**BOWMAN, D.** (Dundee United) (6): 1992 v Fin, US; 1993 v G, Est; 1994 v Sw, I.

**BONE, J.** (Norwich City) (2): 1972 v Y; 1973 v D.

**BOOTH, S.** (Aberdeen, Utrecht) (19): 1993 v G, Est (2); 1994 v Sw, Ma; 1995 v Fi, Ru; 1996 v Fin, Sm, Aus, US, Sw; 1998 v D, Fin, Co, M; 2001 v Pol; 2002 Cro, Bel, La.

**BOWIE, J.** (Rangers) (1): 1920 v E, Ni.

**BOWIE, W.** (Linthouse) (1): 1891 v Ni.

**BOWMAN, G. A.** (Montrose) (1): 1892 v Ni.

**BOYD, J. M.** (Newcastle Utd) (1): 1934 v Ni.

**BOYD, R.** (Mossend Swifts) (2): 1889 v Ni; 1891 v W.

**BOYD, T.** (Motherwell, Chelsea, Celtic) (72): 1991 v R (2), Sw, Bul, USSR; 1992 v Sw, Fin, Ca, N, CIS; 1993 v Sw, Por, I, Ma, G, Est (2); 1994 v I, Ma, Holl, A; 1995 v Fin, Fi, Ru (2), Gr, Sm. 1996 v Gr, Fin, Se, Sm, Aus, D, US, U, Holl, E, Sw; 1997 v A (2), La, Se (2), Est (2), W, Ma, Blr; 1998 v Holl, La, Fr, D, Fin, Co, US, Br, N, M. 1999 v Lth, Est, Fi, CzR (2), G, Fi; 2001 v La, Cro, Aus, Bel, Sm, Pol; 2002 v Bel.

**BOYD, W. G.** (Clyde) (2): 1931 v I, Sw, Fin.

**BRACKENBRIDGE, T.** (Hearts) (1): 1888 v Ni.

**BRADSHAW, T.** (Bury) (1): 1928 v E.

**BRAND, R.** (Rangers) (8): 1961 v Ni, Cz, Ei. (2); 1962 v Ni, W, Cz, U.

**BRANDEN, T.** (Blackburn R.) (1): 1896 v E.

**BRAZIL, A.** (Ipswich Town) (13): 1980 v Pol, H; 1982 v Sp, Holl, Ni, W, E, Nz, USSR; 1983 v EG, Sw, W, E.

**BREMNER, D.** (Hibernian) (1): 1976 v Sw.

**BREMNER, W. J.** (Leeds Utd) (54): 1965 v Sp; 1966 v E, Pol, P, Br, I (2); 1967 v W, Ni, E; 1968 v W, E; 1969 v W, E, Ni, D, A, WG, Cy (2); 1970 v Ei, WG, A; 1971 v W, E; 1972 v Por, Bel, Holl, Ni, W, E, Y, Cz, Br; 1973 v D (2), E (2), Ni, Sw, Br; 1974 v Cz, WG, Ni, W, E, Bel, N, Z, Br, Y; 1975 v Sp (2); 1976 v D.

**BRENNAN, F.** (Newcastle Utd) (7): 1947 v W, Ni; 1953 v W, Ni, E; 1954 v Ni, E.

**BRESLIN, B.** (Hibernian) (1): 1897 v W.

**BREWSTER, G.** (Everton) (1): 1921 v E.

**BROGAN, J.** (Celtic) (4): 1971 v W, Ni, Por, E.

**BROWN, A.** (Middlesbrough) (1): 1904 v E.

**BROWN, A.** (St Mirren) (2): 1890 v W; 1891 v W.

**BROWN, A. D.** (East Fife, Blackpool) (14): 1950 v Sw, Por, Fr; 1952 v USA, D, Se; 1953 v W; 1954 v W, E, N (2), Fin, A, U.

**BROWN, G. C. P.** (Rangers) (19): 1931 v W; 1932 v E, W, Ni; 1933 v E; 1935 v A, E, W; 1936 v E, W; 1937 v G, E, W, Ni, Cz; 1938 v E, W, Cz, Holl.

**BROWN, H.** (Partick Th.) (3): 1947 v W, Bel, L.

**BROWN, J.** (Cambuslang) (1): 1890 v W.

**BROWN, J. B.** (Clyde) (1): 1939 v W.

**BROWN, J. G.** (Sheffield U.) (1): 1975 v R.

**BROWN, R.** (Dumbarton) (2): 1884 v W, Ni.

**BROWN, R.** (Rangers) (3): 1947 v Ni; 1949 v Ni; 1952 v E.

**BROWN, R.** (Dumbarton) (1): 1885 v W.

**BROWN, W. D. F.** (Dundee, Tottenham H.) (28): 1958 v Fr; 1959 v E, W, Ni; 1960 v W, Ni, Pol, A, H, T; 1962 v Ni, W, E, Cz; 1963 v W, Ni, E, A; 1964 v Ni, W, N; 1965 v E, Fin, Pol, Sp; 1966 v Ni, Pol, I.

**BROWNING, J.** (Celtic) (1): 1914 v W.

**BROWNLIE, J.** (Hibernian) (7): 1971 v USSR; 1972 v Pe, Ni, E; 1973 v D (2); 1976 v R.

**BROWNLIE, J.** (Third Lanark) (16): 1909 v E, Ni; 1910 v E, W, Ni; 1911 v W, Ni; 1912 v W, Ni, E; 1913 v W, Ni, E; 1914 v W, Ni, E.

**BRUCE, D.** (Vale of Leven) (1): 1890 v W.

**BRUCE, R. F.** (Middlesbrough) (1): 1934 v A.

**BUCHAN, M. M.** (Aberdeen, Manchester Utd.) (34): 1972 v Por, Bel, W, Y, Cz, Br; 1973 v D (2), E; 1974 v WG, Ni, W, N, Br, Y; 1975 v EG, Sp, Por; 1976 v D, R; 1977 v Fin, Cz, Ch, Arg, Br; 1978 v EG, W, Ni, Pe, Ir, Holl; 1979 v A, N, Por.

**BUCHANAN, J.** (Cambuslang) (1): 1889 v Ni.

**BUCHANAN, J.** (Rangers) (2): 1929 v E; 1930 v E.

**BUCHANAN, P. S.** (Chelsea) (1): 1938 v Cz.

**BUCHANAN, R.** (Abercorn) (1): 1891 v W.

**BUCKLEY, P.** (Aberdeen) (3): 1954 v Ni; 1955 v W, Ni.

**BUICK, A.** (Hearts) (2): 1902 v W, Ni.

**BURCHILL, M.** (Celtic) (6): 2000 v Bos, Lth, E (2), Fr, Holl.

**BURLEY C.** (Chelsea, Celtic, Derby) (45): 1995 v J, Ec, Fi. 1996 v Gr, Se, Aus, D, US, Co, Ho, E, Sw; 1997 v A (2), La, Se (2), Est, Ma, Blr 1998 v Blr, La, Fr, Co, US, Br, N, M. 1999 v Fi, CzR. 2000 v Bos (2), Est, Lth, E (2), Holl, Ei; 2001 v Cro, Aus, Bel, Sm; 2002 v Cro, Bel, La.

**BURLEY, G.** (Ipswich Town) (11): 1979 v W, Ni, E, Arg, N; 1980 v Por, Ni, E, Pol; 1982 v W, E.

**BURNS, F.** (Manchester Utd) (1): 1970 v A.

**BURNS, K.** (Birmingham City, Nottingham F.) (20): 1974 v WG; 1975 v EG, Sp (2); 1977 v Cz, W, (2), Se; 1978 v Ni, W, E, Pe, Ir; 1979 v N; 1980 v Pe, A, Bel; 1981 v Is, Ni, W.

**BURNS, T.** (Celtic) (8): 1981 v Ni; 1982 v Holl, W; 1983 v Bel, Ni, Ca (2); 1988 v E.

**BUSBY, M. W.** (Manchester City) (1): 1934 v W.

**CAIRNS, T.** (Rangers) (8): 1920 v W; 1922 v E; 1923 v E, W; 1924 v Ni; 1925 v W, E, Ni.

**CALDERHEAD, D.** (Q.O.S. Wanderers) (1): 1889 v Ni.

**CALDERWOOD, C.** (Tottenham Hotspur, Aston Villa) (36): 1995 v Ru, Sm, J, Ec, Fi. 1996 v Gr, Fin, Se, Sm, US, U, Holl, E, Sw; 1997 A (2), La, Se (2), Est (2); 1998 v Blr, La, Fr, D, Fin, Co, US, Br, N. 1999 v Lth, Est, Fi, CzR. 2000 v Bos (2).

**CALDERWOOD, R.** (Cartvale) (3): 1885 v Ni, E, W.

**CALDOW, E.** (Rangers) (40): 1957 Sp (2), Sw, WG, E; 1958 v Ni, W, Sw, Par, H, Pol, Y, Fr; 1959 v E, W, Ni, WG, Holl, Por; 1960 v E, W, Ni, A, H, T; 1961 v E, W, Ni, Ei (2), Cz; 1962 v Ni, W, E, Cz (2), U; 1963 v W, Ni, E.

**CALDWELL, G.** (Newcastle) (4): 2002 v Fr, Nig, Skor, SA.

**CALDWELL, S.** (Newcastle) (1): 2001 v Pol.

**CALLAGHAN, P.** (Hibernian) (1): 1900 v Ni.

**CALLAGHAN, W. C.** Dunfermline Ath.) (2): 1970 v Ei, W.

**CAMERON, C.** (Hearts, Wolves) (15): 1999 v G, Fi; 2000 v Lth, Fr, Ei; 2001 v La, Sm, Cro, Aus, Sm, Pol; 2002 v Cro, Bel, La, Fr.

**CAMERON, J.** (Rangers) (1): 1886 v NI.

**CAMERON, J.** (Queen's Park) (1): 1896 v Ni.

**CAMERON, J.** (St Mirren, Chelsea) (2): 1904 v Ni; 1909 v E.

**CAMPBELL, C.** (Queen's Park) (13): 1874 v E; 1876 v W; 1877 v E, W; 1878 v E; 1879 v E; 1880 v E; 1881 v E; 1882 v E, W; 1884 v E; 1885 v E; 1886 v E.

**CAMPBELL, H.** (Renton) (1): 1889 v W.

**CAMPBELL, J.** (Sheffield W.) (1): 1913 v W.

**CAMPBELL, J.** (South Western) (1): 1880 v W.

**CAMPBELL, J.** (Kilmarnock) (2): 1891 v Ni; 1892 v W.

**CAMPBELL, J.** (Celtic) (12): 1893 v E, Ni; 1898 v E, Ni; 1900 v E, Ni; 1901 v E, W, Ni; 1902 v W, Ni; 1903 v W.

**CAMPBELL, J.** (Rangers) (4): 1899 v E, W, Ni; 1901 v Ni.

**CAMPBELL, K.** (Liverpool, Partick Th.) (8): 1920 v E, W, Ni; 1921 v W, Ni; 1922 v W. Ni, E.

**CAMPBELL, P.** (Rangers) (2): 1878 v W; 1879 v W.

**CAMPBELL, P.** (Morton) (1): 1898 v W.

**CAMPBELL, R.** (Falkirk, Chelsea) (5): 1947 v Bel, L; 1950 v Sw, Por, Fr.

**CAMPBELL, W.** (Morton) (5): 1947 v Ni; 1948 v E, Bel, Sw, Fr.

**CARABINE, J.** (Third Lanark) (3): 1938 v Holl; 1939 v E, Ni.

**CARR, W. M.** (Coventry City) (6): 1970 v Ni, W, E; 1971 v D; 1972 v Pe; 1973 v D.

**CASSIDY, J.** (Celtic) (4): 1921 v W, Ni; 1923 v Ni; 1924 v W.

**CHALMERS, S.** (Celtic) (5): 1965 v W, Fin; 1966 v Por, Br; 1967 v Ni.

**CHALMERS, W.** (Rangers) (1): 1885 v Ni.

**CHALMERS, W. S.** (Queen's Park) (1): 1929 v Ni.

**CHAMBERS, T.** (Hearts) (1): 1894 v W.

**CHAPLIN, G. D.** (Dundee) (1): 1908 v W.

**CHEYNE, A. G.** (Aberdeen) (5): 1929 v E, N, G, Holl; 1930 v Fr.

**CHRISTIE, A. J.** (Queen's Park) (3): 1898 v W; 1899 v E, Ni.

**CHRISTIE, R. M.** (Queen's Park) (1): 1884 v E.

**CLARK, J.** (Celtic) (4): 1966 v Br; 1967 v W, Ni, USSR.

**CLARK, R. B.** (Aberdeen) (17): 1968 v W, Holl; 1970 v Ni; 1971 v W, Ni, E, D, Por, USSR; 1972 v Bel, Ni, W, E, Cz, Br; 1973 v D, E.

**CLARKE, S.** (Chelsea) (6): 1988 v H, Bel, Bul, S.Ar, Ma; 1984 v Holl.

**CLELAND, J.** (Royal Albert) (1): 1891 v Ni.

**CLEMENTS, R.** (Leith Ath.) (1): 1891 v Ni.

**CLUNAS, W. L.** (Sunderland) (2): 1924 v E; 1926 v W.

**COLLIER, W.** (Raith R.) (1): 1922 v W.

**COLLINS, J.** (Hibs, Celtic, Monaco, Everton) (58): 1988 v S.Ar; 1990 v EG, Pol, Ma; 1991 v Sw, Bul, Ni, Fin; 1993 v Por (2), Ma, G, Est (2); 1994 v Sw, Holl (2), A; 1995 v Fin, Fi (2), Ru (2), Gr, Sm. 1996 v Gr, Fin, Se, Sm, Aus, D, US, U, Holl, E, Sw; 1997 v A (2), La, Se (2), Est, Ma; 1998 v Blr, La, Fr, Fin, Co, US, Br, M, N. 1999 v Lth. 2000 v Bos (2), Est, E (2).

**COLLINS, R. Y.** (Celtic, Everton, Leeds Utd) (31): 1951 v W, Ni, A; 1955 v Y, A, H; 1956 v Ni, W; 1957 v E, W, Sp (2), Sw, WG; 1958 v Ni, W, Sw, H, Pol, Y, Fr, Par; 1959 v E, W, Ni, WG, Holl, Por; 1965 v E, W, Pol, Sp.

**COLLINS, T.** (Hearts) (1): 1909 v W.

**COLMAN, D.** (Aberdeen) (4): 1911 v E, W, Ni; 1913 v Ni.

**COLQUHOUN, E. P.** (Sheffield Utd) (9): 1972 v Por, Holl, Pe, Y, Cz, Br; 1973 v D (2), E.

**COLQUHOUN, J.** (Hearts) (2): 1988 v S.Ar, Malta.

**COMBE, J. R.** (Hibernian) (3): 1948 v E, Bel, Sw.

**CONN, A.** (Hearts) (1): 1956 v A.

**CONN, A.** (Tottenham H.) (2): 1975 v Ni, E.

**CONNACHAN, E. D.** (Dunfermline Ath.) (2): 1962 v Cz, U.

**CONNELLY, G.** (Celtic) (2): 1974 v Cz, WG.

**CONNOLLY, J.** (Everton) (1): 1973 v Sw.

**CONNOR, J.** (Airdrie) (1): 1886 v Ni.

**CONNOR, J.** (Sunderland) (4): 1930 v Fr; 1932 v Ni; 1934 v E; 1935 v Ni.

**CONNOR, R.** (Dundee, Aberdeen) (4): 1986 v Holl; 1988 v S.Ar; 1989 v E; 1991 v R.

**COOK, W. L.** (Bolton W.) (3): 1934 v E; 1935 v W, Ni.

**COOKE, C.** (Dundee, Chelsea) (16): 1966 v W, I, Por, Br; 1968 v E, Holl; 1969 v W, Ni, A, WG, Cy (2); 1970 v A; 1971 v Bel; 1975 v Sp, Por.

**COOPER, D.** (Rangers, Motherwell) (22): 1980 v Pe, A; 1984 v W, E; 1985 v Y, Ice, Sp (2), W; 1986 v W, EG, Aus (2), Holl, WG, U; 1987 v Bul, L, Ei, Br; 1990 v N, Eg.

**CORMACK, P. B.** (Hibernian, Nottingham F.) (9): 1966 v Br; 1969 v D; 1970 v Ei, WG; 1971 v D, W, Por, E; 1972 v Holl.

**COWAN, J.** (Aston Villa) (3): 1896 v E; 1897 v E; 1898 v E.

**COWAN, J.** (Morton) (25): 1948 v Bel, Sw, Fr; 1949 v E, W, Fr; 1950 v E, W, Ni, Sw, Por, Fr; 1951 v E, W, Ni, A (2), D, Fr, Bel; 1952 v Ni, W, USA, D, Se.

**COWAN, W. D.** (Newcastle Utd) (1): 1924 v E.

**COWIE, D.** (Dundee) (20): 1953 v E, Se; 1954 v Ni, W, Fin, N, A, U; 1955 v W, Ni, A, H; 1956 v W, A; 1957 v Ni, W; 1958 v H, Pol, Y, Par.

**COX, S.** (Rangers) (25): 1948 v Fr; 1949 v E, Fr; 1950 v E, Fr, W, Ni, Sw, Por; 1951 v E, D, Fr, Bel, A; 1952 v Ni, W, USA, D, Se; 1953 v W, Ni, E; 1954 v W, Ni, E.

**CRAIG, A.** (Motherwell) (3): 1929 v Ni, Holl; 1932 v E.

**CRAIG, J.** (Celtic) (1): 1977 v Se.

**CRAIG, J. P.** (Celtic) (1): 1968 v W.

**CRAIG, T.** (Rangers) (8): 1927 v Ni; 1928 v Ni; 1929 v N, G, Holl; 1930 v Ni, E, W.

**CRAIG, T. B.** (Newcastle Utd) (1): 1976 v Sw.

**CRAINEY, S** (Celtic) (2): 2002 v Fr, Nig.

**CRAPNELL, J.** (Airdrie) (9): 1929 v E, N, G; 1930 v Fr; 1931 v Ni, Sw; 1932 v E, Fr; 1933 v Ni.

**CRAWFORD, D.** (St Mirren) (3): 1894 v W, Ni; 1900 v W.

**CRAWFORD, J.** (Queen's Park) (5): 1932 v Fr, Ni; 1933 v E, W, Ni.

**CRAWFORD, S.** (Raith Rovers, Dunfermline) (3): 1995 v Ec; 2001 v Pol; 2002 v Fr.

**CRERAND, P. T.** (Celtic, Manchester Utd) (16): 1961 v Ei (2), Cz; 1962 v Ni, W, E, Cz (2), U; 1963 v W, Ni; 1964 v Ni; 1965 v E, Pol, Fin; 1966 v Pol.

**CRINGAN, W.** (Celtic) (5): 1920 v W; 1922 v E, Ni; 1923 v W, E.

**CROSBIE, J. A.** (Ayr Utd, Birmingham C) (2): 1920 v W; 1922 v E.

**CROAL, J. A.** (Falkirk) (3): 1913 v Ni; 1914 v E, W.

**CROPLEY, A. J.** (Hibernian) (2): 1972 v Por, Bel.

**CROSS, J. H.** (Third Lanark) (1): 1903 v Ni.

**CRUICKSHANK, J.** (Hearts) (6): 1964 v WG; 1970 v W, E; 1971 v D, Bel; 1976 v R.

**CRUM, J.** (Celtic) (2): 1936 v E; 1939 v Ni.

**CULLEN, M. J.** (Luton Town) (1): 1956 v A.

**CUMMING, D. S.** (Middlesbrough) (1): 1938 v E.

**CUMMING, J.** (Hearts) (9): 1955 v E, H, Por, Y; 1960 v E, Pol, A, H, T.

**CUMMINGS, G.** (Partick Th., Aston Villa) (9): 1935 v E; 1936 v W, Ni, E; 1937 v G; 1938 v W, Ni, Cz; 1939 v E.

**CUNNINGHAM, A. N.** (Rangers) (12): 1920 v Ni; 1921 v W, E; 1922 v Ni; 1923 v E, W; 1924 v E, Ni; 1926 v E, Ni; 1927 v E, W.

**CUNNINGHAM, W. C.** (Preston NE) (8): 1954 v N (2), U, Fin, A; 1955 v W, E, H.

**CURRAN, H. P.** (Wolves) (5): 1970 v A; 1971 v Ni, E, D, USSR.

**DAILLY, C.** (Derby, Blackburn, West Ham) (34): 1997 v W, Ma, Blr; 1998 v Blr, La, Fr, D, Fin, Co, US, Br, N, M. 1999 v Lth. 2000 v Bos (2), Est, Lth, E (2), Fr, Holl, Ei; 2001 v La, Sm, Aus, Pol; 2002 v Cro, Bel, La, F, Nig, Skor, SA.

**DALGLISH, K.** (Celtic, Liverpool) (102): 1972 v Bel, Holl; 1973 v D (2), E (2), W, Ni, Sw, Br; 1974 v Cz (2), WG (2), Ni, W, E, Bel, N, Z, Br, Y; 1975 v EG, Sp (2), Se, Por, W, Ni, E, R; 1976 v D (2), R, Sw, Ni, E; 1977 v Fin, Cz, W (2), Se, Ni, E, Ch, Arg, Br; 1978 v EG, Cz, W, Bul, Ni, W, E, Pe, Ir, Holl; 1979 v A, N, Por, W, Ni, E, Arg, N; 1980 v Pe, A, Bel (2), Por, Ni, W, E, Pol, H; 1981 v Se, Por, Is; 1982 v Se, Ni, Por, Sp, Holl, Ni, W, E, Nz, Br; 1983 v Bel, Sw; 1984 v U, Bel, EG; 1985 v Y, Ice, Sp, W; 1986 v EG, Aus, R; 1987 v Bul, L.

**DAVIDSON, C.** (Blackburn Rovers) (15): 1999 v Lth, Est, Fi, CzR (2), G, Fi; 2000 v Est, Bos, Lth, E, Fr; 2001 v La, Pol; 2002, La.

**DAVIDSON, D.** (Queen's Park) (5): 1878 v W; 1879 v W; 1880 v W; 1881 v E, W.

**DAVIDSON, J. A.** (Partick Th.) (8): 1954 v N (2), A, U; 1955 v W, Ni, E, H.

**DAVIDSON, S.** (Middlesbrough) (1): 1921 v E.

**DAWSON, A.** (Rangers) (5): 1980 v Pol, H; 1983 v Ni, Ca (2).

**DAWSON, J.** (Rangers) (14): 1935 v Ni; 1936 v E; 1937 v G, E, W, Ni, A, Cz; 1938 v W, Holl, Ni; 1939 v E, Ni, H.

**DEANS, J.** (Celtic) (2): 1975 v EG, Sp.

**DELANEY, J.** (Celtic, Manchester Utd) (13): 1936 v W, Ni; 1937 v G, E, A, Cz; 1938 v Ni; 1939 v W, Ni; 1947 v E; 1948 v E, W, Ni.

**DEVINE, A.** (Falkirk) (1): 1910 v W.

**DEWAR, G.** (Dumbarton) (2): 1888 v Ni; 1889 v E.

**DEWAR, N.** (Third Lanark) (3): 1932 v E, Fr; 1933 v W.

**DICK, J.** (West Ham Utd) (1): 1959 v E.

**DICKIE, M.** (Rangers) (3): 1897 v Ni; 1899 v Ni; 1900 v W.

**DICKOV, P.** (Manchester City) (3): 2001 v Sm, Cro, Aus.

**DICKSON, W.** (Dumbarton) (1): 1888 v Ni.

**DICKSON, W.** (Kilmarnock) (5): 1970 v Ni, W, E; 1971 v D, USSR.

**DIVERS, J.** (Celtic) (1): 1895 v W.

**DIVERS, J.** (Celtic) (1): 1939 v Ni.

**DOBIE, S.** (WBA) (2): 2002 v Skor, SA.

**DOCHERTY, T. H.** (Preston NE, Arsenal) (25): 1952 v W; 1953 v E, Se; 1954 v N (2), A, U; 1955 v W, E, H (2), A; 1957 v E, Y, Sp (2), Sw, WG; 1958 v Ni, W, E, Sw; 1959 v W, E, Ni.

**DODDS, D.** (Dundee Utd) (2): 1984 v U, Ni.

**DODDS, J.** (Celtic) (3): 1914 v E, W, Ni.

**DODDS, W.** (Aberdeen, Dundee Utd, Rangers) (26): 1997 v La, W, Blr; 1998 v Blr. 1999 v Est, Fi, G, Fi, CzR. 2000 v Bos (2), Est, Lth, E (2), Fr, Holl, Ei; 2001 v La, Sm (2), Aus, Bel, Pol; 2002 v Cro, Bel.

**DOIG, J. E.** (Arbroath, Sunderland) (5): 1887 v Ni; 1889 v Ni; 1896 v E; 1899 v E; 1903 v E.

**DONACHIE, W.** (Manchester City) (35): 1972 v Pe, Ni, E, Y, Cz, Br; 1973 v D, E, W, Ni; 1974 v Ni; 1976 v R, Ni, W, E,; 1977 v Fin, Cz, W (2), Se, Ni, E, Ch, Arg, Br; 1978 v EG, W (2), Bul, E, Ir, Holl; 1979 v A, N, Por.

**DONALDSON, A.** (Bolton) (6): 1914 v E, Ni, W; 1920 v E, Ni; 1922 v Ni.

**DONNACHIE, J.** (Oldham Ath.) (3): 1913 v E; 1914 v E, Ni.

**DONNELLY, S.** (Celtic) (10): 1997 v W, Ma; 1998 La, Fr, D, Fin, Co, US. 1999 v Est. Fi.

**DOUGALL, C.** (Birmingham City) (1): 1947 v W.

**DOUGALL, J.** (Preston NE) (1): 1939 v E.

**DOUGAN, R.** (Hearts) (1): 1950 v Sw.

**DOUGLAS, A.** (Chelsea) (1): 1911 v Ni.

**DOUGLAS, J.** (Renfrew) (1): 1880 v W.

**DOUGLAS, R.** (Celtic) (2): 2002 v Nig, SA.

**DOWDS, P.** (Celtic) (1): 1892 v Ni.

**DOWNIE, R.** (Third Lanark) (1): 1892 v W.

**DOYLE, D.** (Celtic) (8): 1892 v E; 1893 v W; 1894 v E; 1895 v E, Ni; 1897 v E; 1898 v E, Ni.

**DOYLE, J.** (Ayr Utd) (1): 1976 v R.

**DRUMMOND, J.** (Falkirk, Rangers) (14): 1892 v Ni; 1894 v Ni; 1895 v Ni, E; 1896 v E, Ni; 1897 v Ni; 1898 v E; 1900 v E; 1901 v E; 1902 v E, W, Ni; 1903 v Ni.

**DUNBAR, M.** (Cartvale) (1): 1886 v Ni.

**DUNCAN, A.** (Hibernian) (6): 1975 v Por, W, Ni, E, R; 1976 v D.

**DUNCAN, D.** (Derby Co.) (14): 1933 v E, W; 1934 v A, W; 1935 v E, W; 1936 v E, W, Ni; 1937 v G, E, W, Ni; 1938 v W.

**DUNCAN, D. M.** (East Fife) (3): 1948 v Bel, Sw, Fr.

**DUNCAN, J.** (Alexandra Ath.) (2): 1878 v W; 1882 v W.

**DUNCAN, J.** (Leicester City) (1): 1926 v W.

**DUNCANSON, J.** (Rangers) (1): 1947 v Ni.

**DUNLOP, J.** (St Mirren) (1): 1890 v W.

**DUNLOP, W.** (Liverpool) (1): 1906 v E.

**DUNN, J.** (Hibernian, Everton) (6): 1925 v W, Ni; 1927 v Ni; 1928 v Ni, E; 1929 v W.

**DURIE, G. S.** (Chelsea, Tottenham, Rangers) (43): 1988 v Bul; 1989 v I, Cy; 1990 v Y, EG, Eg, Se; 1991 v Sw, Bul (2), USSR, Sm (2), 1992 v Sw, R, Ni, Fin, Ca, N, Holl, G; 1993 v Sw, I; 1994 v Sw, I, Holl (2). 1996 US, Holl, E, Sw; 1997 v A, Se, Ma, Blr; 1998 Blr, La, Fr, Fin, Co, Br, N, M.

**DURRANT, I.** (Rangers, Kilmarnock) (20): 1988 v H, Bel, Ma, Sp; 1989 v N; 1993 v Sw, Por (2), I; 1994 v I, Ma. 1999 v Est, Fi, G, Fi, CzR. 2000 v Bos; Est, Holl, Ei.

**DYKES, J.** (Hearts) (2): 1938 v Holl; 1939 v Ni.
**EASSON, J. F.** (Portsmouth) (3): 1931 v A, Sw; 1934 v W.
**ELLIOTT, M.** (Leicester City) (18): 1998 v Fr, D, Fin. 1999, i Lth, Fi, CzR, Fi, Holl, Ei; 2001 v La, Sm (2), Cro, Aus, Bel; 2002 v Cro, Bel, La.
**ELLIS, J.** (Mossend Swifts) (1): 1892 v Ni.
**EVANS, A.** (Aston Villa) (4): 1982 v Holl, Ni, E, Nz.
**EVANS, R.** (Celtic, Chelsea) (48): 1949 v E, W, Ni, Fr; 1950 v W, Ni, Sw, Por; 1951 v E, A; 1952 v Ni; 1953 v Se; 1954 v Ni, W, E, N, Fin; 1955 v Ni, Por, Y, A, H; 1956 v E, Ni, W, A; 1957 v WG, Sp; 1958 v Ni, W, E, Sw, H, Pol, Y, Par, Fr; 1959 v E, WG, Holl, Por; 1960 v E, Ni, W, Pol; 1960 v A, H, T.
**EWART, J.** (Bradford City) (1): 1921 v E.
**EWING, T.** (Partick Th.) (2): 1958 v W, E.
**FARM, G. N.** (Blackpool) (10): 1953 v W, Ni, E, Se; 1954 v Ni, W, E; 1959 v WG, Holl, Por.
**FERGUSON, B.** (Rangers) (10): 1999 v Lth. 2000 v Bos, Est, E (2), Fr, Ei; 2001 v La, Aus, Bel.
**FERGUSON, D.** (Rangers) (2): 1988 v Ma, Co.
**FERGUSON, D.** (Dundee United, Everton) (7): 1992 v US, Ca, Holl; 1993 v G; 1995 v Gr; 1997 v A, Est.
**FERGUSON, I.** (Rangers) (9): 1989 v I, Cy, Fr; 1993 v Ma, Est; 1994 v Ma, A, Holl; 1997 v Est.
**FERGUSON, J.** (Vale of Leven) (6): 1874 v E; 1876 v E, W; 1877 v E, W; 1878 v W.
**FERGUSON, R.** (Kilmarnock) (7): 1966 v W, E, Holl, Por, Br; 1967 v W, Ni.
**FERNIE, W.** (Celtic) (12): 1954 v Fin, A, U; 1955 v W, Ni; 1957 v E, Ni, W, Y; 1958 v W, Sw, Par.
**FINDLAY, R.** (Kilmarnock) (1): 1898 v W.
**FITCHIE, T. T.** (Woolwich Arsenal, Queen's Park) (4): 1905 v W: 1906 v W, Ni; 1907 v W.
**FLAVEL, R.** (Airdrie) (2): 1947 v Bel, L.
**FLECK, R.** (Norwich City) (4): 1990 v Arg, Se, Br; 1991 v USSR.
**FLEMING, C.** (East Fife) (1): 1954 v Ni.
**FLEMING, J. W.** (Rangers) (3): 1929 v G, Holl; 1930 v E.
**FLEMING, R.** (Morton): 1886 v Ni.
**FORBES, A. R.** (Sheffield Utd, Arsenal) (14): 1947 v Bel, L, E; 1948 v W, Ni; 1950 v E, Por, Fr; 1951 v W, Ni, A; 1952 v W, D, Se.
**FORBES, J.** (Vale of Leven) (5): 1884 v E, W, Ni; 1887 v W, E.
**FORD, D.** (Hearts) (3): 1974 v Cz, WG, W.
**FORREST, J.** (Rangers, Aberdeen) (5): 1966 v W, I; 1971 v Bel, D, USSR.
**FORREST, J.** (Motherwell) (1): 1958 v E.
**FORSYTH, A.** (Partick Th., Manchester Utd) (10): 1972 v Y, Cz, Br; 1973 v D, E; 1975 v Sp, Ni, R, EG; 1976 v D.

**FORSYTH, C.** (Kilmarnock) (4): 1964 v E; 1965 v W, Ni, Fin.

**FORSYTH, T.** (Motherwell, Rangers) (22): 1971 v D; 1974 v Cz; 1976 v Sw, Ni, W, E; 1977 v Fin, Se, W, Ni, E, Ch, Arg, Br; 1978 v Cz, W, Ni, W, E, Pe, Ir, Holl.

**FOYERS, R.** (St Bernards) (2): 1893 v W; 1894 v W.

**FRASER, D. M.** (WBA) (2): 1968 v Holl; 1969 v Cy.

**FRASER, J.** (Moffat) (1): 1891 v Ni.

**FRASER, M. J. E.** (Queen's Park) (5): 1880 v W; 1882 v W, E; 1883 v W, E.

**FRASER, J.** (Dundee) (1): 1907 v Ni.

**FRASER, W.** (Sunderland) (2): 1955 v W, Ni.

**FREEDMAN, D.** (Crystal Palace) (2): 2002 v L1, Fr.

**FULTON, W.** (Abercorn) (1): 1884 v Ni.

**FYFE, J. H.** (Third Lanark) (1): 1895 v W.

**GABRIEL, J.** (Everton) (2): 1961 v W; 1964 v N.

**GALLACHER, K. W.** (Dundee Utd, Coventry, Blackburn R, Newcastle) (53): 1988 v Co, E; 1989 v Ni; I; 1991 v Sm (2); 1992 v R, Ni, N, Holl, G, CIS; 1993 v Sw, Por (2), Est (2); 1994 v I, Ma; 1996 v Aus, D, U, Holl; 1997 v Se (2), Est (2), A, W, Ma, Blr; 1998 v Blr, La, Fr, Fin, US, Br, N, M. 1999 v Lth, Est, Fi, CzR. 2000 v Bos (2), Lth, E, Fr, Ei; 2001 v Sm (2), Cro, Bel.

**GALLACHER, P.** (Sunderland) (1): 1935 v Ni.

**GALLAGHER, H. K.** (Airdrie, Newcastle Utd, Chelsea, Derby C.) (20): 1924 v Ni; 1925 v E, W, Ni; 1926 v W, E, Ni; 1927 v E, W, Ni; 1928 v E, W; 1929 v E, W, Ni; 1930 v W, Ni, Fr; 1934 v E; 1935 v E.

**GALLOWAY, M.** (Celtic) (1): 1992 v R.

**GALT, J. H.** (Rangers) (2): 1908 v W, Ni.

**GARDINER, I.** (Motherwell) (1): 1958 v W.

**GARDNER, D. R.** (Third Lanark) (1): 1897 v W.

**GARDNER, R.** (Queen's Park, Clydesdale) (5): 1872 v E; 1873 v E; 1874 v E; 1875 v E; 1878 v E.

**GEMMELL, T.** (St Mirren) (2): 1955 v Por, Y.

**GEMMELL, T.** (Celtic) (18): 1966 v E; 1967 v W, Ni, E, USSR; 1968 v Ni, E; 1969 v W, Ni, E, D, A, WG, Cy; 1970 v E, Ei, WG; 1971 v Bel.

**GEMMILL, A.** (Derby Co., Nottingham F., Birmingham City) (43): 1971 v Bel; 1972 v Por, Holl, Pe, Ni, W, E; 1976 v D, R, Ni, W, E; 1977 v Fin, Cz, W (2), Ni, E, Ch, Arg, Br; 1978 v EG, Bul, Ni, W, E, Pe, Ir, Holl; 1979 v A, N. Por, N; 1980 v A, Por, Ni, W, E, H; 1981 v Se, Por, Is, Ni.

**GEMMILL, S.** (Nottingham F, Everton) (21): 1995 v J, Ec, Fi; 1996 v Sm, D, US; 1997 v Est, Se, W, Ma, Blr; 1998 v D, Fin; 1999 v G, Fi; 2001 v Sm; 2002 v Cro, Fr, Nig, Skor, SA.

**GIBB, W.** (Clydesdale) (1): 1873 v E.

**GIBSON, D. W.** (Leicester City) (7): 1963 v A, N, Ei, Sp; 1964 v Ni; 1965 v W, Fin.

**GIBSON, J. D.** (Partick Th., Aston Villa) (8): 1926 v E; 1927 v E, W, Ni; 1928 v E, W; 1930 v W. Ni.

**GIBSON, N.** (Rangers, Partick Th.) (14): 1895 v E, Ni; 1896 v E, Ni;

1897 v E, Ni; 1898 v E; 1899 v E, W, Ni; 1900 v E, Ni; 1901 v W; 1905 v Ni.

**GILCHRIST, J. E.** (Celtic) (1): 1922 v E.

**GILHOOLEY, M.** (Hull City) (1): 1922 v W.

**GILLESPIE, G.** (Rangers, Queen's Park) (7): 1880 v E, W; 1882 v E; 1886 v W; 1890 v W; 1891 v Ni.

**GILLESPIE, G. T.** (Liverpool) (13): 1988 v Bel, Bul, Sp; 1989 v N, Fr, Ch; 1990 v Y, EG, Eg, Pol, Ma, Br; 1991 v Bul.

**GILLESPIE, Jas.** (Third Lanark) (1): 1898 v W.

**GILLESPIE, John** (Queen's Park) (1): 1896 v W.

**GILLESPIE, R.** (Queen's Park) (4): 1927 v W; 1931 v W; 1932 v Fr; 1933 v E.

**GILLICK, T.** (Everton) (5): 1937 v A, Cz; 1939 v W, Ni, H.

**GILMOUR, J.** (Dundee) (1): 1931 v W.

**GILZEAN, A. J.** (Dundee, Tottenham H.) (22): 1964 v W, E, N, WG; 1965 v Ni, Sp; 1966 v Ni, W, Pol, I; 1968 v W; 1969 v W, E, WG, Cy (2), A; 1970 v Ni, E, WG, A; 1971 v Por.

**GLAVIN, R.** (Celtic) (1): 1977 v Se.

**GLASS S.** (Aberdeen) (1): 1999 v Fi.

**GLEN, A.** (Aberdeen) (2): 1956 v E, Ni.

**GLEN, R.** (Renton, Hibernian) (3): 1895 v W; 1896 v W; 1900 v Ni.

**GORAM, A. L.** (Oldham, Hibs, Rangers) (42): 1986 v EG, R, Holl; 1987 v Br; 1989 v Y, I; 1990 v EG, Pol, Ma; 1991 v R (2), Sw, Bul (2), USSR, Sm (2); 1992 v Sw, Fin, N, Holl, G, CIS; 1993 v Sw, Por (2), I, Ma; 1994 v Holl; 1995 v Fin, Fi, Ru, Gr; 1996 v Se, D, Holl, Sw, E; 1997 A, La, Est; 1998 v D

**GORDON, J. E.** (Rangers) (10): 1912 v E, Ni; 1913 v E, Ni, W; 1914 v E, Ni; 1920 v W, E, Ni, U.

**GOSSLAND, J.** (Rangers) (1): 1884 v Ni.

**GOUDIE, J.** (Abercorn) (1): 1884 v Ni.

**GOUGH, C. R.** (Dundee Utd, Tottenham H., Rangers) (61): 1983 v Sw, Ni, W, E, Ca (3); 1984 v U, Bel, EG, Ni, W, E, Fr; 1985 v Sp, E, Ice; 1986 v WG, Aus, Is, R, E, D, WG, U; 1987 v Bul, L, Ei (2), Bel, E, Br; 1988 v H, S.Ar, Sp, Co, E; 1989 v Y, I, Cy (2), Fr; 1990 v Fr, Arg, EG, Pol, Ma, Cr; 1991 v USSR, Bul; 1992 v Sm, Ni, Ca, N, Holl, G, CIS; 1993 v Sw, Por.

**GOULD, J.** (Celtic) (2): 2000 v Lth; 2001 v Aus.

**GOURLAY, J.** (Cambuslang) (2): 1886 v Ni; 1888 v W.

**GOVAN, J.** (Hibernian) (6): 1948 v E, W, Bel, Sw, Fr; 1949 v Ni.

**GOW, D. R.** (Rangers) (1): 1888 v E.

**GOW, J. J.** (Queen's Park) (1): 1885 v E.

**GOW, J. R.** (Rangers) (1): 1888 v Ni.

**GRAHAM, A.** (Leeds Utd) (10): 1978 v EG; 1979 v A, N, W, Ni, E, Arg, N; 1980 v A; 1981 v W.

**GRAHAM, G.** (Arsenal, Manchester Utd) (13): 1972 v Por, Sw, Holl, Ni, Y, Cz, Br; 1973 v D (2), E, W, Ni, Br.

**GRAHAM, J.** (Annbank) (1): 1884 v Ni.

**GRAHAM, J. A.** (Arsenal) (1): 1921 v Ni.

**GRANT, J.** (Hibernian) (2): 1959 v W, Ni.

**GRANT, P.** (Celtic) (2): 1989 v E, Ch.

**GRAY, A,** (Hibernian) (1): 1903 v Ni.

**GRAY, A.** (Aston Villa, Wolverhampton W., Everton) (20): 1976 v R, Sw; 1977 v Fin, Cz; 1979 v A, N; 1980 v Por, E; 1981 v Se, Por, Is, Ni; 1982 v Se, Ni; 1983 v Ni, W, E, Ca (2); 1985 v Ice.

**GRAY, D.** (Rangers) (10): 1929 v W, Ni, G, Holl; 1930 v W, E, Ni; 1931 v W; 1933 v W, Ni.

**GRAY, E.** (Leeds Utd) (12): 1969 v E, Cy; 1970 v WG, A; 1971 v W, Ni; 1972 v Bel, Holl; 1976 v W, E; 1977 v Fin, W.

**GRAY, F. T.** (Leeds Utd, Nottingham F.) (32): 1976 v Sw; 1979 v N, Por, W, Ni, E, Arg; 1980 v Bel; 1981 v Se, Por, Is (2), Ni, (2), W, E; 1982 v Se, Ni, Por, Sp, Holl, W, Nz, Br, USSR; 1983 v EG, Sw, (2), Bel, W, E, Ca.

**GRAY, W.** (Pollokshields Ath.) (1): 1886 v E.

**GREEN, A.** (Blackpool) (6): 1971 v Bel, Por, Ni, E; 1972 v W, E.

**GREIG, J.** (Rangers) (44): 1964 v E, WG; 1965 v W, Ni, E, Fin (2), Sp, Pol; 1966 v Ni, W, E, Pol, I (2), Por, Holl, Br; 1967 v W, Ni, E; 1968 v Ni, W, E, Holl; 1969 v W, Ni, E, D, A, WG, Cy (2); 1970 v W, E, Ei, WG, A; 1971 v D, Bel, W, Ni, E; 1976 v D.

**GROVES, W.** (Hibernian, Celtic) (3): 1888 v W; 1889 Ni; 1890 v E.

**GUILLILAND, W.** (Queen's Park) (4): 1891 v W; 1892 v Ni; 1894 v E; 1895 v E.

**GUNN, B.** (Norwich City) (6): 1990 v Eg; 1993 v Est (2); 1994 v Sw, I, Holl.

**HADDOCK, H.** (Clyde) (6): 1955 v E, H (2), Por, Y; 1958 v E.

**HADDOW, D.** (Rangers) (1): 1894 v E.

**HAFFEY, F.** (Celtic) (2): 1960 v E; 1961 v E.

**HAMILTON, A.** (Queen's Park) (4): 1885 v E, W; 1886 v E; 1888 v E.

**HAMILTON, A. W.** (Dundee) (24): 1962 v Cz, U, W, E; 1963 v W, Ni, E, A, N, Ei; 1964 v Ni, W, E, N, WG; 1965 v Ni, W, E, Fin (2), Pol, Sp; 1966 v Pol, Ni.

**HAMILTON, G.** (Aberdeen) (5): 1947 v Ni; 1951 v Bel, A; 1954 v N (2).

**HAMILTON, G.** (Port Glasgow Ath.) (1): 1906 v Ni.

**HAMILTON, J.** (Queen's Park) (3): 1892 v W; 1893 v E, Ni.

**HAMILTON, J.** (St Mirren) (1): 1924 v Ni.

**HAMILTON, R. C.** (Rangers, Dundee) (11): 1899 v E, W, Ni; 1900 v W; 1901 v E, Ni; 1902 v W, Ni; 1903 v E; 1904 v Ni; 1911 v W.

**HAMILTON, T.** (Hurlford) (1): 1891 v Ni.

**HAMILTON, T.** (Rangers) (1): 1932 v E.

**HAMILTON, W. M.** (Hibernian) (1): 1965 v Fin.

**HANNAH, A. B.,** (Renton) (1): 1888 v W.

**HANNAH, J.** (Third Lanark) (1): 1889 v W.

**HANSEN, A. D.** (Liverpool) (26): 1979 v W, Arg; 1980 v Bel, Por; 1981 v Se, Por, Is; 1982 v Se, Ni (2), Por, Sp, W, E, Nz, Br, USSR; 1983 v EG, Sw (2), Bel; 1985 v W; 1986 v R; 1987 v Ei (2), L.

**HANSEN, J.** (Partick Th.) (2): 1972 v Bel, Y.

**HARKNESS, J. D.** (Queen's Park, Hearts) (12): 1927 v E, Ni; 1928 v E; 1929 v W, E, Ni; 1930 v E, W; 1932 v W, Fr; 1934 v W, Ni.

**HARPER, J. M.** (Aberdeen, Hibernian) (4): 1973 v D (2); 1976 v D; 1978 v Ir.

**HARPER, W.** (Hibernian, Arsenal) (11): 1923 v E, Ni, W; 1924 v E, Ni, W; 1925 v E, Ni, W; 1926 v E, Ni.

**HARRIS, J.** (Partick Th.) (2): 1921 v W, Ni.

**HARRIS, N.** (Newcastle Utd) (1): 1924 v E.

**HARROWER, W.** (Queen's Park) (3): 1882 v E; 1884 v Ni; 1886 v W.

**HARTFORD, R. A.** (WBA, Manchester City, Everton) (50): 1972 v Pe, W, E, Y, Cz, Br; 1976 v D, R, Ni; 1977 v Cz, W, (2), Se, Ni, E, Ch, Arg, Br; 1978 v EG, Cz, W (2), Bul, E, Pe, Ir, Holl; 1979 v A, N, Por, W, Ni, E, Arg, N; 1980 v Pe, Bel; 1981 v Ni (2), Is, W, E; 1982 v Se, Ni (2), Por, Sp, W, E, Br.

**HARVEY, D.** (Leeds Utd.) (16): 1973 v D; 1974 v Cz, WG, Ni, W, E, Bel, Z, Br, Y; 1975 v EG, Sp (2); 1976 v D (2); 1977 v Fin.

**HASTINGS, A. C.** (Sunderland) (2): 1936 v Ni; 1938 v Ni.

**HAUGHNEY, M.** (Celtic) (1): 1954 v E.

**HAY, D.** (Celtic) (27): 1970 v Ni, W, E; 1971 v D, Bel, W, Por, Ni; 1972 v Por, Bel, Holl; 1973 v W, Ni, E, Sw, Br; 1974 v Cz (2), WG, Ni, W, E, Bel, N, Z, Br.

**HAY, J.** (Celtic, Newcastle Utd.) (11): 1905 v Ni; 1909 v Ni; 1910 v W, Ni, E; 1911 v Ni, E; 1912 v E, W; 1914 v E, Ni.

**HEGARTY, P.** (Dundee Utd.) (8): 1979 v W, Ni, E, Arg, N; 1980 v E; 1983 v Ni.

**HEGGIE, C.** (Rangers) (1): 1886 v Ni.

**HENDERSON, G. H.** (Rangers) (1): 1904 v Ni.

**HENDERSON, J. G.** (Portsmouth, Arsenal) (7): 1953 v Se; 1954 v Ni, E, N; 1956 v W; 1959 v W, Ni.

**HENDERSON, W.** (Rangers) (30): 1963 v W, Ni, E, A, N, Ei, Sp; 1964 v W, Ni, E, N, WG; 1965 v Fin, Pol, E, Sp; 1966 v Ni, W, Pol, I, Holl; 1967 v W, Ni; 1968 v Holl; 1969 v Ni, E, Cy; 1970 v Ei; 1971 v Por.

**HENDRY C.** (Blackburn R., Rangers, Bolton) (51): 1993 v Est (2); 1994 v Ma, Holl (2), A; 1995 v Fin, Fi, Gr, Ru, Sm; 1996 v Fin, Se, Sm, Aus, D, US, U, Holl, E, Sw; 1997 A (2), Se (2), Est (2); 1998 v La, D, Fin, Co, US, Br, N, M. 1999 v Lth, Est, Fi, G. 2000 v Bos (2), Est, E (2), Fr; 2001 v La, Sm (2), Cro, Aus, Bel.

**HEPBURN, J.** (Alloa Ath.) (1) 1891 v W.

**HEPBURN, R.** (Ayr Utd) (1): 1932 v Ni.

**HERD, A. C.** (Hearts) (1): 1935 v Ni.

**HERD, D. G.** (Arsenal) (5): 1959 v E, Ni; 1961 v E, Cz.

**HERD, G.** (Clyde) (5): 1958 v E; 1960 v H, T; 1961 v W, Ni.

**HERRIOT, J.** (Birmingham City) (8): 1969 v Ni, E, D, Cy (2), W; 1970 v Ei, WG.

**HEWIE, J. D.** (Charlton Ath.) (19): 1956 v E, A; 1957 v E, Ni, W, Y, Sp (2), Sw, WG; 1958 v H, Pol, Y, Fr; 1959 v Holl, Por; 1960 v Ni, W, Pol.

**HIGGINS, A.** (Kilmarnock) (1): 1885 v Ni.

**HIGGINS, A.** (Newcastle Utd.) (4): 1910 v E, Ni; 1911 v E, Ni.

**HIGHET, T. C.** (Queen's Park) (4): 1875 v E; 1876 v E, W; 1878 v E.

**HILL, D.** (Rangers) (3): 1881 v E, W; 1882 v W.

**HILL, D. A.** (Third Lanark) (1): 1906 v Ni.

**HILL, F. R.** (Aberdeen) (3): 1930 v Fr; 1931 v W, Ni.

**HILL, J.** (Hearts) (2): 1891 v E; 1892 v W.

**HOGG, G.** (Hearts) (2): 1896 v E, Ni.

**HOGG, J.** (Ayr Utd.) (1): 1922 v Ni.

**HOGG, R. M.** (Celtic) (1): 1937 v Cz.

**HOLM, A. H.** (Queen's Park) (3): 1882 v W; 1883 v E, W.

**HOLT, D. D.** (Hearts) (5): 1963 v A, N, Ei, Sp; 1964 v WG.

**HOLT, G.** (Kilmarnock, Norwich) (3): 2001 v La, Cro; 2002 v Fr.

**HOLTON, J. A.** (Manchester Utd.) (15): 1973 v W, Ni, E, Sw, Br; 1974 v Cz, WG, Ni, W, E, N, Z, Br, Y; 1975 v EG.

**HOPE, R.** (WBA) (2): 1968 v Holl; 1969 v D.

**HOPKIN, D.** (Crystal Palace, Leeds) (7): 1997 v Ma, Blr; 1998 v Blr, La; 1999 v CzR. 2000 v Bos (2).

**HOULISTON, W.** (Queen of the South) (3): 1949 v E, Ni, Fr.

**HOUSTON, S. M.** (Manchester Utd.) (1): 1976 v D.

**HOWDEN, W.** (Partick Th.) (1): 1905 v Ni.

**HOWE, R.** (Hamilton Accies) (2): 1929 v N, Holl.

**HOWIE, J.** (Newcastle Utd.) (3): 1905 v E; 1906 v E; 1908 v E.

**HOWIE, H.** (Hibernian) (1): 1949 v W.

**HOWIESON, J.** (St Mirren) (1): 1927 v Ni.

**HUGHES, J.** (Celtic) (8): 1965 v Pol, Sp; 1966 v Ni, I (2); 1968 v E; 1969 v A; 1970 v Ei.

**HUGHES, W.** (Sunderland) (1): 1975 v Se.

**HUMPHRIES, W.** (Motherwell) (1): 1952 v Se.

**HUNTER, A.** (Kilmarnock, Celtic) (4): 1972 v Pe, Y; 1973 v E; 1974 v Cz.

**HUNTER, J.** (Dundee) (1): 1909 v W.

**HUNTER, J.** (Third Lanark, Eastern) (4): 1874 v E, 1875 v E, 1876 v E, 1877 v W.

**HUNTER, R.** (St Mirren) (1): 1890 v Ni.

**HUNTER, W.** (Motherwell) (3): 1960 v H, T; 1961 v W.

**HUSBAND, J.** (Partick Th.) (1): 1947 v W.

**HUTCHISON, D.** (Everton, Sunderland) (19): 1999 v CzR, G; 2000 v Bos, Est, Lth, E (2), Fr, Holl, Ei; 2001 v La, Sm (2), Cro, Aus, Bel; 2002 v Cro, Bel, La.

**HUTCHISON, T.** (Coventry City) (17): 1974 v Cz (2), WG (2), Ni, W, Bel, N, Z, Y; 1975 v EG, Sp (2), Por, E, R; 1976 v D.

**HUTTON, J.** (Aberdeen, Blackburn R.) (10): 1923 v E, W, Ni; 1924 v

Ni; 1926 v W, E, Ni; 1927 v Ni; 1928 v W, Ni.

**HUTTON, J.** (St Bernards) (1): 1887 v Ni.

**HYSLOP, T.** (Stoke City, Rangers) (2): 1896 v E; 1897 v E.

**IMLACH, J. J. S.** (Nottingham F.) (4): 1958 v H, Pol, Y. Fr.

**IMRIE, W. N.** (St Johnstone) (2): 1929 v N, G.

**INGLIS, J.** (Kilmarnock Ath.) (1): 1884 v Ni.

**INGLIS, J.** (Rangers) (2): 1883 v E, W.

**IRONS, J. H.** (Queen's Park) (1): 1900 v W.

**IRVINE, B.** (Aberdeen) (9): 1991 v R; 1993 v G, Est (2); 1994 v Sw, I, Ma, A, Holl.

**JACKSON, A.** (Cambuslang) (2): 1886 v W, 1888 v Ni.

**JACKSON, A.** (Aberdeen, Huddersfield Town) (17): 1925 v E, W, Ni; 1926 v E, W, Ni; 1927 v W, Ni; 1928 v E, W; 1929 v E, W, Ni; 1930 v E, W, Ni, Fr.

**JACKSON, C.** (Rangers) (8): 1975 v Se, Por, W; 1976 v D, R, Ni, W, E.

**JACKSON D.** (Hibs, Celtic) (28): 1995 v Ru, Sm, J, Ec, Fi. 1996 v Gr, Fin, Se, Sm, Aus, D, US; 1997 v La, Se (2), Est, A, W, Ma, Blr; 1998 v D, Fin, Co, US, Br, N. 1999 v Lth, Est.

**JACKSON, J.** (Partick Th., Chelsea) (8): 1931 v A, I, Sw; 1933 v E; 1934 v E; 1935 v E; 1936 v W, Ni.

**JACKSON, T. A.** (St Mirren) (6): 1904 v W, E, Ni; 1905 v W; 1907 v W, Ni.

**JAMES, A.** (Preston NE, Arsenal) (8): 1926 v W; 1928 v E; 1929 v E, Ni; 1930 v E, W, Ni; 1933 v W.

**JARDINE, A.** (Rangers) (38): 1971 v D; 1972 v Por, Bel, Holl; 1973 v E, Sw, Br; 1974 v Cz (2), WG (2), Ni, W, E, Bel, N, Z, Br, Y; 1975 v EG, Sp (2), Se, Por, W, Ni, E; 1977 v Se, Ch, Br; 1978 v Cz, W, Ni, Ir; 1980 v Pe, A. Bel (2).

**JARVIE, A.** (Airdrie) (3): 1971 v Por, Ni, E.

**JESS, E.** (Aberdeen) (18): 1993 v I, Ma; 1994 v Sw, I, Holl (2), A; 1995 v Fin; 1996 v Se, Sm, US, U, E; 1998 v D; 1999 v CzR (2), G, Fi.

**JENKINSON, T.** (Hearts) (1): 1887 v Ni.

**JOHNSTON, A.** (Sunderland, Rangers, Middlesbrough) (15): 1999 v Est, Fi, CzR (2), G, Fi; 2000 v Est, Fr, Ei; 2001 v Sm (2), Cro; 2002 v Nig, Skor, SA.

**JOHNSTON, L. H.** (Clyde) (2): 1948 v Bel, Sw.

**JOHNSTON, M.** (Watford, Celtic, Nantes, Rangers) (38): 1984 v W, E, Fr; 1985 v Y, Ice, Sp (2), W; 1986 v EG; 1987 v Bul, Ei (2), L; 1988 v H, Bel, L. S.Ar, Sp, Co, E; 1989 v N, Y, I, Cy (2), Fr, E, Ch; 1990 v Fr, N, EG, Pol, Ma, Cr, Se, Br; 1992 v Sw, Sm.

**JOHNSTON, R.** (Sunderland) (1): 1938 v Cz.

**JOHNSTON, W.** (Rangers, WBA) (22): 1966 v W, E, Pol, Holl; 1968 v W, E; 1969 v Ni; 1970 v Ni; 1971 v D; 1977 v Se, W, Ni, E, Ch, Arg, Br; 1978 v EG, Cz, W (2), E, Pe.

**JOHNSTONE, D.** (Rangers) (14): 1973 v W, Ni, E, Sw, Br; 1975 v EG, Se; 1976 v Sw, Ni, E; 1978 v Bul, Ni, W; 1980 v Bel.

**JOHNSTONE, J.** (Abercorn) (1): 1888 v W.
**JOHNSTONE, J.** (Celtic) (23): 1965 v W, Fin; 1966 v E; 1967 v W, USSR; 1968 v W; 1969 v A, WG; 1970 v E, WG; 1971 v D, E; 1972 v Por, Bel, Holl, Ni, E; 1974 v W, E, Bel, N; 1975 v EG, Sp.
**JOHNSTONE, JAS.** (Kilmarnock) (1): 1894 v W.
**JOHNSTONE, J.** (Hearts) (3): 1930 v W; 1933 v W, Ni.
**JOHNSTONE, J. A.** (Hearts) (3): 1930 v W; 1933 v W, Ni.
**JOHNSTONE, R.** (Hibernian, Manchester City) (17): 1951 v E, D, Fr; 1952 v Ni, E; 1953 v E, Se; 1954 v W, E, N, Fin; 1955 v Ni, H, E; 1956 v E, Ni, W.
**JOHNSTONE, W.** (Third Lanark) (3): 1887 v Ni; 1889 v W; 1890 v E.
**JORDAN, J.** (Leeds Utd, Manchester Utd, AC Milan) (52): 1973 v E, Sw, Br; 1974 v Cz (2), WG, Ni, W, E, Bel, N, Z, Br, Y; 1975 v EG, Sp (2); 1976 v Ni, W, E; 1977 v Cz, W, Ni, E; 1978 v EG, Cz, W, Bul, Ni, E, Pe, Ir, Holl; 1979 v A, Por, W, Ni, E, N; 1980 v Bel, Ni, W, E, Pol; 1981 v Is, W, E; 1982 v Se, Holl, W, E, USSR.
**KAY, J. L.** (Queen's Park) (6): 1880 v E; 1882 v E, W; 1883 v E, W; 1884 v W.
**KEILLOR, A.** (Montrose, Dundee) (6): 1891 v W; 1892 v Ni; 1894 v Ni; 1895 v W; 1896 v W; 1897 v E.
**KEIR, L.** (Dumbarton) (5): 1885 v W: 1886 v Ni; 1887 v E, W; 1888 v E.
**KELLY, H. T.** (Blackpool) (1): 1952 v USA.
**KELLY, J.** (Renton, Celtic) (8): 1888 v E; 1889 v E; 1890 v E; 1892 v E; 1893 v E, Ni; 1894 v W; 1896 v Ni.
**KELLY, J. C.** (Barnsley) (1): 1949 v W, Ni.
**KELSO, R.** (Renton, Dundee) (8): 1885 v W, Ni; 1886 v W; 1887 v E, W; 1888 v E, Ni; 1898 v Ni.
**KELSO, T.** (Dundee) (1): 1914 v W.
**KENNAWAY, J.** (Celtic) (1): 1934 v A.
**KENNEDY, A.** (Eastern, Third Lanark) (6): 1875 v E; 1876 v E, W; 1878 v E; 1882 v W; 1884 v W.
**KENNEDY, J.** (Celtic) (1): 1964 v W, Fr, WG; 1965 v W, Ni, Fin.
**KENNEDY, J.** (Hibernian) (1): 1897 v W.
**KENNEDY, S.** (Aberdeen) (8): 1978 v Bul, W, E, Pe, Holl; 1979 v A, Por; 1982 v Por.
**KENNEDY, S,** (Partick Th.) (1): 1905 v W.
**KENNEDY, S.** (Rangers) (5): 1975 v Se, Por, W, Ni, E.
**KER, G.** (Queen's Park) (5): 1880 v E; 1881 v E, W; 1882 v W, E.
**KER, W.** (Granville, Queen's Park) (2): 1872 v E; 1873 v E.
**KERR, A.** (Partick Th.) (2): 1955 v A, H.
**KERR, P.** (Hibernian) (1): 1924 v Ni.
**KEY, G.** (Hearts) (1): 1902 v Ni.
**KEY, W.** (Queen's Park) (1): 1907 v Ni.
**KING, A.** (Hearts, Celtic) (6): 1896 v E, W; 1897 v E; 1898 v Ni; 1899 v Ni, W.
**KING, J.** (Hamilton Accies) (2): 1933 v Ni; 1934 v Ni.
**KING, W. S.** (Queen's Park) (1): 1929 v W.

**KINLOCH, J. D.** (Partick Th.) (1): 1922 v Ni.

**KINNAIRD, A. F.** (Wanderers) (1): 1873 v E.

**KINNEAR, D.** (Rangers) (1): 1938 v Cz.

**KYLE, K.** (Sunderland) (2): 2002 v Skor, SA.

**LAMBERT, P.** (Motherwell, Borussia Dortmund, Celtic) (30): 1995 v J, Ec; 1997 v La, Se (2), A, Blr; 1998 v Blr, La, Fin, Co, US, Br, N, M. 1999 v Lth, CzR (2), G, Fi; 2000 v Bos, Lth, Holl, Ei; 2001 v Bel, Sm; 2002 v Cro, Bel, Fr, Nig.

**LAMBIE, J. A.** (Queen's Park) (3): 1886 v Ni; 1887 v Ni; 1888 v E.

**LAMBIE, W. A.** (Queen's Park) (9): 1892 v Ni; 1893 v W; 1894 v E; 1895 v E, Ni; 1896 v E, Ni; 1897 v E, Ni.

**LAMONT, D.** (Pilgrims) 1885 v Ni.

**LANG, A.** (Dumbarton) (1): 1880 v W.

**LANG, J. J.** (Clydesdale, Third Lanark) (2): 1876 v W; 1878 v W.

**LATTA, A.** (Dumbarton) (2): 1888 v W; 1889 v E.

**LAW, D.** (Huddersfield Town, Manchester Utd, Torino, Manchester City) (55): 1959 v W, Ni, Holl, Por; 1960 v Ni, W; 1960 v E, Pol, A; 1961 v E, Ni; 1962 v Cz (2), E; 1963 v W, Ni, E, A, N, Ei, Sp; 1964 v W, E, N, WG;1965 v W, Ni, E, Fin (2), Pol, Sp; 1966 v Ni, E, Pol; 1967 v W, E, USSR; 1968 v Ni; 1969 v Ni, A, WG; 1972 v Pe, Ni, W, E, Y, Cz, Br; 1974 v Cz (2), WG (2), Ni, Z.

**LAW, G.** (Rangers) (3): 1910 v E, Ni, W.

**LAW, T.** (Chelsea) (2): 1928 v E, 1930 v E.

**LAWRENCE, J.** (Newcastle Utd.) (1): 1911 v E.

**LAWRENCE, T.** (Liverpool) (3): 1963 v Ei; 1969 v W, WG.

**LAWSON, D.** (St Mirren) (1): 1923 v E.

**LECKIE, R.** (Queen's Park) (1): 1872 v E.

**LEGGAT, G.** (Aberdeen, Fulham) (18): 1956 v E; 1957 v W; 1958 v Ni, H, Pol, Y, Par; 1959 v E, W, Ni, WG, Holl; 1960 v E, Ni, W, Pol, A, H.

**LEIGHTON, J.** (Aberdeen, Manchester Utd, Hibernian, Aberdeen) (91): 1983 v EG, Sw (2), Bel, W, E, Ca (2); 1984 v U, Bel, Ni, W, E, Fr; 1985 v Y, Ice, Sp (2), W, E, Ice; 1986 v W, EG, Aus (2), Is, D, WG, U; 1987 v Bul, Ei (2), L, Bel; 1988 v H, Bel, Bul, L, S.Ar, Ma, Sp, Co, E; 1989 v N, Cy (2), Fr, E, Ch; 1990 v Y, Fr, N, Arg, Ma, Cr, Se, Br; 1994 v Ma, A, Holl; 1995 v Gr, Ru, Sm, J, Ec, Fi. 1996 v Gr, Fin, Se, Sm, Aus, D, US;1997 v Se (2), Est, A, W, Ma, Blr.1998 v Blr, La, D, Fin, US, Br, N, M. 1999 v Lth, Est.

**LENNIE, W.** (Aberdeen) (2): 1908 v W, Ni.

**LENNOX, R.** (Celtic) (10): 1967 v Ni, E, USSR; 1968 v W, L; 1969 v D, A. WG, Cy; 1970 v W.

**LESLIE, L. G.** (Airdrie) (5): 1961 v W, Ni, Ei (2), Cz.

**LEVEIN, C.** (Hearts) (16): 1990 v Arg, EG, Eg, Pol, Ma, Se; 1991 R, Sm; 1993 v Por (2), G; 1994 v Sw, Holl; 1995 v Fin, Fa, Ru.

**LIDDELL, W.** (Liverpool) (28): 1947 v W, Ni; 1948 v E, W, Ni; 1950 v E, W, Por, Fr; 1951 v W, Ni, E, A; 1952 v W, Ni, E, USA, D, Se; 1953 v W, Ni, E; 1954 v W; 1955 v Por, Y, A, H; 1956 v Ni.

**LIDDLE, D.** (East Fife) (3): 1931 v A, I, Sw.

**LINDSAY, D.** (St Mirren) (1): 1903 v Ni.

**LINDSAY, J.** (Dumbarton) (8): 1880 v W; 1881 v W, E; 1884 v W, E; 1885 v W, E; 1886 v E.

**LINDSAY, J.** (Renton) (3): 1888 v E; 1893 v E, Ni.

**LINWOOD, A. B.** (Clyde) (1): 1950 v W.

**LITTLE, R. J.** (Rangers) (1): 1953 v Se.

**LIVINGSTONE, G. T.** (Man City, Rangers) (2): 1906 v E; 1907 v W.

**LOCHHEAD, A.** (Third Lanark) (1): 1889 v W.

**LOGAN, J.** (Ayr Utd) (1): 1891 v W.

**LOGAN, T.** (Falkirk) (1): 1913 v Ni.

**LOGIE, J. T.** (Arsenal) (1): 1953 v Ni.

**LONEY, W.** (Celtic) (2): 1910 v W, Ni.

**LONG, H.** (Clyde) (1): 1947 v Ni.

**LONGAIR, W.** (Dundee) (1): 1894 v Ni.

**LORIMER, P.** (Leeds Utd) (21): 1970 v A; 1971 v W, Ni; 1972 v Ni, W, E; 1973 v D (2), E (2); 1974 v WG, E, Bel, N, Z, Br, Y; 1975 v Sp; 1976 v D (2), R.

**LOVE, A.** (Aberdeen) (3): 1931 v A, I, Sw.

**LOW, A.** (Falkirk) (1): 1934 v Ni.

**LOW, T. P.** (Rangers) (1): 1897 v Ni.

**LOW, W. L.** (Newcastle U) (5): 1911 v E, W; 1912 v Ni; 1920 v E, Ni.

**LOWE, J.** (Cambuslang) (1): 1891 v Ni.

**LOWE, J.** (St Bernards) (1): 1887 v Ni.

**LUNDIE, J.** (Hibernian) (1): 1886 v W.

**LYALL, J.** (Sheffield W.) (1): 1905 v E.

**McADAM, J.** (Third Lanark) (1): 1880 v W.

**McALLISTER, B.** (Wimbledon) (3): 1997 v W, Ma, Blr.

**McALLISTER, G.** (Leicester City, Leeds Utd, Coventry) (57): 1990 v EG, Pol, Ma; 1991 v R, Sw (2), Bul, USSR, Sm, (2); 1992 v Ni, Fin, US, Ca, N, Holl, G, CIS; 1993 v Sw, Por, I, Ma; 1994 v Sw, I, Ma, Holl (2), A; 1995 v Fin, Ru (2), Gr, Sm. 1996 v Gr, Fin, Se, Sm, Aus, D, US, U, Holl, E, Sw; 1997 v A (2), La, Est (2), Se, W, Ma, Blr; 1998 v Blr, La, Fr; 1999 v CzR.

**McARTHUR, D.** (Celtic) (3): 1895 v E, Ni; 1899 v W.

**McATEE, A.** (Celtic) (1): 1913 v W.

**McAULAY, J.** (Dumbarton, Arthurlie) (2): 1882 v W; 1884 v Ni.

**McAULAY, J.** (Dumbarton) (8): 1883 v E, W; 1884 v E; 1885 v E, W; 1886 v E; 1887 v E, W.

**McAULEY, R.** (Rangers) (2): 1932 v Ni, W.

**McAVENNIE, F.** (West Ham Utd., Celtic) (5): 1986 v Aus (2), D, WG; 1988 v S.Ar.

**McBAIN, E.** (St Mirren) (1): 1894 v W.

**McBAIN, N.** (Manchester Utd., Everton) (3): 1922 v E; 1923 v Ni; 1924 v W.

**McBRIDE, J.** (Celtic) (2): 1967 v W, Ni.

**McBRIDE, P.** (Preston NE) (6): 1904 v E; 1906 v E; 1907 v E, W; 1908 v E; 1909 v W.

**McCALL, J.** (Renton) (5): 1886 v W; 1887 v E, W; 1888 v E; 1890 v E.

**McCALL, S. M.** (Everton, Rangers) (40) 1990 v Arg, EG, Eg, Pol, Ma, Cr, Se, Br; 1991 v Sw, USSR, Sm (2); 1992 v Sw, R, US, Ca, N, Holl, G, CIS; 1993 v Sw, Por (2); 1994 v I, Holl (2), A; 1995 v Fin, Ru, Gr; 1996 v Gr, D, US, U, Holl, E, Sw; 1997 v A, La; 1998 v D.

**McCALLIOG, J.** (Sheffield W., Wolverhampton W.) (5): 1967 v E, USSR; 1968 v Ni; 1969 v D; 1971 v Por.

**McCALLUM, N.** (Renton) (1): 1888 v Ni.

**McCANN, R. J.** (Motherwell) (5): 1959 v WG; 1960 v E, Ni, W; 1961 v E.

**McCANN, N.** (Hearts, Rangers) (14): 1999 v Lth, CzR. 2000 v Bos; Est, E, Fr, Holl, Ei; 2001 v La, Sm, Aus; 2002 v Cro, Fr, Nig.

**McCARTNEY, W.** (Hibernian) (1): 1902 v Ni.

**McCLAIR, B.** (Celtic, Manchester Utd) (30): 1987 v L, Ei, E, Br; 1988 v Bul, Ma, Sp; 1989 v N, I, Cy, Fr; 1990 v N, Arg; 1991 v Bul (2), Sm; 1992 v Sw, R, Ni, US, Ca, N, Holl, G, CIS; 1993 v Sw, Por, Est (2).

**McCLORY, A.** (Motherwell) (3): 1927 v W; 1928 v Ni; 1935 v W.

**McCLOY, P.** (Ayr Utd) (2): 1924 v E; 1925 v E.

**McCLOY, P.** (Rangers) (4): 1973 v W, Ni, Sw, Br.

**McCOIST, A.** (Rangers, Kilmarnock) (61): 1986 v Holl; 1987 v L, Ei, Bel, E, Br; 1988 v H, Bel, Ma, Sp, Co, E; 1989 v Y, Fr, Cy, E; 1990 v Y, Fr, N, EG, Eg, Pol, Ma, Cr, Se, Br; 1991 v R, Sw, Bul (2), USSR; 1992 v Sw, Sm, Ni, Fin, US, Ca, N, Holl, G, CIS; 1993 v Sw, Por (2), I, Ma. 1996 v Gr, Fin, Sm, Aus, D, U, E, Sw; 1997 v A (2), Se, Est; 1998 v Blr. 1999 v Lth, Est.

**McCOLL, A.** (Renton) (1): 1888 v Ni.

**McCOLL, I. M.** (Rangers) (14): 1950 v E, Fr; 1951 v W, Ni, Bel; 1957 v E, Ni, W, Y, Sp, Sw, WG; 1958 v Ni, E.

**McCOLL, R. S.** (Queen's Park, Newcastle Utd.) (13): 1896 v W, Ni; 1897 v Ni; 1898 v Ni; 1899 v Ni; E, W; 1900 v E, W; 1901 v E, W; 1902 v E; 1908 v Ni.

**McCOLL, W.** (Renton) (1): 1895 v W.

**McCOMBIE, A.** (Sunderland, Newcastle Utd.) (4): 1903 v E, W; 1905 v E, W.

**McCORKINDALE, J.** (Partick Th.) (1): 1891 v W.

**McCORMICK, R.** (Abercorn) (1): 1886 v W.

**McCRAE, D.** (St Mirren) (2): 1929 v N, G.

**McCREADIE, A.** (Rangers) (2): 1893 v W; 1894 v E.

**McCREADIE, E. G.** (Chelsea) (23): 1965 v E, Sp, Fin, Pol; 1966 v Por, Ni, W, Pol, I; 1967 v E, USSR; 1968 v Ni, W, E, Holl; 1969 v Ni, E, D, A, WG, Cy (2).

**McCULLOCH, D.** (Hearts, Brentford, Derby Co.) (7): 1935 v W; 1936 v E; 1937 v W, Ni; 1938 v Cz; 1939 v H, W.

**MacDONALD, A.** (Rangers) (1): 1976 v Sw.

**McDONALD, J.** (Edinburgh University) (1): 1886 v E.

**McDONALD, J.** (Sunderland) (2): 1956 v W, Ni.

**MacDOUGALL, E. J.** (Norwich City) (7): 1975 v Se, Por, W, Ni, E; 1976 v D, R.

**McDOUGALL, J.** (Liverpool) (2): 1931 v I, A.

**McDOUGALL, J.** (Airdrie) (1): 1926 v Ni.

**McDOUGALL, J.** (Vale of Leven) (5): 1877 v E, W; 1878 v E; 1879 v E, W.

**McFADDEN, J.** (1): 2002 v SA.

**McFADYEN, W.** (Motherwell) (2): 1934 v A, W.

**MACFARLANE, A.** (Dundee) (5): 1904 v W; 1906 v W; 1908 v W; 1909 v Ni; 1911 v W.

**McFARLANE, R.** (Morton) (1): 1896 v W.

**MACFARLANE, W.** (Hearts) (1): 1947 v L.

**McGARR, E.** (Aberdeen) (2): 1970 v Ei, A.

**McGARVEY, F.** (Liverpool, Celtic) (7): 1979 v Ni, Arg; 1984 v U, Bel, EG, Ni, W.

**McGEOCH, A.** (Dumbreck) (4): 1876 v E, W; 1877 v E, W.

**McGHEE, J.** (Hibernian) (1): 1886 v W.

**McGHEE, M.** (Aberdeen) (4): 1983 v Ca (2); 1984 v Ni, E.

**McGINLAY, J.** (Bolton W.) (13): 1994 v A, Holl; 1995 v Fi (2), Ru (2), Gr, Sm; 1996 v Se; 1997 v Se, Est (2), A.

**McGONAGLE, W.** (Celtic) (6): 1933 v E; 1934 v A, E, Ni; 1935 v Ni, W.

**McGRAIN, D.** (Celtic) (62): 1973 v W, Ni, E, Sw, Br; 1974 v Cz (2), WG, W, E, Bel, N, Z, Br, Y; 1975 v Sp, Se, Por, W, Ni, E, R; 1976 v D (2), Sw, Ni, W, E; 1977 v Fin, Cz, W (2), Se, Ni, E, Ch, Arg, Br; 1978 v EG, Cz; 1980 v Bel, Por, Ni, W, E, Pol, H; 1981 v Se, Por, Is, (2), Ni (2), W, E; 1982 v Se, Sp, Holl, Ni, E, Nz, USSR.

**McGREGOR, J. C.** (Vale of Leven) (4): 1877 v E, W; 1878 v E; 1880 v E.

**McGRORY, J. E.** (Kilmarnock) (3): 1965 v Ni, Fin; 1966 v Por.

**McGRORY, J.** (Celtic) (7): 1928 v Ni; 1931 v E; 1932 v Ni, W; 1933 v E, Ni; 1934 v Ni.

**McGUIRE, W.** (Beith) (2): 1881 v E, W.

**McGURK, F.** (Birmingham City) (1): 1934 v W.

**McHARDY, H.** (Rangers) (1): 1885 v Ni.

**McINALLY, A.** (Aston Villa, Bayern Munich) (8): 1989 v Cy, Ch; 1990 v Y, Fr, Arg, Pol, Ma, Cr.

**McINALLY, J.** (Dundee Utd) (10): 1987 v Bel, Br; 1988 v Ma; 1991 v Bul (2); 1992 v US, N, CIS; 1993 v G, Por.

**McINALLY, T. B.** (Celtic) (2): 1926 v Ni; 1927 v W.

**McINALLY, T.** (Cowlairs) (1): 1889 v Ni.

**McINNES, J.** (Cowlairs) (1): 1889 v Ni.

**McINTOSH, W.** (Third Lanark) (1): 1905 v Ni.

**McINTYRE, A.** (Vale of Leven) (2): 1878 v E; 1882 v E.

**McINTYRE, H.** (Rangers) (1): 1880 v W.

**McINTYRE, J.** (Rangers) (1): 1884 v W.

**McKAY, D.** (Celtic) (14): 1959 v E, WG, Holl, Por; 1960 v E, Pol, A, H, T; 1961 v W, Ni; 1962 v Ni, Cz, U.

**MACKAY, D. C.** (Hearts, Tottenham H.) (22): 1957 v Sp; 1958 v Fr; 1959 v W, Ni, WG, E; 1960 v W, Ni, A, Pol, H, T; 1961 v W, Ni, E; 1963 v E, A, N; 1964 v Ni, W, N; 1966 v N.

**MACKAY, G.** (Hearts) (4): 1988 v Bul, L, S.Ar, Ma.

**McKAY, J.** (Blackburn R.) (1): 1924 v W.

**McKAY, R.** (Newcastle Utd.) (1): 1928 v W.

**McKEAN, R.** (Rangers) (1): 1976 v Sw.

**McKENZIE, D.** (Brentford) (1): 1938 v Ni.

**MACKENZIE, J. A.** (Partick Th.) (9): 1954 v W, E, N, Fin, A, U; 1955 v E, H; 1956 v A.

**McKEOWN, M.** (Celtic) (2): 1889 v Ni; 1890 v E.

**McKIE, J.** (East Stirling) (1): 1898 v W.

**McKILLOP, T. R.** (Rangers) (1): 1938 v Holl.

**McKIMMIE, S.** (Aberdeen) (40): 1989 v E, Ch; 1990 v Arg, Eg, Cr, Br; 1991 v R (2), Sw, Bul, Sm; 1992 v Sw, Ni, Fin, US, Ca, N, Holl, G, CIS. 1993 v Por, Est; 1994 v Sw, I, Holl (2), A; 1995 v Fin, Fi (2), Ru (2), Gr. 1996 v Gr, Fin, Se, D, U, Holl, E.

**McKINLAY, D.** (Liverpool) (2): 1922 v W, Ni.

**McKINLAY, T.** (Celtic) (22): 1996 v Gr, Fin, D, U, E, Sw; 1997 v A (2), La, Se (2), Est (2), W, Ma, Blr; 1998 v Blr, La, Fr, US, Br, M.

**McKINLAY, W.** (Dundee Utd, Blackburn R.) (29): 1994 v Ma, Holl (2), A; 1995 v Fi (2), Ru (2), Gr, Sm, J, Ec; 1996 v Fin, Se, Sm, Aus, D, Holl; 1997 v Se, Est; 1998 v La, Fr, D, Fin, Co, US, Br. 1999 v Est, Fi.

**McKINNON, A.** (Queen's Park) (1): 1874 v E.

**McKINNON, R.** (Rangers) (28): 1966 v W, E, I (2), Holl, Br; 1967 v W, Ni, E; 1968 v Ni, W, E, Holl; 1969 v D, A, WG, Cy; 1970 v Ni, W, E, Ei, WG, A; 1971 v D, Bel, Por, USSR, D.

**McKINNON, R.** (Motherwell) (3): 1994 v Ma; 1995 v J, Fi.

**MACKINNON, N.** (Dumbarton) (4): 1883 v E, W; 1884 v E, W.

**McKINNON, W. W.** (Queen's Park) (9): 1872 v E; 1873 v E; 1874 v E; 1875 v E; 1876 v E, W; 1877 v E; 1878 v E; 1879 v E.

**McLAREN, A.** (St Johnstone) (5): 1929 v N, G, Holl; 1933 v W, Ni.

**McLAREN, A.** (Preston NE) (4): 1947 v E, Bel, L; 1948 v W.

**McLAREN, A.** (Hearts, Rangers) (24): 1992 v US, Ca, N; 1993 v I, Ma, G, Est (2); 1994 v I, Ma, Holl, A; 1995 v Fin, Fi (2), Ru (2), Gr, Sm, J, Ec; 1996 v Fin, Se, Sm.

**McLAREN, A.** (Kilmarnock) (1): 2001 v Pol.

**McLAREN, J.** (Hibernian, Celtic) (3): 1888 v W; 1889 v E; 1890 v E.

**McLEAN, A.** (Celtic) (4): 1926 v W, Ni; 1927 v W, E.

**McLEAN, D.** (St Bernards) (2): 1896 v W; 1897 v Ni.

**McLEAN, D.** (Sheffield W.) (1): 1912 v E.

**McLEAN, G.** (Dundee) (1): 1968 v Holl.

**McLEAN, T.** (Kilmarnock) (6): 1969 v D. Cy, W; 1970 v Ni, W; 1971 v D.

**McLEISH, A.** (Aberdeen) (77): 1980 v Por, Ni, W, E, Pol, H; 1981 v Se, Is (2), Ni (2), E; 1982 v Se, Sp, Ni, Br; 1983 v Bel, Sw, W, E, Ca (3); 1984 v U, Bel, EG, Ni, W, E, Fr; 1985 v Y, Ice, (2), Sp (2), W, E; 1986 v W, EG, Aus (2), E, Holl, D; 1987 v Bel, E, Br; 1988 v Bel, Bul, L, S.Ar, Ma, Sp, Co, E; 1989 v N, Y, I, Cy (2), Fr, E, Ch; 1990 v Y, Fr, N, Arg, EG, Eg, Cr, Se, Br; 1991 v R, Sw, USSR, Bul; 1993 v Ma.

**McLEOD, D.** (Celtic) (4): 1905 v Ni; 1906 v E, W, Ni.

**McLEOD, J.** (Dumbarton) (5): 1888 v Ni; 1889 v W; 1890 v Ni; 1892 v E; 1893 v W.

**MacLEOD, J. M.** (Hibernian) (4): 1961 v E, Ei (2), Cz.

**MACLEOD, M.** (Celtic, Borussia Dort., Hibernian) (20): 1985 v E; 1987 v Ei, L, E, Br; 1988 v Co, E; 1989 v I, Ch; 1990 v Y, Fr, N, Arg, EG, Pol, Se, Br; 1991 v R, Sw, USSR.

**McLEOD, W.** (Cowlairs) (1): 1886 v Ni.

**McLINTOCK, A.** (Vale of Leven) (3): 1875 v E; 1876 v E; 1880 v E.

**McLINTOCK, F.** (Leicester City, Arsenal) (9): 1963 v N, Ei, Sp; 1965 v Ni; 1967 v USSR; 1970 v Ni; 1971 v W, Ni, E.

**McLUCKIE, J. S.** (Manchester City) (1): 1934 v W.

**McMAHON, A.** (Celtic) (6): 1892 v E; 1893 v E, Ni; 1894 v E; 1901 v Ni. 1902 v W.

**McMENEMY, J.** (Celtic) (12): 1905 v Ni; 1909 v Ni; 1910 v E, W; 1911 v Ni, W, E; 1912 v W; 1914 v W, Ni, E; 1920 v Ni.

**McMENEMY, J.** (Motherwell) (1): 1934 v W.

**McMILLAN, J.** (St Bernards) (1): 1897 v W.

**McMILLAN, I. L.** (Airdrie, Rangers) (6): 1952 v E, USA, D; 1955 v E; 1956 v E; 1961 v Cz.

**McMILLAN, T.** (Dumbarton) (1): 1887 v Ni.

**McMULLAN, J.** (Partick Th., Manchester City) (16): 1920 v W; 1921 v W, Ni, E; 1924 v E, Ni; 1925 v E; 1926 v W, E; 1927 v E, W; 1928 v E, W; 1929 v W, E, Ni.

**McNAB, A.** (Morton) (2): 1921 v E, Ni.

**McNAB, A.** (Sunderland, WBA) (2): 1937 v A; 1939 v E.

**McNAB, C. D.** (Dundee) (6): 1931 v E, W, A, I, Sw; 1932 v E.

**McNAB, J. S.** (Liverpool) (1): 1923 v W.

**McNAIR, A.** (Celtic) (15): 1906 v W; 1907 v Ni; 1908 v E, W; 1909 v E; 1910 v W; 1912 v E, W, Ni; 1913 v E; 1914 v E, Ni; 1920 v E, W, Ni.

**McNAMARA J.** (Celtic) (13): 1997 v La, Se, Est, W; 1998 v D, Co, US, N, M; 2000 v Holl; 2001 v Sm; 2002 v Bel, Fr.

**J. McNAUGHT, W.** (Raith R.) (5): 1951 v A, W, Ni; 1952 v E; 1955 v Ni.

**McNAUGHTON, K.** (Aberdeen) (1): 2002 v Nig.

**McNEIL, H.** (Queen's Park) (10): 1874 v E; 1875 v E; 1876 v E, W; 1877 v W; 1878 v E; 1879 v E, W; 1881 v E, W.

**McNEIL, M.** (Rangers) (2): 1876 v W; 1880 v E.

**McNEILL, W.** (Celtic) (29): 1961 v E, Ei (2), Cz; 1962 v Ni, E, Cz, U; 1963 v Ei, Sp; 1964 v W, E, WG; 1965 v E, Fin, Pol, Sp; 1966 v Ni, Pol; 1967 v USSR; 1968 v E; 1969 v Cy (2), W, E; 1970 v WG; 1972 v Ni, W, E.

**McPHAIL, J.** (Celtic) (5): 1950 v W; 1951 v W, Ni, A; 1954 v Ni.

**McPHAIL, R.** (Airdrie, Rangers) (17): 1927 v E; 1929 v W; 1931 v E, Ni; 1932 v W, Ni, Fr; 1933 v E, Ni; 1934 v A, Ni; 1935 v E; 1937 v G, E, Cz; 1938 v W, Ni.

**McPHERSON, D.** (Kilmarnock) (1): 1892 v Ni.

**McPHERSON, D.** (Hearts, Rangers) (27): 1989 v Cy, E; 1990 v N, Ma, Cr, Se, Br; 1991 v Sw, Bul (2), USSR, Sm (2); 1992 v Sw, R, Ni, Fin, US, Ca, N, Holl, G, CIS; 1993 v Sw, I, Ma, Por.

**McPHERSON, J.** (Clydesdale) (1): 1875 v E.

**McPHERSON, J.** (Vale of Leven) (8): 1879 v E, W; 1880 v E; 1881 v W; 1883 v E, W; 1884 v E; 1885 v Ni.

**McPHERSON, J.** (Kilmarnock, Cowlairs, Rangers) (9): 1888 v W; 1889 v E; 1890 v Ni, E; 1892 v W; 1894 v E; 1895 v E, Ni; 1897 Ni.

**McPHERSON, J.** (Hearts) (1): 1891 v E.

**McPHERSON, R.** (Arthurlie) (1): 1882 v E.

**McQUEEN, G.** (Leeds Utd., Manchester Utd.) (30): 1974 v Bel; 1975 v Sp (2), Por, W, Ni, E, R; 1976 v D; 1977 v Cz, W (2), Ni, E; 1978 v EG, Cz, W, Bul, Ni, W; 1979 v A, N, Por, Ni, E, N; 1980 v Pe, A, Bel; 1981 v W.

**McQUEEN, M.** (Leith Ath.) (2): 1890 v W; 1891 v W.

**McRORIE, D. M.** (Morton) (1): 1931 v W.

**McSPADYEN, A.** (Partick Th.) (2): 1939 v E, H.

**McSTAY, P.** (Celtic) (76): 1984 v U, Bel, EG, Ni, W, E; 1985 v Ice, Sp (2), W; 1986 v EG, Aus, Is, U, Y; 1987 v Bul, Ei (2), L, Bel, E, Br; 1988 v H, Bel, Bul, L, S.Ar, Sp, Co, E; 1989 v N, Y, I, Cy (2), Fr, E, Ch; 1990 v Y, Fr, N, Arg, EG, Eg, Pol, Ma, Cr, Se, Br; 1991 v R, USSR, Bul; 1992 v Sm, Fin, US, Ca, N, Holl, G, CIS; 1993 v Sw, Por (2), I, Ma, Est (2); 1994 v I, Holl; 1995 v Fin, Fi, Ru; 1996 v Aus, 1997 v Est (2), A.

**McSTAY, W.** (Celtic) (13): 1921 v W, Ni; 1925 v E, Ni, W; 1926 v E, Ni, W; 1927 v E, Ni, W; 1928 v W, Ni.

**McSWEGAN, G.** (Hearts) (2): 2000 v Bos, Lth.

**McTAVISH, J.** (Falkirk) (1): 1910 v Ni.

**McWHATTIE, G. C.** (Queen's Park) (2): 1901 v W, Ni.

**McWILLIAM, P.** (Newcastle Utd.) (8): 1905 v E; 1906 v E; 1907 v E, W; 1909 v E, W; 1910 v E; 1911 v W.

**MACARI, L.** (Celtic, Manchester Utd.) (24): 1972 v W, E, Y, Cz, Br; 1973 v D, E (2), W, Ni; 1975 v Se, Por, W, E, R; 1977 v Ni, E, Ch, Arg; 1978 v EG, W, Bul, Pe, Ir.

**MACAULEY, A. R.** (Brentford, Arsenal) (7): 1947 v E; 1948 v E, W, Ni, Bel, Sw, Fr.

**MADDEN, J.** (Celtic) (2): 1893 v W; 1895 v W.

**MAIN, F. R.** (Rangers) (1): 1938 v W.

**MAIN, J.** (Hibernian) (1): 1909 v Ni.

**MALEY, W.** (Celtic) (2): 1893 v E, Ni.

**MALPAS, M.** (Dundee Utd.) (55): 1984 v Fr; 1985 v E, Ice; 1986 v W, Aus (2), Is, R, E, Holl, D, WG; 1987 v Bul, Ei, Bel; 1988 v Bel, Bul, L, S.Ar, Ma; 1989 v N, Y, I, Cy (2), Fr, E, Ch; 1990 v Y, Fr, N, Eg, Pol, Ma, Cr, Se, Br; 1991 v R (2), Bul (2), USSR, Sm (2); 1992 v Sw, Ni, Fin, US, Ca, N, Holl, G; 1993 v Sw, Por, I.

**MARSHALL, H.** (Celtic) (2): 1899 v W; 1900 v Ni.

**MARSHALL, G.** (Celtic) (1): 1992 v US.

**MARSHALL, J.** (Middlesbrough, Llanelly) (7): 1921 v E, W, Ni; 1922 v E, W, Ni; 1924 v W.

**MARSHALL, J.** (Third Lanark) (4): 1885 v Ni; 1886 v W; 1887 v E, W.

**MARSHALL, J.** (Rangers) (3): 1932 v E; 1933 v E; 1934 v E.

**MARSHALL, R. W.** (Rangers) (2): 1892 v Ni; 1894 v Ni.

**MARTIN, B.** (Motherwell) (2): 1995 v. J, Ec.

**MARTIN, F.** (Aberdeen) (6): 1954 v N (2), A, U; 1955 v E, H.

**MARTIN, N.** (Hibernian, Sunderland) (3): 1965 v Fin, Pol; 1966 v I.

**MARTIS, J.** (Motherwell) (1): 1961 v W.

**MASON, J.** (Third Lanark) (7): 1949 v E, W, Ni; 1950 v Ni; 1951 v Ni, Bel, A.

**MASSIE, A.** (Hearts, Aston Villa) (18): 1932 v Ni, W, Fr; 1933 v Ni; 1934 v E, Ni; 1935 v E, Ni, W; 1936 v W, Ni, E; 1937 v G, E, W, Ni, A; 1938 v W.

**MASSON, D. S.** (QPR, Derby Co.) (17): 1976 v Ni, W, E; 1977 v Fin, Cz, W, Ni, E, Ch, Arg, Br; 1978 v EG, Cz, W, Ni, E, Pe.

**MATHERS, D.** (Partick Th.) (1): 1954 v Fin.

**MATTEO, D.** (Leeds Utd) (6): 2001 v Aus, Sm, Bel; 2002 v Cro, Bel, Fr.

**MAXWELL, W. S.** (Stoke City) (1): 1898 v E.

**MAY, J.** (Rangers) (5): 1906 v W, Ni; 1908 v E, Ni; 1909 v W.

**MEECHAN, P.** (Celtic) (1): 1896 v Ni.

**MEIKLEJOHN, D. D.** (Rangers) (15): 1922 v W; 1924 v W; 1925 v W, Ni, E; 1928 v W, Ni; 1929 v E, Ni; 1930 v E, Ni; 1931 v E; 1932 v W, Ni; 1934 v A.

**MENZIES, A.** (Hearts) (1): 1906 v E.

**MERCER, R.** (Hearts) (2): 1912 v W; 1913 v Ni.

**MIDDLETON, R.** (Cowdenbeath) (1): 1930 v Ni.

**MILLAR, A.** (Hearts) (1): 1939 v W.

**MILLAR, J.** (Rangers) (3): 1897 v E; 1898 v E, W.

**MILLAR, J.** (Rangers) (2): 1963 v A, Ei.

**MILLER, C.** (Dundee United) (1): 2001 v Pol.

**MILLER, K.** (Rangers) (1): 2001 v Pol.

**MILLER, J.** (St Mirren) (5): 1931 v E, I, Sw; 1932 v Fr; 1934 v E.

**MILLER, P.** (Dumbarton) (3): 1882 v E; 1883 v E, W.

**MILLER, T.** (Liverpool, Manchester Utd.) (3): 1920 v E; 1921 v E, Ni.

**MILLER, W.** (Third Lanark) (1): 1876 v E.

**MILLER, W.** (Celtic) (6): 1947 v E, W, Bel, L; 1948 v W, Ni.

**MILLER, W.** (Aberdeen) (65): 1975 v R; 1978 v Bul; 1980 v Bel, W, E, Pol, H; 1981 v Se, Por, Is, Ni (2), W, E; 1982 v Ni, Por, Holl, Br, USSR; 1983 v EG, Sw (2), W, E, Ca (3); 1984 v U, Bel, EG, W, E, Fr; 1985 v Y, Ice, Sp (2), W, E, Ice; 1986 v W, EG, Aus (2), Is, R, E, Holl, D, WG, U; 1987 v Bul, E, Br; 1988 v H, L, S.Ar, Ma, Sp, Co, E; 1989 v N, Y; 1990 Y, N.

**MILLS, W.** (Aberdeen) (3): 1936 v W, Ni; 1937 v W.

**MILNE, J. V.** (Middlesbrough) (2): 1938 v E; 1939 v E.

**MITCHELL, D.** (Rangers) (5): 1890 v Ni; 1892 v E; 1893 v E, Ni; 1894 v E.

**MITCHELL, J.** (Kilmarnock) (3): 1908 v Ni; 1910 v Ni, W.

**MITCHELL, R. C.** (Newcastle Utd.) (2): 1951 v D, Fr.

**MOCHAN, N.** (Celtic) (3): 1954 v N, A, U.

**MOIR, W.** (Bolton) (1): 1950 v E.

**MONCUR, R.** (Newcastle Utd.) (16): 1968 v Holl; 1970 v Ni, W, E, Ei; 1971 v D, Bel, W, Por, Ni, E, D; 1972 v Pe, Ni, W, E.

**MORGAN, H.** (St Mirren, Liverpool) (2): 1898 v W; 1899 v E.

**MORGAN, W.** (Burnley, Manchester Utd.) (21): 1968 v Ni; 1972 v Pe, Y, Cz, Br; 1973 v D (2), E (2), W, Ni, Sw, Br; 1974 v Cz (2), WG (2), Ni, Bel, Br, Y.

**MORRIS, D.** (Raith R.) (6): 1923 v Ni; 1924 v E, Ni; 1925 v E, W, Ni.

**MORRIS, H.** (East Fife) (1): 1950 v Ni.

**MORRISON, T.** (St Mirren) (1): 1927 v E.

**MORTON, A. L.** (Queen's Park, Rangers) (31): 1920 v W, Ni; 1921 v E; 1922 v E, W; 1923 v E, W, Ni; 1924 v E, W, Ni; 1925 v E, W, Ni; 1927 v E, Ni; 1928 v E, W, Ni; 1929 v E, W, Ni; 1930 v E, W, Ni; 1931 v E, W, Ni; 1932 v E, W, Fr.

**MORTON, H. A.** (Kilmarnock) (2): 1929 v G, Holl.

**MUDIE, J. K.** (Blackpool) (17): 1957 v W, Ni, E, Y, Sw, Sp (2), WG; 1958 v Ni, E, W, Sw, H, Pol, Y, Par, Fr.

**MUIR, W.** (Dundee) (1): 1907 v Ni.

**MUIRHEAD, T. A.** (Rangers) (8): 1922 v Ni; 1923 v E; 1924 v W; 1927 v Ni; 1928 v Ni; 1929 v W, Ni; 1930 v W.

**MULHALL, G.** (Aberdeen, Sunderland) (3): 1960 v Ni; 1963 v Ni; 1964 v Ni.

**MUNRO, A. D.** (Hearts, Blackpool) (3): 1937 v W, Ni; 1938 v Holl.

**MUNRO, F. M.** (Wolverhampton W.) (9): 1971 v Ni, E, D, USSR; 1975 v Se, W, Ni, E, R.

**MUNRO, I.** (St Mirren) (7): 1979 v Arg, N; 1980 v Pe, A, Bel, W, E.

**MUNRO, N.** (Abercorn) (2): 1888 v W; 1889 v E.

**MURDOCH, J.** (Motherwell) (1): 1931 v Ni.

**MURDOCH, R.** (Celtic) (12): 1966 v W, E, I (2); 1967 v Ni; 1968 v Ni; 1969 v W, Ni, E, WG, Cy; 1970 v A.

**MURPHY, F.** (Celtic) (1): 1938 v Holl.

**MURRAY, J.** (Renton) (1): 1895 v W.

**MURRAY, J.** (Hearts) (5): 1958 v E, H, Pol, Y, Fr.

**MURRAY, J. W.** (Vale of Leven) (1): 1890 v W.

**MURRAY, P.** (Hibernian) (2): 1896 v Ni; 1897 v W.

**MURRAY, S.** (Aberdeen) (1): 1972 v Bel.

**MUTCH, G.** (Preston NE) (1): 1938 v E.

**NAPIER, C. E.** (Celtic, Derby County) (5): 1932 v E; 1935 v E, W; 1937 v Ni, A.

**NAREY, D.** (Dundee Utd.) (35): 1977 v Se; 1979 v Psor, Ni, Arg; 1980 v Por, Ni, Pol, H; 1981 v W, E; 1982 v Holl, W, E, Nz, Br, USSR; 1983 v EG, Sw, Bel, Ni, W, E, Ca (3); 1986 v Is, R, Holl, WG, U; 1987 v Bul, E, Bel; 1989 v I, Cy.

**NAYSMITH, G.** (Hearts, Everton) (6): 2000 v Ei; 2001 v La, Sm, Cro, 2002 v Cro, Bel.

**NEIL, R. G.** (Hibernian, Rangers) (2): 1896 v W; 1900 v W.

**NEILL, R. W.** (Queen's Park) (5): 1876 v W; 1877 v E, W; 1878 v W; 1880 v E.

**NELLIES, P.** (Hearts) (2): 1914 v W, Ni.

**NELSON, J.** (Cardiff C.) (4): 1925 v W, Ni; 1928 v E; 1930 v Fr.

**NEVIN, P.** (Chelsea, Everton, Tranmere) (28): 1986 v R, E; 1987 v L, Ei, Bel; 1988 v L; 1989 v Cy, E; 1991 v R, Bul, Sm; 1992 v US, G, CIS; 1993 v Ma, Por, Est; 1994 v Sw, Ma, Holl (2), A. 1995 v Fi, Ru, Sm; 1996 v Se, Sm, Aus.

**NIBLO, T.** (Aston Villa) (1): 1904 v E.

**NIBLOE, J.** (Kilmarnock) (11): 1929 v E, N, Holl; 1930 v W; 1931 v E, Ni, A, I, Sw; 1932 v E, Fr.

**NICHOLAS, C.** (Celtic, Arsenal, Aberdeen) (20): 1983 v Sw, Ni, E, Ca (3); 1984 v Bel, Fr; 1985 v Y, Ice, Sp, W; 1986 v Is, R, E, D, U; 1987 v Bul, E; 1989 v Cy.

**NICOL, S.** (Liverpool) (27): 1985 v Y, Ice, Sp, W; 1986 v W, EG, Aus, E, D, WG, U; 1988 v H, Bul, S.Ar, Sp, Co, E; 1989 v N, Y, Cy, Fr; 1990 v Y, Fr; 1991 v USSR, Sm; 1992 Sw.

**NICOLSON, B.** (Dunfermline) (2): 2001 v Pol; 2002 v La.

**NISBET, J.** (Ayr Utd.) (3): 1929 v N, G, Holl.

**NIVEN, J. B.** (Moffat) (1): 1885 v Ni.

**O'CONNOR, G.** (Hibernian) (2): 2002 v Nig, Skor.

**O'DONNELL, F.** (Preston NE, Blackpool) (6): 1937 v E, A, Cz; 1938 v E, W, Holl.

**O'DONNELL, P.** (Motherwell) (1): 1994 v Sw.

**OGILVIE, D. H.** (Motherwell) (1): 1934 v A.

**O'HARE, J.** (Derby County) (13): 1970 v W, Ni, E; 1971 v D, Bel, W, Ni; 1972 v Por, Bel, Holl, Pe, Ni, W.

**O'NEIL, J.** (Hibs) (1): 2001 v Pol.

**O'NEIL, B.** (Celtic, Wolfsburg) (6): 1996 v Aus; 1999 v G; 2000 v Lth, Holl, Ei; 2001 v Aus.

**ORMOND, W. E.** (Hibernian) (6): 1954 v E, N, Fin, A, U; 1959 v E.

**O'ROURKE, F.** (Airdrie) (1): 1907 v Ni.

**ORR, J.** (Kilmarnock) (1): 1892 v W.

**ORR, R.** (Newcastle Utd.) (2): 1902 v E; 1904 v E.

**ORR, T.** (Morton) (2): 1952 v Ni, W.

**ORR, W.** (Celtic) (3): 1900 v Ni; 1903 v Ni; 1904 v W.

**ORROCK, R.** (Falkirk) (1): 1913 v W.

**OSWALD, J.** (Third Lanark, St Bernards, Rangers) (3): 1889 v E; 1895 v E; 1897 v W.

**PARKER, A. H.** (Falkirk, Everton) (15): 1955 v Por, Y, A; 1956 v E, Ni, W, A; 1957 v Ni, W, Y; 1958 v Ni, W, E, Sw, Par.

**PARLANE, D.** (Rangers) (12): 1973 v W, Sw, Br; 1975 v Sp, Se, Por, W, Ni, E, R; 1976 v D; 1977 v W.

**PARLANE, R.** (Vale of Leven) (3): 1878 v W; 1879 v E, W.

**PATERSON, G. D.** (Celtic) (1): 1939 v Ni.

**PATERSON, J.** (Leicester City) (1): 1920 v E.

**PATERSON, J.** (Cowdenbeath) (3): 1931 v A, I, Sw.

**PATON, A.** (Motherwell) (2): 1952 v D, Se.

**PATON, D.** (St Bernards) (1): 1896 v W.

**PATON, M.** (Dumbarton) (5): 1883 E; 1884 v W; 1885 v W, E; 1886 v E.

**PATON, R.** (Vale of Leven) (2): 1879 v E, W.

**PATRICK, J.** (St Mirren) (2): 1897 E, W.

**PAUL, J. McD.** (Queen's Park) (3): 1909 v E, W, Ni.

**PAUL, W.** (Partick Th.) (3): 1888 v W; 1889 v W; 1890 v W.

**PAUL, W.** (Dykebar) (1891 v W.

**PEARSON, T.** (Newcastle Utd.) (2): 1947 v E, Bel.

**PENMAN, A.** (Dundee) (1): 1966 v Holl.

**PETTIGREW, W.** (Motherwell) (5): 1976 v Sw, Ni, W; 1977 v W, Se.

**PHILLIPS, J.** (Queen's Park) (3): 1877 v E, W; 1878 v W.

**PLENDERLEITH, J. B.** (Manchester City) (1): 1961 v Ni.

**PORTEOUS, W.** (Hearts) (1): 1903 v Ni.

**PRESSLEY, S.** (Hearts) (2): 2000 v Fr, Ei.

**PRINGLE, C.** (St Mirren) (1): 1921 v W.

**PROVAN, D.** (Rangers) (5): 1964 v Ni, N; 1966 v I (2), Holl.

**PROVAN, D.** (Celtic) (10): 1980 v Bel (2), Por, Ni; 1981 v Is, W, E; 1982 v Se, Por, Ni.

**PURSELL, P.** (Queen's Park) (1): 1914 v W.

**QUINN, J.** (Celtic) (11): 1905 v Ni; 1906 v Ni, W; 1908 v Ni, E; 1909 v E; 1910 v E, Ni, W; 1912 v E, W.

**QUINN, P.** (Motherwell) (4): 1961 v E, Ei (2); 1962 v U.

**RAE, G.** (Dundee) (2): 2001 v Pol; 2002 v La.

**RAE, J.** (Third Lanark) (2): 1889 v W; 1890 v Ni.

**RAESIDE, J. S.** (Third Lanark) (1): 1906 v W.

**RAISBECK, A. G.** (Liverpool) (8): 1900 v E; 1901 v E; 1902 v E; 1903 v E, W; 1904 v E; 1906 v E; 1907 v E.

**RANKIN, G.** (Vale of Leven) (2): 1890 v Ni; 1891 v E.

**RANKIN, R.** (St Mirren) (3): 1929 v N, G, Holl.

**REDPATH, W.** (Motherwell) (9): 1949 v W, Ni; 1951 v E, D, Fr, Bel, A; 1952 v Ni, E.

**REID, J, G.** (Airdrie) (3): 1914 v W; 1920 v W; 1924 v Ni.

**REID, R.** (Brentford) (2): 1938 v E, Ni.

**REID, W.** (Rangers) (9): 1911 v E, W, Ni; 1912 v Ni; 1913 v E, W, Ni; 1914 v E, Ni.

**REILLY, L.** (Hibernian) (38): 1949 v E, W, Fr; 1950 v W, Ni, Sw, Fr; 1951 v W, E, D, Fr, Bel, A; 1952 v Ni, W, E, USA, D, Se; 1953 v Ni, W, E, Se; 1954 v W; 1955 v H (2), Por, Y, A, E; 1956 v E, W, Ni, A; 1957 v E, Ni, W, Y.

**RENNIE, H. G.** (Hearts, Hibs) (13): 1900 v E, Ni; 1901 v E; 1902 v E, Ni, W; 1903 v Ni, W; 1904 v Ni; 1905 v W; 1906 v Ni; 1908 v Ni, W.

**RENNY-TAILYOUR, H. W.** (Royal Engineers) (1): 1873 v E.

**RHIND, A.** (Queen's Park) (1): 1872 v E.

**RICHMOND, A.** (Queen's Park) (1): 1906 v W.

**RICHMOND, J. T.** (Clydesdale, Queen's Park) (3): 1877 v E; 1878 v E; 1882 v W.

**RING, T.** (Clyde) (12): 1953 v Se; 1955 v W, Ni, E, H; 1957 v E, Sp (2), Sw, WG; 1958 v Ni, Sw.

**RIOCH, B. D.** (Derby County, Everton) (24): 1975 v Por, W, Ni, E, R; 1976 v D (2), R, Ni, W, E; 1977 v Fin, Cz, W (2), Ni, E, Ch, Br; 1978 v Cz, Ni, E, Pe, Holl.

**RITCHIE, A.** (East Stirling) (1): 1891 v W.

**RITCHIE, H.** (Hibernian) (2): 1923 v W; 1928 v Ni.

**RITCHIE, J.** (Queen's Park) (1): 1897 v W.

**RITCHIE, P.** (Hearts, Bolton) (6): 1999 v G, Czr, E; 2000 v Lth, Fr, Holl.

**RITCHIE, W.** (Rangers) (1): 1962 v U.

**ROBB, D. T.** (Aberdeen) (5): 1971 v W, E, Por, D, USSR.

**ROBB, W.** (Rangers, Hibernian) (2): 1926 v W; 1928 v W.

**ROBERTSON, A.** (Clyde) (5): 1955 v Por, A, H; 1958 v Sw, Par.

**ROBERTSON, D.** (Rangers) (3): 1991 v Ni; 1994 v Sw, Holl.

**ROBERTSON, G.** (Motherwell, Sheffield W.) (4): 1910 v W; 1912 v W; 1913 v E, Ni.

**ROBERTSON, G.** (Kilmarnock) (1): 1938 v Cz.

**ROBERTSON, H.** (Dundee) (1): 1962 v Cz.

**ROBERTSON, J.** (Dundee) (2): 1931 v A, I.

**ROBERTSON, J.** (Hearts) (16): 1991 v R, Sw, Bul, Sm (2); 1992 v Ni, Fin; 1993 v I, Ma, G, Est; 1995 v J, Ec, Fi. 1996 v Gr, Se.

**ROBERTSON, J. N.** (Nottingham F., Derby County) (28): 1978 v Ni, W, Ir; 1979 v Por, N; 1980 v Pe, A, Bel (2), Por; 1981 v Se, Por, Is, Ni (2), E; 1982 v Se, Ni (2), E, Nz, Br, USSR; 1983 v EG, Sw; 1984 v U, Bel.

**ROBERTSON, J. G.** (Tottenham H.) (1): 1965 v W.

**ROBERTSON, J. T.** (Everton, Southampton, Rangers) (16): 1898 v E; 1899 v E; 1900 v E, W; 1901 v W, Ni, E; 1902 v W, Ni, E; 1903 v E, W; 1904 v E, W, Ni; 1905 v W.

**ROBERTSON, P.** (Dundee) (1): 1903 v Ni.

**ROBERTSON, T.** (Queen's Park) (4): 1889 v Ni; 1890 v E; 1891 v W; 1892 v Ni.

**ROBERTSON, T.** (Hearts) (1): 1898 v Ni.

**ROBERTSON, W.** (Dumbarton) (2): 1887 v E, W.

**ROBINSON, R.** (Dundee) (4): 1974 v WG; 1975 v Se, Ni, R.

**ROSS, M.** (Rangers) (2): 2002 v Skor, SA.

**ROUGH, A.** (Partick Th, Hibernian) (53): 1976 v Sw, Ni, W, E; 1977 v Fin, Cz, W (2), Se, Ni, E, Ch, Arg, Br; 1978 v Cz, W, Ni, E, Pe, Ir, Holl; 1979 v A, Por, W, Arg, N; 1980 v Pe, A, Bel (2), Por, W, E, Pol, H; 1981 v Se, Por, Is (2), Ni, W, E; 1982 v Se, Ni, Sp, Holl, W, E, Nz, Br, USSR; 1986 v W, E.

**ROUGVIE, D.** (Aberdeen) (1): 1984 v Ni.

**ROWAN, A.** (Caledonian, Queen's Park) (2): 1880 v E; 1882 v W.

**RUSSELL, D.** (Hearts, Celtic) (6): 1895 v E, Ni; 1897 v W; 1898 v Ni; 1901 v W, Ni.

**RUSSELL, J.** (Cambuslang) (1): 1890 v Ni.

**RUSSELL W. F.** (Airdrie) (2): 1924 v W; 1925 v E.

**RUTHERFORD, E.** (Rangers) (1): 1948 v F.

**ST JOHN, I.** (Motherwell, Liverpool) (21): 1959 v WG; 1960 v E, Ni, W, Pol, A; 1961 v E; 1962 v Ni, W, E, Cz (2), U; 1963 v W, Ni, E, N, Ei, Sp; 1964 v Ni; 1965 v E.

**SAWERS, W.** (Dundee) (1): 1895 v W.

**SCARFF, P.** (Celtic) (1): 1931 v Ni.

**SCHAEDLER, E.** (Hibernian) (1): 1974 v WG.

**SCOTT, A. S.** (Rangers, Everton) (16): 1957 v Ni, Y, WG; 1958 v W, Sw; 1959 v Por; 1962 v Ni, W, E, Cz, U; 1964 v W, N; 1965 v Fin; 1966 v Por, Br.

**SCOTT, J.** (Hibernian) (1): 1966 v Holl.

**SCOTT, J.** (Dundee) (2): 1971 v D, USSR.

**SCOTT, M.** (Airdrie) (1): 1898 v W.

**SCOTT, R.** (Airdrie) (1): 1894 v Ni.

**SCOULAR, J.** (Portsmouth) (9): 1951 v D, Fr, A; 1952 v E, USA, D, Se; 1953 v W, Ni.

**SELLAR, W.** (Battlefield, Queen's Park) (9): 1885 v E; 1886 v E; 1887 v E, W; 1888 v E; 1891 v E; 1892 v E; 1893 v E, Ni.

**SEMPLE, J.** (Cambuslang) (1): 1886 v W.

**SEVERIN, S.** (Hearts) (3): 2002 v La, Skor, SA.

**SHANKLY, W.** (Preston NE) (5): 1938 v E; 1939 v E, W, Ni, H.

**SHARP, G. M.** (Everton) (12): 1985 v Ice; 1986 v W, Aus (2), Is, R, U; 1987 v Ei; 1988 v Bel, Bul, L, Ma.

**SHARP, J.** (Dundee, Woolwich Arsenal, Fulham) (5): 1904 v W; 1907 v W, E; 1908 v E; 1909 v W.

**SHAW, D.** (Hibernian) (8): 1947 v W, Ni; 1948 v E, Bel, Sw, Fr; 1949 v W, Ni.

**SHAW, F. W.** (Pollokshields Ath.) (2): 1884 v E, W.

**SHAW, J.** (Rangers) (4): 1947 v E, Bel, L; 1948 v Ni.

**SHEARER, D.** (Aberdeen) (7) 1994 v A, Holl; 1995 v Fin, Ru, Sm, Fi. 1996 v Gr.

**SHEARER, R.** (Rangers) (4): 1961 v E, Ei (2), Cz.

**SILLARS, D. C.** (Queen's Park) (5): 1891 v Ni; 1892 v E; 1893 v W; 1894 v E; 1895 v W.

**SIMPSON, J.** (Third Lanark) (3): 1895 v E, W, Ni.

**SIMPSON, J.** (Rangers) (14): 1935 v E, W, Ni; 1936 v E, W, Ni; 1937 v G, E, W, Ni, A, Cz; 1938 v W, Ni.

**SIMPSON, N.** (Aberdeen) (4): 1983 v Ni; 1984 v Fr; 1987 v E; 1988 v E.

**SIMPSON, R. C.** (Celtic) (5): 1967 v E, USSR; 1968 v Ni, E; 1969 v A.

**SINCLAIR, G. L.** (Hearts) (3): 1910 v Ni; 1912 v W, Ni.

**SINCLAIR, J. W. E.** (Leicester City) (1): 1966 v Por.

**SKENE, L. H.** (Queen's Park) (1): 1904 v W.

**SLOAN, T.** (Third Lanark) (1): 1904 v W.

**SMELLIE, R.** (Queen's Park) (6): 1887 v Ni; 1888 v W; 1889 v E; 1891 v E; 1893 v E, Ni.

**SMITH, A.** (Rangers) (20): 1898 v E; 1900 v E, Ni, W; 1901 v E, Ni, W; 1902 v E, Ni, W; 1903 v E, Ni, W; 1904 v Ni; 1905 v W; 1906 v E, Ni; 1907 v W; 1911 v E, Ni.

**SMITH, D.** (Aberdeen, Rangers) (2): 1966 v Holl; 1968 v Holl.

**SMITH, G.** (Hibernian) (18): 1947 v E, Ni; 1948 v W, Bel, Sw, Fr; 1952 v E, USA; 1955 v Por, Y, A, H; 1956 v E, Ni, W; 1957 v Sp (2), Sw.

**SMITH, H. G.** (Hearts) (3): 1988 v S.Ar; 1991 Ni; 1992 v Ca.

**SMITH, J.** (Rangers) (2): 1935 v Ni; 1938 v Ni.

**SMITH, J.** (Ayr United) (1): 1924 v E.

**SMITH, J.** (Aberdeen, Newcastle Utd.) (4): 1968 v Holl; 1974 v WG, Ni, W.

**SMITH, J. E.** (Celtic) (2); 1959 v H, Por.

**SMITH, Jas** (Queen's Park) (1): 1872 v E.

**SMITH, J.** (Mauchline, Edinburgh University, Queen's Park) (10): 1877 v E, W; 1879 v E, W; 1880 v E; 1881 v W, E; 1883 v E, W; 1884 v E.

**SMITH, N.** (Rangers) (12): 1897 v E; 1898 v W; 1899 v E, W, Ni; 1900 v E, W, Ni; 1901 v Ni, W; 1902 v E, Ni.

**SMITH, R,** (Queen's Park) (2): 1872 v E; 1873 v E.

**SMITH, T. M.** (Kilmarnock, Preston NE) (2): 1934 v E; 1938 v E.

**SOMERS, P.** (Celtic) (4): 1905 v E, Ni; 1907 v Ni; 1909 v W.

**SOMERS, W. S.** (Third Lanark, Queen's Park) (3): 1879 v E, W; 1880 v W.

**SOMERVILLE, G.** (Queen's Park) (1): 1886 v E.

**SOUNESS, G. J.** (Middlesbrough, Liverpool, Sampdoria) (54): 1975 v EG, Sp, Se; 1978 v Bul, W, E, Holl; 1979 v A. N, W, Ni, E; 1980 v Pe, A, Bel, Por, Ni; 1981 v Por, Is (2); 1982 v Ni, Por, Sp, W, E, Nz, Br, USSR; 1983 v EG, Sw (2), Bel, W, E, Ca (3); 1984 v U, Ni, W; 1985 v Y, Ice (2), Sp (2), W, E; 1986 v EG, Aus (2), R, E, D, WG.

**SPEEDIE, D. R.** (Chelsea, Coventry City) (10): 1985 v E; 1986 v W, EG, Aus, E; 1989 v Y, I, Cy (2), Ch.

**SPEEDIE, F.** (Rangers) (3): 1903 v E, W, Ni.

**SPENCER, J.** (Chelsea) (14): 1995 v Ru, Gr, Sm, J; 1996 v Fin, Aus, D, US, U, Holl, E, Sw; 1997 v La, W.

**SPIERS, J. H.** (Rangers) (1): 1908 v W.

**STANTON, P.** (Hibernian) (16): 1966 v Holl; 1969 v Ni; 1970 v Ei, A; 1971 v D, Bel, Por, USSR, D; 1972 v Por, Bel, Holl, W; 1973 v W, Ni; 1974 v WG.

**STARK. J.** (Rangers) (2): 1909 v E, Ni.

**STEEL, W.** (Morton, Derby County, Dundee) (30): 1947 v E, Bel, L; 1948 v Fr, E, W, Ni; 1949 v E, W, Ni, Fr; 1950 v E, W, Ni, Sw, Por, Fr; 1951 v W, Ni, E, A (2), D, Fr, Bel; 1952 v W; 1953 v W, E, Ni, Se.

**STEELE, D. M.** (Huddersfield) (3): 1923 v E, W, Ni.

**STEIN, C.** (Rangers, Coventry City) (21): 1969 v W, Ni, D, E, Cy (2); 1970 v A, Ni, W, E, Ei, WG; 1971 v D, USSR, Bel, D; 1972 v Cz; 1973 v E (2), W, Ni.

**STEPHEN, J. F.** (Bradford) (2): 1947 v W; 1948 v W.

**STEVENSON, G.** (Motherwell) (12): 1928 v W, Ni; 1930 v Ni, E, Fr; 1931 v E, W; 1932 v W, Ni; 1933 v W; 1934 v E; 1935 v Ni.

**STEWART, A.** (Queen's Park) (2): 1888 v Ni; 1889 v W.

**STEWART, A.** (Third Lanark) (1): 1894 v W.

**STEWART, D.** (Dumbarton) (1): 1888 v Ni.

**STEWART, D.** (Queen's Park) (3): 1893 v W; 1894 v Ni; 1897 v Ni.

**STEWART, D. S.** (Leeds Utd.) (1): 1978 v EG.

**STEWART, G.** (Hibernian, Man City) (4): 1906 v W, E; 1907 v E, W.

**STEWART, J.** (Kilmarnock, Middlesbrough) (2): 1977 v Ch; 1979 v N.

**STEWART, M.** (Manchester Utd) (3): 2002 v Nig, Skor, SA.

**STEWART, R.** (West Ham Utd.) (10): 1981 v W, Ni, E; 1982 v Ni, Por, W; 1984 v Fr; 1987 v Ei (2), L.

**STEWART, W. E.** (Queen's Park) (2): 1898 v Ni; 1900 v Ni.

**STOCKDALE, R.** (Middlesbrough) (3): 2002 v Nig, Skor, SA.

**STORRIER, D.** (Celtic) (3): 1899 v E, W, Ni.

**STRACHAN, G.** (Aberdeen, Manchester Utd., Leeds Utd.) (50): 1980 v Ni, W, E, Pol, H; 1981 v Se, Por; 1982 v Ni, Por, Sp, Holl, Nz, Br, USSR; 1983 v EG, Sw (2), Bel, Ni, W, E, Ca (3); 1984 v EG, Ni, E, Fr; 1985 v Sp, E, Ice; 1986 v W, Aus, R, D, WG, U; 1987 v Bul, Ei (2); 1988 v H; 1989 v Fr; 1990 v Fr; 1991 v USSR, Bul, Sm; 1992 v Sw, R, Ni, Fin.

**STURROCK, P.** (Dundee Utd.) (20): 1981 v W, Ni, E; 1982 v Por, Ni, W, E; 1983 v EG, Sw, Bel, Ca (3); 1984 v W; 1985 v Y; 1986 v Is, Holl, D, U; 1987 v Bel.

**SULLIVAN, N.** (Wimbledon, Spurs) (27): 1997 v W; 1998 Fr, Co. 1999 v Fi (2), CzR (2), G. 2000 v Bos (2), Est, E (2) Fr, Holl, Ei; 2001 v La, Sm (2), Cro, Bel, Pol; 2002 v Cro, Bel, La, Fr, Skor.

**SUMMERS, W.** (St Mirren) (1): 1926 v E.

**SYMON, J. S.** (Rangers) (1): 1939 v H.

**TAIT, T. S.** (Sunderland) (1): 1911 v W.

**TAYLOR, J.** (Queen's Park) (6): 1872 v E; 1873 v E; 1874 v E; 1875 v E; 1876 v E, W.

**TAYLOR, J. D.** (Dumbarton, St Mirren) (4): 1892 v W; 1893 v W; 1894 v Ni; 1895 v Ni.

**TAYLOR, W.** (Hearts) (1): 1892 v E.

**TELFER, P.** (Coventry) (1): 2000 v Fr.

**TELFER, W.** (Motherwell) (2): 1933 v Ni; 1934 v Ni.

**TELFER, W. D.** (St Mirren) (1): 1954 v W.

**TEMPLETON, R.** (Aston Villa, Newcastle Utd., Woolwich Arsenal, Kilmarnock) (11): 1902 v E; 1903 v E, W; 1904 v E; 1905 v W; 1908 v Ni; 1910 v E, Ni; 1912 v E, Ni; 1913 v W.

**THOMPSON, S.** (Dundee United) (2): 2002 v Fr, Nig.

**THOMSON, A.** (Arthurlie) (1): 1886 v Ni.

**THOMSON, A.** (Third Lanark) (1): 1889 v W.

**THOMSON, A.** (Airdrie) (1): 1909 v Ni.

**THOMSON, A.** (Celtic) (3): 1926 v E; 1932 v Fr; 1933 v W.

**THOMSON, C.** (Hearts, Sunderland) (21): 1904 v Ni; 1905 v E, Ni, W; 1906 v W, Ni; 1907 v E, W, Ni; 1908 v E, W, Ni; 1909 v W; 1910 v E; 1911 v Ni; 1912 v E, W; 1913 v E, W; 1914 v E, Ni.

**THOMSON, C.** (Sunderland) (1): 1937 v Cz.

**THOMSON, D.** (Dundee) (1): 1920 v W.

**THOMSON, J.** (Celtic) (4): 1930 v Fr; 1931 v E, W, Ni.

**THOMSON, J. J.** (Queen's Park) (3): 1872 v E; 1873 v E; 1874 v E.

**THOMSON, J. R.** (Everton) (1): 1933 v W.

**THOMSON, R.** (Celtic) (1): 1932 v W.

**THOMSON, R. W.** (Falkirk) (1): 1927 v E.

**THOMSON, S.** (Rangers) (2): 1884 v W, Ni.

**THOMSON, W.** (Dumbarton) (4): 1892 v W; 1893 v W; 1898 v Ni, W.

**THOMSON, W.** (Dundee) (1): 1896 v W.

**THOMSON, W.** (St Mirren) (7): 1980 v Ni; 1981 v Ni (2); 1982 v Por; 1983 v Ni, Ca; 1984 v EG.

**THORNTON, W.** (Rangers) (7): 1947 v W, Ni; 1948 v E, Ni; 1949 v Fr; 1952 v D, Se.

**TONER, W.** (Kilmarnock) (2): 1959 v W, Ni.

**TOWNSLEY, T.** (Falkirk) (1926 v W.

**TROUP, A.** (Dundee, Everton) (5): 1920 v E; 1921 v W, Ni; 1922 v Ni; 1926 v E.

**TURNBULL, E. F.** (Hibernian) (8): 1948 v Bel, Sw; 1951 v A; 1958 v H, Pol, Y, Par, Fr.

**TURNER, T.** (Arthurlie) (1): 1884 v W.

**TURNER, W.** (Pollokshields Ath.) (2): 1885 v Ni; 1886 v Ni.

**URE, J. F.** (Dundee, Arsenal) (11): 1962 v W, Cz; 1963 v W, Ni, E, A, N, Sp; 1964 v Ni, N; 1968 v Ni.

**URQUHART, D.** (Hibernian) (1): 1934 v W.

**VALLANCE, T.** (Rangers) (7): 1877 v E, W; 1878 v E; 1879 v E, W; 1881 v E, W.

**VENTERS, A.** (Cowdenbeath, Rangers) (3): 1934 v Ni; 1936 v E; 1939 v E.

**WADDELL, T. S.** (Queen's Park) (6): 1891 v Ni; 1892 v E; 1893 v E, Ni; 1895 v E, Ni.

**WADDELL, W.** (Rangers) (17): 1947 v W; 1949 v E, W, Ni, Fr; 1950 v E, Ni; 1951 v E, D, Fr, Bel, A; 1952 v Ni, W; 1954 v Ni; 1955 v W, Ni.

**WALES, H. M.** (Motherwell) (1): 1933 v W.

**WALKER, A.** (Celtic) (3): 1988 v Co; 1995 v Fin, Fi.

**WALKER, F.** (Third Lanark) (1): 1922 v W.

**WALKER, G.** (St Mirren) (4): 1930 v Fr; 1931 v Ni, A, Sw.

**WALKER, J.** (Hearts, Rangers) (5): 1895 v Ni; 1897 v W; 1898 v Ni; 1904 v W, Ni.

**WALKER, J.** (Swindon T.) (9): 1911 v E, W, Ni; 1912 v E, W, Ni; 1913 v E, W, Ni.

**WALKER, N.** (Hearts) (2): 1993 v G, 1996 US.

**WALKER, R.** (Hearts) (29): 1900 v E, Ni; 1901 v E, W; 1902 v E, W, Ni; 1903 v E, W, Ni; 1904 v E, W, Ni; 1905 v E, W, Ni; 1906 v Ni; 1907 v E, Ni; 1908 v E, W, Ni; 1909 v E, W; 1912 v E, W, Ni; 1913 v E, W.

**WALKER, T.** (Hearts) (20): 1935 v E, W; 1936 v E, W, Ni; 1937 v G, E, W, Ni, A, Cz; 1938 v E, W, Ni, Cz, Holl; 1939 v E, W, Ni, H.

**WALKER, W.** (Clyde) (2): 1909 v Ni; 1910 v Ni.

**WALLACE, I. A.** (Coventry City) (3): 1978 v Bul; 1979 v Por, W.

**WALLACE, W. S. B.** (Hearts, Celtic) (7): 1965 v Ni; 1966 v E, Holl; 1967 v E, USSR; 1968 v Ni; 1969 v E.

**WARDHAUGH, J.** (Hearts) (2): 1955 v H; 1957 v Ni.

**WARK, J.** (Ipswich Town, Liverpool) (29): 1979 v W, Ni, E, Arg, N; 1980 v Pe, A, Bel (2); 1981 v Is, Ni; 1982 v Se, Sp, Holl, Ni, Nz, Br, USSR; 1983 v EG, Sw (2), Ni, E; 1984 v U, Bel, EG, E, Fr; 1985 v Y.

**WATSON, A.** (Queen's Park) (3): 1881 v E, W; 1882 v E.

**WATSON, J.** (Sunderland, Middlesbrough) (6): 1903 v E, W; 1904 v E; 1905 v E; 1909 v E, Ni.

**WATSON, J.** (Motherwell, Huddersfield Town) (2): 1948 v Ni; 1954 v Ni.

**WATSON, J. A. K.** (Rangers) (1): 1878 v W.

**WATSON, P. R.** (Blackpool) (1): 1934 v A.

**WATSON, R.** (Motherwell) (1): 1971 v USSR.

**WATSON, W.** (Falkirk) (1): 1898 v W.

**WATT, F.** (Kilbirnie) (4): 1889 v W, Ni; 1890 v W; 1891 v E.

**WATT, W. W.** (Queen's Park) (1): 1887 v Ni.

**WAUGH, W.** (Hearts) (1): 1938 v Cz.

**WEIR, A.** (Motherwell) (6): 1959 v WG; 1960 v E, Por, A, H, T.

**WEIR, D.** (Hearts, Everton) (34): 1997 v W, Ma; 1998 Fr, D, Fin, N, M. 1999 v Est, Fi, CzR (2), G, Fi. 2000 v Bos (2), Est, Lth, E (2), Holl; 2001 v La, Sm (2), Cro, Aus, Bel, Pol; 2002 v Cro, Bel, La, Fr, Nig, Skor, SA.

**WEIR, J.** (Third Lanark) (1): 1887 v Ni.

**WEIR, J. B.** (Queen's Park) (4): 1872 v E; 1874 v E; 1875 v E; 1878 v W.

**WEIR, P.** (St Mirren, Aberdeen) (6): 1980 v N, W, Pol, H; 1983 v Sw; 1984 v Ni.

**WHITE, J.** (Albion Rovers, Hearts) (2): 1922 v W; 1923 v Ni.

**WHITE, J. A.** (Falkirk, Tottenham H.) (22): 1959 v WG, Holl, Por; 1960 v Ni, W, Pol, A, T; 1961 v W; 1962 v Ni, W, E, Cz (2); 1963 v W, Ni, E; 1964 v Ni, W, E, N, WG.

**WHITE, W.** (Bolton W.) (2): 1907 v E; 1908 v E.

**WHITELAW, A.** (Vale of Leven) (2): 1887 v Ni; 1890 v W.

**WHYTE, D.** (Celtic, Middlesbrough, Aberdeen) (12): 1988 v Bel; L; 1989 v Ch; 1992 v US; 1993 v Por, I; 1995 v J, Ec, US; 1997 v La; 1998 v Fin: 1999 v G.

**WILKIE, L.** (Dundee) (1): 2002 v SA.

**WILLIAMS, G.** (Nottingham Forest) (3): 2002 v Nig, Skor, SA.

**WILSON, A.** (Sheffield W.) (6): 1907 v E; 1908 v E; 1912 v I; 1913 v E, W; 1914 v Ni.

**GARETH WILLIAMS won his first Scotland cap against Nigeria in April, 2002**

**WILSON, A.** (Portsmouth) (1): 1954 v Fin.

**WILSON, A. N.** (Dunfermline, Middlesbrough) (12): 1920 v E, W, Ni; 1921 v E, W, Ni; 1922 v E, W, Ni; 1923 v E, W, Ni.

**WILSON, D.** (Queen's Park) (1): 1900 v W.

**WILSON, D.** (Oldham) (1): 1913 v E.

**WILSON, D.** (Rangers) (22): 1961 v E, W, Ni, Ei (2), Cz; 1962 v Ni, W, E, Cz, U; 1963 v W, E, A, N, Ei, Sp; 1964 v E, WG; 1965 v Ni, E, Fin.

**WILSON, G. W.** (Hearts, Everton, Newcastle Utd.) (6): 1904 v W; 1905 v E, Ni; 1906 v W; 1907 v E; 1909 v E.

**WILSON, H.** (Newmilns, Sunderland, Third Lanark) (4): 1890 v W; 1897 v E; 1902 v W; 1904 v Ni.

**WILSON, I. A.** (Leicester City, Everton) (5): 1987 v E, Br; 1988 v Bel, Bul, L.

**WILSON, J.** (Vale of Leven) (4): 1888 v W; 1889 v E; 1890 v E; 1891 v E.

**WILSON, P.** (Celtic) (4): 1926 v Ni; 1930 v Fr; 1931 v Ni; 1933 v E.

**WILSON, P.** (Celtic) (1): 1975 v Sp.

**WILSON, R. P.** (Arsenal) (2): 1972 v Por, Holl.

**WINTERS, R.** (Aberdeen) (1): 1999 v G.

**WISEMAN, W.** (Queen's Park) ( 2): 1927 v W; 1930 v Ni.

**WOOD, G.** (Everton, Arsenal) (4): 1979 v Ni, E, Arg; 1982 v Ni.

**WOODBURN, W. A.** (Rangers) (24): 1947 v E, Bel, L; 1948 v W, Ni; 1949 v E, Fr; 1950 v E, W, Ni, Por, Fr; 1951 v E, W, Ni, A (2), D, Fr, Bel; 1952 v E, W, Ni, USA.

**WOTHERSPOON, D. N.** (Queen's Park) (2): 1872 v E; 1873 v E.

**WRIGHT, K.** (Hibs) (1): 1992 v Ni.

**WRIGHT, S.** (Aberdeen) (2): 1993 v G, Est.

**WRIGHT, T.** (Sunderland) (3): 1953 v W, Ni, E.

**WYLIE, T. G.** (Rangers) (1): 1890 v Ni.

**YEATS, R.** (Liverpool) (2): 1965 v W; 1966 v I.

**YORSTON, B. C.** (Aberdeen) (1): 1931 v Ni.

**YORSTON, H.** (Aberdeen) (1): 1955 v W.

**YOUNG, A.** (Hearts, Everton) (8): 1960 v E, A, H, T; 1961 v W, Ni, Ei; 1966 v Por.

**YOUNG, A.** (Everton) (2): 1905 v E; 1907 v W.

**YOUNG, G. A.** (Rangers) (53): 1947 v E, Ni, Bel, L; 1948 v E, Ni, Bel, Sw, Fr; 1949 v E, W, Ni, Fr; 1950 v E, W, Ni, Sw, Por, Fr; 1951 v E, W, Ni, A (2), D, Fr, Bel; 1952 v E, W, Ni, USA, D, Se; 1953 v W, E, Ni, Se; 1954 v Ni, W; 1955 v W, Ni, Por, Y; 1956 v Ni, W, E, A; 1957 v E, Ni, W, Y, Sp, Sw.

**YOUNG, J.** (Celtic) (1): 1906 v Ni.

**YOUNGER, T.** (Hibernian, Liverpool) (24): 1955 v Por, Y, A, H; 1956 v E, Ni, W, A: 1957 v E, Ni, W, Y, Sp (2), Sw, WG; 1958 v Ni, W, E, Sw, H, Pol, Y, Par.

## EUROPEAN CHAMPIONSHIPS

| Year | Winners | | Runners-up | | Venue |
|------|---------|---|------------|---|-------|
| 1960 | RUSSIA | 2 | Yugoslavia | 1 | France |
| 1964 | SPAIN | 2 | Russia | 1 | Spain |
| 1968 | ITALY | 2 | Yugoslavia | 0 | Italy |
| | (aet in replay after 1-1 draw) | | | | |
| 1972 | W GERMANY | 3 | Russia | 0 | Belgium |
| 1976 | CZECH | 2 | W Germany | 2 | Yugoslavia |
| | (Czechs won 5-3 on penalties) | | | | |
| 1980 | W GERMANY | 2 | Belgium | 1 | Italy |
| 1984 | FRANCE | 2 | Spain | 0 | France |
| 1988 | HOLLAND | 2 | Russia | 0 | West Germany |
| 1992 | DENMARK | 2 | Germany | 0 | Sweden |
| 1996 | GERMANY | 2 | Czech Rep | 1 | Wembley |
| | (1-1 full time. Germany scored Golden Goal in extra time) | | | | |
| 2000 | FRANCE | 2 | Italy | 1 | Holland |
| | (1-1 full time. France scored Golden Goal in extra time) | | | | |

**THE DRAW: Uefa chief executive Gerhard Aigner shows Scotland's name after Portuguese legend Eusebio had drawn us for Group Five of the Euro 2004 Championships qualification at the Congress Center in Porto, Portugal.**

# EUROPEAN SUPER CUP
### (Champions Cup v Cup-Winners' Cup winners)

| Year | Home | Score | Away | Score |
|------|------|-------|------|-------|
| 1972 | AJAX | 3 | Rangers | 2 |
| | Rangers | 1 | AJAX | 3 |
| 1973 | AC Milan | 0 | AJAX | 1 |
| | AJAX | 6 | AC Milan | 0 |

**1974 – Not contested**

| Year | Home | Score | Away | Score |
|------|------|-------|------|-------|
| 1975 | Bayern Munich | 0 | DYNAMO KIEV | 1 |
| | DYNAMO KIEV | 2 | Bayern Munich | 0 |
| 1976 | Bayern Munich | 2 | ANDERLECHT | 1 |
| | ANDERLECHT | 4 | Bayern Munich | 1 |
| 1977 | Hamburg | 1 | LIVERPOOL | 1 |
| | LIVERPOOL | 6 | Hamburg | 0 |
| 1978 | ANDERLECHT | 3 | Liverpool | 1 |
| | Liverpool | 2 | ANDERLECHT | 1 |
| 1979 | NOTTS FOREST | 1 | Barcelona | 0 |
| | Barcelona | 1 | NOTTS FOREST | 1 |
| 1980 | Nottingham Forest | 2 | VALENCIA | 1 |
| | VALENCIA | 1 | Nottingham Forest | 0 |

**1981 – Not contested**

| Year | Home | Score | Away | Score |
|------|------|-------|------|-------|
| 1982 | Barcelona | 1 | ASTON VILLA | 0 |
| | ASTON VILLA | 3 | Barcelona | 0 |
| 1983 | Hamburg | 0 | ABERDEEN | 0 |
| | ABERDEEN | 2 | Hamburg | 0 |
| 1984 | JUVENTUS | 2 | Liverpool | 0 |

**1985 Juventus v Everton not played due to UEFA ban on English clubs**

| Year | Home | Score | Away | Score |
|------|------|-------|------|-------|
| 1986 | ST BUCHAREST | 1 | Dynamo Kiev | 0 |
| 1987 | Ajax | 0 | FC PORTO | 1 |
| | FC PORTO | 1 | Ajax | 0 |
| 1988 | MECHELEN | 3 | PSV Eindhoven | 1 |
| | PSV Eindhoven | 1 | MECHELEN | 0 |
| 1989 | Barcelona | 1 | AC MILAN | 1 |
| | AC MILAN | 1 | Barcelona | 0 |
| 1990 | Sampdoria | 1 | AC MILAN | 1 |
| | AC MILAN | 2 | Sampdoria | 0 |
| 1991 | MANCHESTER UTD | 1 | Red Star Belgrade | 0 |
| 1992 | Werder Bremen | 1 | BARCELONA | 1 |
| | BARCELONA | 2 | Werder Bremen | 1 |
| 1993 | PARMA | 0 | AC Milan | 1 |
| | AC Milan | 0 | PARMA | 2 |

(aet, 90 min. 0-1, agg.1-2 for Parma)

| Year | Home | Score | Away | Score |
|------|------|-------|------|-------|
| 1994 | Arsenal | 0 | AC MILAN | 0 |
| | AC MILAN | 2 | Arsenal | 0 |
| 1995 | Real Zaragoza | 1 | AJAX | 1 |
| | AJAX | 4 | Real Zaragoza | 0 |
| 1996 | Paris St Germain | 0 | JUVENTUS | 1 |
| | JUVENTUS | 6 | Paris St Germain | 1 |
| 1997 | BARCELONA | 0 | Borussia Dortmund | 0 |
| | Borussia Dortmund | 1 | BARCELONA | 1 |
| 1998 | Real Madrid | 0 | CHELSEA | 1 |
| 1999 | LAZIO | 1 | Manchester United | 0 |
| 2000 | GALATASARAY | 2 | Real Madrid | 1 |

(1-1 full time. Galatasaray scored golden goal in extra time)

| Year | Home | Score | Away | Score |
|------|------|-------|------|-------|
| 2001 | LIVERPOOL | 3 | BAYERN MUNICH | 2 |

## EUROPEAN CUP FINALS

| Year | Winners | Runners-up |
|------|---------|-----------|
| 1956 | REAL MADRID . . . . . . 4 | Rheims . . . . . . . . . . . . . . . . . . . . 3 |
| | (Paris, 38,000) | |
| 1957 | REAL MADRID . . . . . 2 | Fiorentina . . . . . . . . . . . . . . . . . . 0 |
| | (Madrid, 124,000) | |
| 1958 | REAL MADRID . . . . . . 3 | AC Milan . . . . . . . . . . . . . . . . . . . 2 |
| | After extra time (Brussels, 67,000) | |
| 1959 | REAL MADRID . . . . . . 2 | Rheims . . . . . . . . . . . . . . . . . . . . 0 |
| | (Stuttgart, 80,000) | |
| 1960 | REAL MADRID . . . . . . 7 | Eintracht . . . . . . . . . . . . . . . . . . . 3 |
| | (Glasgow, 127,261) | |
| 1961 | BENFICA . . . . . . . . . . 3 | Barcelona . . . . . . . . . . . . . . . . . . 2 |
| | (Berne, 28,000) | |
| 1962 | BENFICA . . . . . . . . . . 5 | Real Madrid . . . . . . . . . . . . . . . . 3 |
| | (Amsterdam, 65,000) | |
| 1963 | AC MILAN . . . . . . . . 2 | Benfica . . . . . . . . . . . . . . . . . . . . 1 |
| | (Wembley, 45,000) | |
| 1964 | INTER MILAN . . . . . . 3 | Real Madrid . . . . . . . . . . . . . . . . 1 |
| | (Vienna, 74,000) | |
| 1965 | INTER MILAN . . . . . . 1 | Benfica . . . . . . . . . . . . . . . . . . . . 0 |
| | (Milan, 80,000) | |
| 1966 | REAL MADRID . . . . . . 2 | Partisan Belgrade . . . . . . . . . . . 1 |
| | (Brussels, 55,000) | |
| 1967 | CELTIC . . . . . . . . . . . 2 | Inter Milan . . . . . . . . . . . . . . . . . 1 |
| | (Lisbon, 56,000) | |
| 1968 | MAN UNITED . . . . . . 4 | Benfica . . . . . . . . . . . . . . . . . . . . 1 |
| | (Wembley, 100,000) | |
| 1969 | AC MILAN . . . . . . . . 4 | Ajax . . . . . . . . . . . . . . . . . . . . . . 1 |
| | (Madrid, 50,000) | |
| 1970 | FEYENOORD . . . . . . . 2 | Celtic . . . . . . . . . . . . . . . . . . . . . 1 |
| | (Milan, 50,000) | |
| 1971 | AJAX . . . . . . . . . . . . . 2 | Panathinaikos . . . . . . . . . . . . . . 0 |
| | (Wembey, 90,000) | |
| 1972 | AJAX . . . . . . . . . . . . . 2 | Inter Milan . . . . . . . . . . . . . . . . . 0 |
| | (Rotterdam, 67,000) | |
| 1973 | AJAX . . . . . . . . . . . . . 1 | Juventus . . . . . . . . . . . . . . . . . . 0 |
| | (Belgrade, 93,500) | |
| 1974 | BAYERN MUNICH . . . . . . 4 | Atletico Madrid . . . . . . . . . . . . . 0 |
| | (Brussels, 65,000) (after 1-1 draw) | |
| 1975 | BAYERN MUNICH . . . . . . 2 | Leeds . . . . . . . . . . . . . . . . . . . . . 0 |
| | (Paris, 50,000) | |
| 1976 | BAYERN MUNICH . . . . . . 1 | St Etienne . . . . . . . . . . . . . . . . . 0 |
| | (Glasgow, 54,864) | |

# Want to stop smoking?

## You can do it . . . We can help.

---

## Contact Smoking Concerns - 0141 201 9825 -

---

Smoking Concerns is Greater Glasgow NHS Board's specialist tobacco project

**NHS** Greater Glasgow

## EUROPEAN CUP FINALS (continued)

| 1977 | LIVERPOOL...............3 | Borussia MG...................1 |
|------|---------------------------|--------------------------------|

(Rome, 57,000)

| 1978 | LIVERPOOL...............1 | Bruges .........................0 |
|------|---------------------------|------------------------------------|

(Wembley, 92,000)

| 1979 | NOTTS FOREST ........1 | Malmo...........................0 |
|------|------------------------|----------------------------------|

(Munich, 57,500)

| 1980 | NOTTS FOREST ........1 | Hamburg........................0 |
|------|------------------------|---------------------------------|

(Madrid, 50,000)

| 1981 | LIVERPOOL...............1 | Real Madrid ..................0 |
|------|---------------------------|--------------------------------|

(Paris, 48,360)

| 1982 | ASTON VILLA.............1 | Bayern Munich...............0 |
|------|---------------------------|------------------------------|

(Rotterdam, 46,000)

| 1983 | HAMBURG.................1 | Juventus .......................0 |
|------|---------------------------|-----------------------------------|

(Athens, 75,000)

| 1984 | LIVERPOOL...............1 | Roma ............................1 |
|------|---------------------------|-----------------------------------|

(Rome, 69,693)

Liverpool won 4-2 on penalties

| 1985 | JUVENTUS................1 | Liverpool ......................0 |
|------|---------------------------|-----------------------------------|

(Brussels, 58,000)

| 1986 | STEAU BUCHAREST.0 | Barcelona......................0 |
|------|--------------------|-------------------------------|

Steau Bucharest won 2-0 on penalties (Seveille, 70,000)

| 1987 | PORTO .....................2 | Bayern Munich...............1 |
|------|-----------------------------|------------------------------|

(Vienna, 59,000)

| 1988 | PSV .........................0 | Benfica.........................0 |
|------|-----------------------------|-----------------------------------|

(Stuttgart, 70,000)

PSV Eindhoven won 6-5 on penalties

| 1989 | AC MILAN .................4 | Steau Bucharest ............0 |
|------|-----------------------------|------------------------------|

(Barcelona, 97,000)

| 1990 | AC MILAN .................1 | Benfica.........................0 |
|------|-----------------------------|-----------------------------------|

(Vienna, 57,500)

| 1991 | R.S. BELGRADE ........0 | Marseille.......................0 |
|------|-------------------------|-----------------------------------|

(Bari, 56,000)

Red Star won 5-3 on penalties

| 1992 | BARCELONA .............1 | Sampdoria ....................0 |
|------|--------------------------|--------------------------------|

After extra time

(Wembley, 70,000)

| 1993 | MARSEILLE................1 | AC Milan ......................0 |
|------|----------------------------|------------------------------|

(Munich, 65,000)

| 1994 | AC MILAN .................4 | Barcelona......................0 |
|------|-----------------------------|-------------------------------|

(Athens, 75,000)

| 1995 | AJAX .......................1 | AC Milan ......................0 |
|------|-----------------------------|------------------------------|

(Vienna, 49,000)

| 1996 | JUVENTUS................1 | Ajax....................................1 |
|---|---|---|

(Rome, 67,000)

(1-1 full time. Juventus won 4-2 on penalties)

| 1997 | B DORTMUND...........3 | Juventus .........................1 |
|---|---|---|

(Munich, 55,500 )

| 1998 | REAL MADRID ..........1 | Juventus .........................0 |
|---|---|---|

(Amsterdam, 45,000)

| 1999 | MANCHESTER UTD ..2 | Bayern Munich................1 |
|---|---|---|

(Barcelona, 90,000)

| 2000 | REAL MADRID ...........3 | Valencia............................0 |
|---|---|---|

(Paris, 73,000)

| 2001 | BAYERN MUNICH......1 | Valencia............................1 |
|---|---|---|

(Milan, 80,000)

(1-1 full-time. Bayern won 5-4 on penalties)

| 2002 | REAL MADRID ..........2 | Bayer Leverkusen ...........1 |
|---|---|---|

(Glasgow, 52,000)

**Real Madrid players hold the Champions League trophy aloft after a 2-1 win over Bayer Leverkusen at Hampden**

## EUROPEAN CUP-WINNERS' CUP FINALS

| 1961 | Rangers . . . . . . . . 0 | FIORENTINA . . . . . . . . . . . . . . . . . 2 |
|---|---|---|

(Ibrox, 80,000)

| | FIORENTINA . . . . . . 2 | Rangers . . . . . . . . . . . . . . . . . . . . . 1 |

(Florence, 50,000)

Aggregate 4-1

| 1962 | ATLETICO MADRID . 1 | Fiorentina . . . . . . . . . . . . . . . . . . . 1 |

(Glasgow, 27,389)

| | ATLETICO MADRID . 3 | Fiorentina . . . . . . . . . . . . . . . . . . . 0 |

(Stuttgart, 45,000)

| 1963 | SPURS . . . . . . . . . 5 | Atletico Madrid . . . . . . . . . . . . . . 1 |

(Rotterdam, 25,000)

| 1964 | SPORTING LISBON . 1 | MTK Budapest . . . . . . . . . . . . . . . . 0 |

(Antwerp, 18,000)

*After 3-3 draw in Brussels*

| 1965 | WEST HAM . . . . . . 2 | Munich 1860 . . . . . . . . . . . . . . . . . 0 |

(Wembley, 100,000)

| 1966 | BOR. DORTMUND. . 2 | Liverpool . . . . . . . . . . . . . . . . . . . . 1 |

(Hampden, 41,657)

| 1967 | BAYERN MUNICH . . 1 | Rangers . . . . . . . . . . . . . . . . . . . . . 0 |

(Nuremberg, 69,480 aet)

| 1968 | AC MILAN . . . . . . . 2 | S.V. Hamburg . . . . . . . . . . . . . . . . 0 |

(Rotterdam, 60,000)

| 1969 | S BRATISLAVIA. . . . 3 | Barcelona . . . . . . . . . . . . . . . . . . . 2 |

(Basle, 40,000)

| 1970 | MANCHESTER CITY 2 | Gornik . . . . . . . . . . . . . . . . . . . . . . 1 |

(Vienna, 10,000)

| 1971 | CHELSEA. . . . . . . . 2 | Real Madrid . . . . . . . . . . . . . . . . . 1 |

(Athens, 24,000, after 1-1 draw)

| 1972 | RANGERS. . . . . . . . 3 | Moscow Dynamo . . . . . . . . . . . . . 2 |

(Barcelona, 35,000)

| 1973 | AC MILAN. . . . . . . . 1 | Leeds United . . . . . . . . . . . . . . . . 0 |

(Salonika, 45,000)

| 1974 | AC MAGDEBURG. . . 2 | AC Milan . . . . . . . . . . . . . . . . . . . . 0 |

(Rotterdam, 5,000)

| 1975 | DYNAMO KIEV . . . . 3 | Ferencvaros . . . . . . . . . . . . . . . . . 0 |

(Basle, 13,000)

| 1976 | ANDERLECHT . . . . 4 | West Ham . . . . . . . . . . . . . . . . . . . 2 |

(Brussels, 58,000)

| 1977 | SV HAMBURG . . . . 2 | Anderlecht . . . . . . . . . . . . . . . . . . 0 |

(Amsterdam, 65,000)

| 1978 | ANDERLECHT . . . . 4 | Austria Wein . . . . . . . . . . . . . . . . 0 |

(Amsterdam, 48,679)

| 1979 | BARCELONA . . . . . . 4 | Fortuna Dusseldorf . . . . . . . . . . .3 |
| | (Basle, 58,000) | |
| 1980 | VALENCIA. . . . . . . . . 0 | Arsenal . . . . . . . . . . . . . . . . . . . . . . . . .0 |
| | (Brussels, 40,000, Valencia won 5-4 on penalties) | |
| 1981 | DYNAMO TBILISI . . . 2 | Carl Zeiss Jena . . . . . . . . . . . . . . . .1 |
| | (Dusseldorf, 9,000) | |
| 1982 | BARCELONA . . . . . . 2 | Standard Liege. . . . . . . . . . . . . . . . . .1 |
| | (Barcelona, 100,000) | |
| 1983 | ABERDEEN. . . . . . . . 2 | Real Madrid. . . . . . . . . . . . . . . . . . . . .1 |
| | (Gothenburg, 17,804) | |
| 1984 | JUVENTUS . . . . . . . . 2 | FC Porto. . . . . . . . . . . . . . . . . . . . . . . .1 |
| | (Basle, 60,000) | |
| 1985 | EVERTON . . . . . . . . . 3 | Vienna Rapide . . . . . . . . . . . . . . . . . .1 |
| | (Rotterdam, 30,000) | |
| 1986 | DYNAMO KIEV . . . . . 3 | Atletico Madrid. . . . . . . . . . . . . . . .0. |
| | (Lyon, 39,300) | |
| 1987 | AJAX. . . . . . . . . . . . . 1 | Lokomotiv Leipzig. . . . . . . . . . . . . .0 |
| | (Athens, 35,000) | |
| 1988 | MICHELEN . . . . . . . . 1 | Ajax . . . . . . . . . . . . . . . . . . . . . . . . . . .0 |
| | (Strasbourg, 39,446) | |
| 1989 | BARCELONA . . . . . . 2 | Sampdoria . . . . . . . . . . . . . . . . . . . . .0 |
| | (Berne, 45,000) | |
| 1990 | SAMPDORIA. . . . . . . 2 | Anderlecht . . . . . . . . . . . . . . . . . . . . .0 |
| | (Gothenburg, 20,103) | |
| 1991 | MANCHESTER UTD . 2 | Barcelona. . . . . . . . . . . . . . . . . . . . . .1 |
| | (Rotterdam, 50,000) | |
| 1992 | WERDER BREMEN. . 2 | Monaco . . . . . . . . . . . . . . . . . . . . . . . .0 |
| | (Lisbon, 50,000) | |
| 1993 | Antwerp . . . . . . . . . . 1 | PARMA. . . . . . . . . . . . . . . . . . . . . . . . .3 |
| | (Wembley, 50,000) | |
| 1994 | Parma . . . . . . . . . . . . 0 | ARSENAL. . . . . . . . . . . . . . . . . . . . . . .1 |
| | (Copenhagen, 33,765) | |
| 1995 | Arsenal . . . . . . . . . . . 1 | REAL SARAGOZA. . . . . . . . . . . . . .2 |
| | (aet, 90 minutes 1-1)(Paris, 42,000) | |
| 1996 | PARIS ST GERMAIN . 1 | Rapid Vienna . . . . . . . . . . . . . . . . . . .0 |
| | (Brussels, 50,000) | |
| 1997 | BARCELONA . . . . . . 1 | Paris St Germain . . . . . . . . . . . . . . .0 |
| | (Rotterdam, 40,000) | |
| 1998 | CHELSEA . . . . . . . . . 1 | VfB Stuttgart . . . . . . . . . . . . . . . . . . .0 |
| | (Stockholm) | |
| 1999 | LAZIO . . . . . . . . . . . . 2 | Real Mallorca . . . . . . . . . . . . . . . . . .1 |
| | Villa Park, 30,000 | |

# UEFA CUP FINALS

*(FORMERLY FAIRS CITIES CUP)*

| 1958 | London . . . . . . . . 2 | BARCELONA . . . . . . . . . . . . . . . . . 2 |
|------|---------------------------|-----------------------------------------|
| | BARCELONA . . . . . 6 | London . . . . . . . . . . . . . . . . . . . . . 0 |
| | (agg: 8-2) | |
| 1960 | Birmingham . . . . . . 0 | BARCELONA . . . . . . . . . . . . . . . . . 0 |
| | BARCELONA . . . . . 4 | Birmingham . . . . . . . . . . . . . . . . 1 |
| | (agg: 4-1) | |
| 1961 | Birmingham . . . . . . 2 | ROMA . . . . . . . . . . . . . . . . . . . . . . 2 |
| | ROMA . . . . . . . . . . . 2 | Birmingham . . . . . . . . . . . . . . . . 0 |
| | (agg: 4-2) | |
| 1962 | VALENCIA . . . . . . . 6 | Barcelona . . . . . . . . . . . . . . . . . . . 2 |
| | Barcelona . . . . . . . 1 | VALENCIA . . . . . . . . . . . . . . . . . . 1 |
| | (agg 7-3) | |
| 1963 | Dynamo Zagreb . . . 1 | VALENCIA . . . . . . . . . . . . . . . . . . 2 |
| | VALENCIA . . . . . . . 2 | Dynamo Zagreb . . . . . . . . . . . . . 0 |
| | (agg: 4-1) | |
| 1964 | REAL ZARAGOSSA . 2 | Valencia . . . . . . . . . . . . . . . . . . . . 1 |
| | (Barcelona) | |
| 1965 | FERENCVAROS . . . . 1 | Juventus . . . . . . . . . . . . . . . . . . . . 0 |
| | (Turin) | |
| 1966 | BARCELONA . . . . . 0 | Real Zaragossa . . . . . . . . . . . . . . 1 |
| | Real Zaragossa . . . . 2 | BARCELONA . . . . . . . . . . . . . . . . 4 |
| | (agg: 4-3) | |
| 1967 | DINAMO ZAGREB . . 2 | Leeds United . . . . . . . . . . . . . . . . 0 |
| | Leeds United . . . . . . 0 | DINAMO ZAGREB . . . . . . . . . . . 0 |
| | (agg: 2-0) | |
| 1968 | LEEDS UNITED . . . . 1 | Ferencvaros . . . . . . . . . . . . . . . . . 0 |
| | Ferencvaros . . . . . . . 0 | LEEDS UNITED . . . . . . . . . . . . . . 0 |
| | (agg: 1-0) | |
| 1969 | NEWCASTLE UTD . . 3 | Ujpest Dozsa . . . . . . . . . . . . . . . . 0 |
| | Ujpest Dozsa . . . . . . 2 | NEWCASTLE UTD . . . . . . . . . . . 3 |
| | (agg: 6-2) | |
| 1970 | Anderlecht . . . . . . . . 3 | ARSENAL . . . . . . . . . . . . . . . . . . . 1 |
| | ARSENAL . . . . . . . . 3 | Anderlecht . . . . . . . . . . . . . . . . . . 0 |
| | (agg: 4-3) | |
| 1971 | Juventus . . . . . . . . . . 2 | LEEDS UNITED . . . . . . . . . . . . . . 2 |
| | LEEDS UNITED . . . . . 1 | Juventus . . . . . . . . . . . . . . . . . . . . 1 |
| | (agg: 3-3) | |
| | *Leeds won on away goals* | |
| 1972 | Wolves . . . . . . . . . . . 1 | TOTTENHAM . . . . . . . . . . . . . . . . 2 |
| | TOTTENHAM . . . . . . 1 | Wolves . . . . . . . . . . . . . . . . . . . . . 1 |
| | (agg: 3-2) | |

| 1973 | LIVERPOOL . . . . . . . 3 | Borussia M . . . . . . . . . . . . . . . . . . . . . 0 |
|------|---------------------------|--------------------------------------------------------|
|      | Borussia M . . . . . . . . 2 | LIVERPOOL . . . . . . . . . . . . . . . . . . . 0 |

(agg: 3-2)

| 1974 | Tottenham Hostpur. . 2 | FEYENOORD . . . . . . . . . . . . . . . . . . . 2 |
|------|------------------------|---------------------------------------------------|
|      | FEYENOORD . . . . . . 2 | Tottenham Hotspur . . . . . . . . . . . 0 |

(agg: 4-2)

| 1975 | BORUSSIA M | 0 | Twente | 0 |
|------|------------|---|--------|---|
|      | Twente | 1 | BORUSSIA M | 5 |

(agg: 5-1)

| 1976 | LIVERPOOL | 3 | FC Bruges | 2 |
|------|-----------|---|-----------|---|
|      | Bruges | 1 | LIVERPOOL | 1 |

(agg 4-3)

| 1977 | JUVENTUS | 1 | Athletic Bilbao | 0 |
|------|----------|---|-----------------|---|
|      | Athletic Bilbao | 2 | JUVENTUS | 1 |

(agg: 2-2)

*Juventus won on away goals*

| 1978 | Bastia | 0 | PSV EINDHOVEN | 0 |
|------|--------|---|---------------|---|
|      | PSV EINDHOVEN | 3 | Bastia | 0 |

(agg: 3-0)

| 1979 | Red Star Belgrade | 1 | BORUSSIA M | 1 |
|------|-------------------|---|------------|---|
|      | BORUSSIA M | 1 | Red Star Belgrade | 0 |

(agg: 2-1)

| 1980 | Borussia M | 3 | EINTRACHT | 2 |
|------|------------|---|-----------|---|
|      | EINTRACHT | 1 | Borussia M | 0 |

(agg: 3-3)

*Eintracht won on away goals*

| 1981 | IPSWICH | 3 | AZ 67 | 0 |
|------|---------|---|-------|---|
|      | AZ 67 | 4 | IPSWICH | 2 |

(agg: 5-4)

| 1982 | GOTHENBURG | 1 | Hamburg | 0 |
|------|------------|---|---------|---|
|      | Hamburg | 0 | GOTHENBURG | 3 |

(agg: 4-0)

| 1983 | ANDERLECHT | 1 | Benfica | 0 |
|------|------------|---|---------|---|
|      | Benfica | 1 | ANDERLECHT | 1 |

(agg: 2-1)

| 1984 | Anderlecht | 1 | TOTTENHAM | 1 |
|------|------------|---|-----------|---|
|      | TOTTENHAM | 1 | Anderlecht | 1 |

(agg: 2-2)

*Tottenham won 4-3 on penalties*

| 1985 | Videoton | 0 | REAL MADRID | 3 |
|------|----------|---|-------------|---|
|      | REAL MADRID | 0 | Videoton | 1 |

(agg: 3-1)

| 1986 | REAL MADRID | 5 | Cologne | 1 |
|---|---|---|---|---|
| | Cologne | 2 | REAL MADRID | 0 |
| | | (agg: 5-3) | | |
| 1987 | GOTHENBURG | 1 | Dundee United | 0 |
| | Dundee United | 1 | GOTHENBURG | 1 |
| | | (agg: 2-1) | | |
| 1988 | Espanol | 3 | BAYER LEVERKUSEN | 0 |
| | BAYER LEVERKUSEN | 3 | Espanol | 0 |
| | (agg: 3-3 *Leverkusen won 3-2 on penalties*) | | | |
| 1989 | NAPOLI | 2 | Stuttgart | 1 |
| | Stuttgart | 3 | NAPOLI | 3 |
| | | (agg: 5-4) | | |
| 1990 | JUVENTUS | 3 | Fiorentina | 1 |
| | Fiorentina | 0 | JUVENTUS | 0 |
| | | (agg: 3-1) | | |
| 1991 | INTER MILAN | 2 | Roma | 0 |
| | Roma | 1 | INTER MILAN | 0 |
| | | (agg: 2-1) | | |
| 1992 | Torino | 2 | AJAX | 2 |
| | AJAX | 0 | Torino | 0 |
| | (agg: 2-2. Ajax win on away goals rule) | | | |
| 1993 | Borussia Dortmund | 1 | JUVENTUS | 3 |
| | JUVENTUS | 3 | Borussia Dortmund | 0 |
| | | (agg: 6-1) | | |
| 1994 | Salsburg | 0 | INTER MILAN | 1 |
| | INTER MILAN | 1 | Salsburg | 0 |
| | | (agg: 2-0) | | |
| 1995 | PARMA | 1 | Juventus | 0 |
| | Juventus | 1 | PARMA | 1 |
| | | (agg: 2-1) | | |
| 1996 | BAYERN MUNICH | 2 | Bordeaux | 0 |
| | Bordeaux | 1 | BAYERN MUNICH | .3 |
| | | (agg: 5-1) | | |
| 1997 | Schalke | 1 | INTER MILAN | 0 |
| | INTER MILAN | 1 | Schalke | 0 |
| | (agg: 1-1. Schalke win 4-1 on penalties) | | | |
| 1998 | INTER MILAN | 3 | Lazio | 0 |
| | | (Paris) | | |
| 1999 | PARMA | 3 | Marseille | 0 |
| | | (Moscow) | | |
| 2000 | GALATASARAY | 0 | Arsenal | 0 |
| | (Galatasaray won 4-1 on penalties) | | | |
| | | (Copenhagen) | | |
| 2001 | LIVERPOOL | 5 | Alaves | 4 |
| | (4-4 full-time. Liverpool win with golden goal) | | | |
| | | (Dortmund) | | |
| 2002 | Borussia Dortmund | 2 | FEYENOORD | 3 |
| | | (Rotterdam) | | |

# GAMES TO REMEMBER

**1967 CELTIC ......... 2 Inter Milan ..........................1**
**(European Cup Final, Lisbon, May 25. Attendance 56,000)**
CELTIC: Simpson, Craig, Gemmell, Murdoch, McNeill, Clark, Johnstone, Wallace, Chalmers, Auld, Lennox.
Scorers: Gemmell (63), Chalmers (85).
INTER MILAN: Sarti, Burgnich, Facchetti, Bedin, Guarneri, Picchi, Domenghini, Cappellini, Mazzola, Bicicli, Corso.
Scorer: Mazzola (7 pen).

**1967 England......... 2 SCOTLAND.......................3**
**(Home Internationals, Wembley, April 15. Att: 100,000)**
SCOTLAND: Simpson, Gemmell, McCreadie, Greig, McKinnon, Baxter, Wallace, Bremner, McCalliog, Law, Lennox.
Scorers: Law, Lennox, McCalliog.
ENGLAND: Banks, Cohen, Wilson, Stiles, J Charlton, Moore, Ball, Greaves, R Charlton, Hurst, Peters.
Scorers: J. Charlton, Hurst.

**1972 RANGERS........ 3 Moscow Dynamo.............2**
**(Cup-Winner's Cup Final, Barcelona, May 24. Att: 35,000)**
RANGERS: McCloy, Jardine, Mathieson, Greig, D Johnstone, Smith, McLean, Conn, Stein, MacDonald, W Johnston.
Scorers: Stein (24), Johnston (40, 49).
MOSCOW DYNAMO: Pilgui, Basalev, Dolmatov, Zykov, Dobbonosov, (Gerschkovitch), Zhukov, Baidatchini, Jakubik (Eschtrekov), Sabo, Makovikov, Evryuzhikbin.
Scorers: Eschtrekov (55) Makovikov (87).

**1983 ABERDEEN........ 2 Real Madrid.....................1**
**(Cup-Winner's Cup Final, Gothenburg, May 11. Att: 17,804)**
ABERDEEN: Leighton, Rougvie, McMaster, Cooper, McLeish, Miller, Strachan, Simpson, McGhie, Black (Hewitt), Weir. Subs: Kennedy, Gunn, Watson, Hewitt, Angus.
Scorers: Black (7), Hewitt (112).
REAL MADRID: Agustin, Jan jose, Camacho, Metgod, Bonet, Gallego, Juanito, Angel, Santillana, Stielike, Isidro.
Scorer: Juanito (14 pen).

**1983 SV HAMBURG .... 0 ABERDEEN.........................0**
**(Super Cup (1st leg) Hamburg, November 22. Att: 15,000)**
HAMBURG: Stein, Schroder, Wehmeyer, Jacobs, Hieronymus, Hartwig, (Wuttke), Roff, Groh, Schatzschneider, Magath, Von Heeson.
ABERDEEN: Leighton, Cooper, Rougvie, Simpson, McLeish, Miller, Strachan, Hewitt, McGhee, Bell, Weir.

**1983 ABERDEEN........ 2 HAMBURG.........................0**
**(Super Cup (2nd leg), Aberdeen, December 20. Att: 22,500)**
ABERDEEN: Leighton, McKimmie, McMaster, Simpson, McLeish, Miller, Strachan, Hewitt (Black), McGhee, Bell, Weir.
Scorers: Simpson (47) McGhee (64).
HAMBURG: Stein, Kaltz (Hanson) Wehmeyer, Jacobs, Hieronymus, Hartwig, Schroder, Groh, Schatzschneider (Wuttke), Magath, Roff.

# SCOTTISH CLUBS IN EUROPE
# A COMPLETE HISTORY
Abbreviations EC (European Champions Cup), ECWC
(European Cup Winners Cup), FC (Fair Cities Cup) UEFA
(UEFA Cup) w (won) l (lost)

## ABERDEEN
### 1967-68 ECWC

| Opponents | Venue | Res | Scorers | Rnd |
|---|---|---|---|---|
| KR Reykjavic | H | W10-1 | Munro 3, Storrie 2 | 1 |
| Iceland | | | Smith 2, McMillan, | |
| | | | Petersen,Taylor | |
| | A | W4-1 | Storrie 2 Buchan, Munro | |
| Standard Liege | A | L0-3 | | 2 |
| Belgium | H | W2-0 | Munro, Melrose | |
| **1968-69 FC** | | | | |
| Slavia Sofia | A | D0-0 | | 1 |
| Bulgaria | H | W2-0 | Robb, Taylor | |
| Real Zaragossa | H | W2-1 | Forrest, Smith | 2 |
| Spain | A | L0-3 | | |
| **1970-71 ECWC** | | | | |
| Honved | H | W3-1 | Graham, Harper, S Murray | 1 |
| Hungary | A | L1-3 | S Murray | |
| **1971-72 UEFA CUP** | | | | |
| Celta Vigo | A | W2-0 | Harper, o.g. | 1 |
| Spain | H | W1-0 | Harper | |
| Juventus | A | L0-2 | | 2 |
| Italy | H | D1-1 | Harper | |
| **1972-73 UEFA CUP** | | | | |
| Borussia Munch. | H | L2-3 | Harper, Jarvie | 1 |
| W Germany | A | L3-6 | Harper 2, Jarvie | |
| **1973-74 UEFA CUP** | | | | |
| Finns Harp | H | W4-1 | R Miller, Jarvie 2, | 1 |
| Eire | | | Graham | |
| | A | W3-1 | Robb, Graham, R Miller | |
| Tottenham H | H | D1-1 | Hermiston pen | 2 |
| England | A | L1-4 | Jarvie | |
| **1977-78 UEFA CUP** | | | | |
| RWD Molenbeek | A | D0-0 | | 1 |
| Belgium | H | L1-2 | Jarvie | |
| **1978-79 ECWC** | | | | |
| Marek Stanke | A | L2-3 | Jarvie, Harper | 1 |
| Bulgaria | H | W3-0 | Strachan, Jarvie, Harper | |
| Fortuna Dusseldorf | A | L0-3 | | 2 |
| West Germany | H | W2-0 | McLelland, Jarvie | |

| Opponents | Venue | Res | Scorers | Rnd |
|---|---|---|---|---|
| | | **1979-80 UEFA CUP** | | 1 |
| Eintracht Frankfurt | H | D1-1 | Harper | |
| W Germany | A | L0-1 | | |
| | | **1980-81 EC** | | |
| Austria Vienna | H | W1-0 | McGhee | 1 |
| Austria | A | D0-0 | | |
| Liverpool | H | L0-1 | | 2 |
| England | A | L0-4 | | |
| | | **1981-82 UEFA CUP** | | |
| Ipswich Town | A | D1-1 | Hewitt | 1 |
| England | H | W3-1 | Strachan, pen, Weir 2 | |
| Arges Pitesti | H | W3-0 | Strachan, Weir, Hewit t | 2 |
| Romania | A | D2-2 | Strachan, pen, Hewitt | |
| SV Hamburg | H | W3-2 | Black, Watson, Hewitt | 3 |
| Germany | A | L1-3 | McGhee | |
| | | **1982-83 ECWC** | | |
| Sion | H | W7-0 | Black 2, Strachan, | Pr |
| Switzerland | | | Hewitt, Simpson, | |
| | | | McGhee, Kennedy | |
| | A | W4-1 | Hewitt, Miller, McGhee 2 | |
| Dinamo Tirana | H | W1-0 | Hewitt | 1 |
| Albania | A | D0-0 | | |
| Lech Poznan | H | W2-0 | McGhee, Weir | 2 |
| Poland | A | W1-0 | Bell | |
| Bayern Munich | A | D0-0 | | QF |
| Germany | H | W3-2 | Simpson, McLeish, Hewitt | |
| Waterschei | H | W5-1 | Black, Simpson | SF |
| Belgium | | | McGhee 2, Weir | |
| | A | L0-1 | | |
| Real Madrid | N | W2-1 | Black, Hewitt | F |
| | | **1983-94 (European Super Cup)** | | |
| Hamburg | A | D0-0 | | |
| Germany | H | W2-0 | Simpson, McGhee | |
| | | **1983-84 ECWC** | | |
| Akranes | A | W2-1 | McGhee 2 | 1 |
| Iceland | H | D1-1 | Strachan, pen | |
| Beveren | A | D0-0 | | 2 |
| Belgium | | W4-1 | Strachan 2, 1 pen, | |
| | | | Simpson, Weir | |
| Ujpest Dozsa | A | L0-2 | | QF |
| Hungary | H | W3-0 | McGhee 3 | |
| Porto | A | L0-1 | | SF |
| Portugal | H | L0-1 | | |
| | | **1984-85 EC** | | |
| Dynamo Berlin | H | W2-1 | Black 2 | 1 |
| E. Germany | A | L1-2 | Angus | |

| Opponents | Venue | Res | Scorers | Rnd |
|---|---|---|---|---|
| **1985-86 EC** | | | | |
| Akranes | A | W3-1 | Black, Hewitt, Stark | 1 |
| Iceland | H | W4-1 | Simpson, Hewitt Gray, Falconer | |
| Servette | A | D0-0 | | 2 |
| Switz. | H | W1-0 | McDougall | |
| IFK Gothenburg | H | D2-2 | J Miller, Hewitt | QF |
| Sweden | A | D0-0 | | |
| **1986-87 ECWC** | | | | |
| Sion | H | W2-1 | Bett (pen), Wright | 1 |
| Switzerland | A | L0-3 | | |
| **1987-88 UEFA CUP** | | | | |
| Bohemians | A | D0-0 | | 1 |
| Eire | H | W1-0 | Bett pen | |
| Feyenoord | H | W2-1 | Falconer, J Miller | 2 |
| Holland | A | L0-1 | | |
| **1988-89 UEFA CUP** | | | | |
| Dynamo Dresden | H | D0-0 | | 1 |
| East Germany | A | L0-2 | | |
| **1989-90 UEFA CUP** | | | | |
| Rapid Vienna | H | W2-1 | C Robertson, Grant | 1 |
| Austria | A | L0-1 | | |
| **1990-91 ECWC** | | | | |
| Salamis | A | W2-0 | Mason, Gillhaus | 1 |
| | H | W3-0 | C Robertson, Gillhaus, Jess | |
| Legia Warsaw | H | D0-0 | | 2 |
| Poland | A | L0-1 | | |
| **1991-92 UEFA CUP** | | | | |
| BK Copenhagen | H | L0-1 | | 1 |
| Denmark | A | L0-2 | | |
| **1993-94 ECWC** | | | | |
| Valur | A | W3-0 | Shearer, Jess 2 | 1 |
| Iceland | H | W4-0 | Jess 2, Miller, Irvine | |
| Torino | A | L2-3 | Paatelainen, Jess | |
| Italy | H | L1-3 | Richardson | |
| **1994-95 UEFA CUP** | | | | |
| Skonto Riga | A | D0-0 | | P |
| Latvia | H | D1-1 | Kane | |
| **1996-97 UEFA CUP** | | | | |
| Vilnius | A | W4-1 | Dodds 2, Glass, Shearer | Q |
| Latvia | H | L1-3 | Irvine | |
| Barry Town | A | W3-1 | Windass, Glass, Young | 1 |
| Wales | A | D3-3 | Dodds 2, Rowson | |
| Brondby | H | L0-2 | | 2 |
| Denmark | A | D0-0 | | |
| **2000-01 UEFA CUP** | | | | |
| Bohemians | H | L1-2 | Winters | Q |
| Ireland | A | W1-0 | Morrison og | |

# AIRDRIE

## 1992-93 ECWC

| Opponents | Venue | Res | Scorers | Rnd |
|---|---|---|---|---|
| Sparta Prague | H | L0-1 | | 1 |
| Czechoslovakia | A | L1-2 | Black | |

# CELTIC

| Opponents | Venue | Res | Scorers | Rnd |
|---|---|---|---|---|
| **1962-63 FC** | | | | |
| Valencia | A | L2-4 | Carrol 2 | 1 |
| Spain | H | D2-2 | Crerand, o.g. | |
| **1963-64 ECWC** | | | | |
| Basle | A | W5-1 | Divers, Hughes 3, Lennox | 1 |
| Switzerland | H | W5-0 | Johnstone, Divers 2 Murdoch, Chalmers | |
| Dynamo Zagreb | H | W3-0 | Chalmers 2, Hughes | 2 |
| Yugoslavia | A | L1-2 | Murdoch | |
| Slovan Bratislava | H | W1-0 | Murdoch pen | QF |
| Czechoslovakia | A | W1-0 | Hughes | |
| MTK Budapest | H | W3-0 | Johnstone, Chalmers 2 | SF |
| Hungary | A | L0-4 | | |
| **1964-65 FC** | | | | |
| Leixoes | A | D1-1 | Murdoch | 1 |
| Portugal | H | W3-0 | Murdoch, pen, Chalmers | |
| Barcelona | A | L1-3 | Hughes | 2 |
| Spain | H | D0-0 | | |
| **1965-66 ECWC** | | | | |
| Go Ahead | A | W6-0 | Gallacher 2, Hughes Johnstone 2 Lennox | 1 |
| Holland | H | W1-0 | McBride | |
| Aarhus | A | W1-0 | McBride | 2 |
| Denmark | H | W2-0 | McNeill, Johnstone | |
| Dynamo Kiev | H | W3-0 | Gemmell, Murdoch 2 | QF |
| USSR | A | D1-1 | Gemmell | |
| Liverpool | H | W1-0 | Lennox | SF |
| England | A | L0-2 | | |
| **1966-67 EC** | | | | |
| Zurich | H | W2-0 | Gemmell, McBride | 1 |
| Switzerland | A | W3-0 | Gemmell 2, 1 pen, McBride | |
| Nantes | A | W3-1 | McBride, Lennox, Chalmers | 2 |
| France | H | W3-1 | Johnstone, Lennox, Chalmers | |
| Vojvodina | A | L0-1 | | QF |
| Yugoslavia | H | W2-0 | Chalmers, McNeill | |
| Dukla Prague | H | W3-1 | Johnstone, Wallace, 2 | SF |
| Czechoslovakia | A | D0-0 | | |
| Inter Milan | N | W2-1 | Gemmell, Chalmers | F |

| Opponents | Venue | Res | Scorers | Rnd |
|---|---|---|---|---|
| | | **1967-68 EC** | | |
| Dymano Kiev | H | L1-2 | Lennox | 1 |
| USSR | A | D1-1 | Lennox | |
| | | **1968-69 EC** | | |
| St Etienne | A | L0-2 | | 1 |
| France | H | W4-0 | Gemmell pen, Craig | |
| | | | Chalmers, McBride | |
| Red Star Belgrade | H | W5-1 | Murdoch, Johnstone 2, | 2 |
| Yugoslavia | | | Lennox, Wallace | |
| | A | D1-1 | Wallace | |
| AC Milan | A | D0-0 | | QF |
| Italy | H | L0-0 | | |
| | | **1969-70 EC** | | |
| Basle | A | D0-0 | | 1 |
| Switzerland | H | W2-0 | Hood, Gemmell | |
| Benfica | H | W3-0 | Gemmell, Wallace, Hood | 2 |
| Portugal | A | L0-3 | | |
| Fiorentina | H | W3-0 | Auld, Wallace, o.g. | QF |
| Italy | A | L0-1 | | |
| Leeds United | A | W1-0 | Connelly | SF |
| England | H | W2-1 | Hughes, Murdoch | |
| Feyenoord | N | L1-2 | Gemmell | F |
| | | **1970-71 EC** | | |
| KPV Kokkola | H | W9-0 | Hood 3, Wilson 2, Hughes | 1 |
| Finland | | | McNeill, Johnstone, | |
| | | | Davidson | |
| | A | W5-0 | Wallace 2, Callaghan | |
| | | | Davidson, Lennox | |
| Waterford | A | W7-0 | Wallace 3, Murdoch 2 | 2 |
| Eire | | | Macari 2 | |
| | H | W3-2 | Hughes, Johnstone 2 | |
| Ajax | A | L0-3 | | QF |
| Holland | H | W1-0 | Johnstone | |
| | | **1971-72 EC** | | |
| BK 1903 | A | L1-2 | Macari | 1 |
| Copenhagen | H | W3-0 | Wallace 2, | |
| Denmark | | | Callaghan | |
| Sliema W | H | W5-0 | Gemmell, Macari 2 | 2 |
| Malta | | | Hood, Brogan | |
| | A | W2-1 | Hood, Lennox | |
| Ujpest Dozsa | A | W2-1 | Macari, o.g. | QF |
| Hungary | H | D1-1 | Macari | |
| Inter Milan | A | D0-0 | | SF |
| Italy | H | D0-0 | lost on penalties | |

| Opponents | Venue | Res | Scorers | Rnd |
|---|---|---|---|---|
| | | **1972-73 EC** | | |
| Rosenborg | H | W2-1 | Macari, Deans | 1 |
| Norway | A | W3-1 | Macari, Hood, Dalglish | |
| Ujpest Dozsa | H | W2-1 | Dalglish 2 | 2 |
| Hungary | A | L0-3 | | |
| | | **1973-74 EC** | | |
| Turun | A | W6-1 | Callaghan 2, Hood, | 1 |
| Finland | | | Johnstone, Deans, | |
| | | | Connelly, pen | |
| | H | W3-0 | Deans, Johnstone 2 | |
| Vejle | H | D0-0 | | 2 |
| Denmark | A | W1-0 | Lennox | |
| Basle | A | L2-3 | Wilson, Dalglish | QF |
| Switzerland | H | W4-2 | Dalglish, Deans, | |
| | | | Callaghan, Murray | |
| Atletico Madrid | H | D0-0 | | SF |
| Spain | A | L0-2 | | |
| | | **1974-75 EC** | | |
| Olympiakos | H | D1-1 | Wilson | 1 |
| Greece | A | L0-2 | | |
| | | **1975-76 ECWC** | | |
| Valur | A | W2-0 | Wilson McDonald | 1 |
| Iceland | H | W7-0 | Edvaldsson, Dalglish | |
| | | | McCluskey, pen, Deans | |
| | | | Hood 2, Callaghan | |
| Boavista | A | D0-0 | | 2 |
| Portugal | H | W3-1 | Dalglish, Edvaldsson, Deans | |
| Zwickau | H | D1-1 | Dalglish | QF |
| East Germany | A | L0-1 | | |
| | | **1976-77 UEFA CUP** | | |
| Wisla Krakow | H | D2-2 | McDonald, Dalglish | 1 |
| Poland | A | L0-2 | | |
| | | **1977-78 EC** | | |
| Jeunesse D'Esch | H | W5-0 | McDonald, Wilson, | 1 |
| Luxembourg | | | Craig 2, McLaughlin | |
| | A | W6-1 | Lennox 2, Glavin | |
| | | | Edvaldsson 2, Craig | |
| SW Innsbruck | H | W2-1 | Craig, Burns | 2 |
| Austria | A | L0-3 | | |
| | | **1979-80 EC** | | |
| Partizan Tirana | A | L0-1 | | 1 |
| Albania | H | W4-1 | McDonald, Aitken 2 | |
| | | | Davidson | |
| Dundalk | H | W3-2 | McDonald, Burns | 2 |
| Eire | | | McCluskey | |
| | A | D0-0 | | |

| Opponents | Venue | Res | Scorers | Rnd |
|---|---|---|---|---|
| Real Madrid | H | W2-0 | McCluskey, Doyle | QF |
| Spain | A | L0-3 | | |

**1980-81 ECWC**

| | | | | |
|---|---|---|---|---|
| Diosgyor | H | W6-0 | McGarvey 2, Sullivan | P |
| Hungary | | | McCluskey 2, o.g. | |
| | A | L1-2 | Nicholas | |
| Timisorara | H | W2-1 | Nicholas 2 | 1 |
| Romania | A | L0-1 | lost on away goals | |

**1981-82 EC**

| | | | | |
|---|---|---|---|---|
| Juventus | H | W1-0 | MacLeod | 1 |
| Italy | A | L0-2 | | |

**1982-83 EC**

| | | | | |
|---|---|---|---|---|
| Ajax | H | D2-2 | Nicholas, McGarvey | 1 |
| Holland | A | W2-1 | Nicholas, McCluskey | |
| Real Sociedad | A | L0-2 | | 2 |
| Spain | H | W2-1 | MacLeod 2 | |

**1983-84 UEFA CUP**

| | | | | |
|---|---|---|---|---|
| Aarhus | H | 1-0 | Aitken | 1 |
| Denmark | A | W4-1 | MacLeod, McGarvey, | |
| | | | Aitken, Provan | |
| Sporting Lisbon | A | L0-2 | | 2 |
| Portugal | H | W5-0 | Burns, McAdam, McClair | |
| | | | MacLeod, McGarvey | |
| Notts Forest | A | D0-0 | | 3 |
| England | H | L1-2 | MacLeod | |

**1984-85 ECWC**

| | | | | |
|---|---|---|---|---|
| Gent | A | L0-1 | | 1 |
| Belgium | H | W3-0 | McGarvey 2, McStay | |
| Rapid Vienna | A | L1-3 | McClair | 2 |
| Austria | H | W3-0 | McClair, MacLeod, Burns | |
| (UEFA ordered match to be replayed) | | | | |
| | N | L0-1 | | |

**1985-86 ECWC**

| | | | | |
|---|---|---|---|---|
| Atletico Madrid | A | D1-1 | Johnston | 1 |
| Spain | H | L1-2 | Aitken | |

**1986-87 EC**

| | | | | |
|---|---|---|---|---|
| Shamrock Rov | A | W1-0 | MacLeod | 1 |
| Ireland | H | W2-0 | Johnston 2 | |
| Dymano Kiev | H | D1-1 | Johnston | 2 |
| USSR | A | L1-3 | McGhee | |

**1987-88 UEFA CUP**

| | | | | |
|---|---|---|---|---|
| Bor Dortmund | H | W2-1 | Walker, Whyte | 1 |
| W Germany | A | L0-2 | | |

| Opponents | Venue | Res | Scorers | Rnd |
|---|---|---|---|---|
| | | **1988-89 EC** | | |
| Honved | A | L0-1 | | 1 |
| Hungary | H | W4-0 | Stark, Walker, McAvennie, McGhee | |
| Werder Bremen | H | L0-2 | | 2 |
| W Germany | A | D0-0 | | |
| | | **1989-90 ECWC** | | |
| *Part Belgrade | A | L1-2 | Galloway | 1 |
| Yugoslavia | H | W5-4 | Dziekanowski 4 Walker | |
| | | **1991-92 UEFA CUP** | | |
| Ekeren | H | W2-0 | Nicholas 2, 1 pen | 1 |
| Belgium | A | D1-1 | Galloway | |
| Neuchatel Xamax | A | L1-5 | O'Neill | 2 |
| Switzerland | H | W1-0 | Miller | |
| | | **1992-93 UEFA CUP** | | |
| Cologne | A | L0-2 | | 1 |
| Germany | H | W3-0 | McStay, Creaney, Collins | |
| Bor Dortmund | A | L0-1 | | 2 |
| Germany | H | L1-2 | Creaney | |
| | | **1993-94 UEFA CUP** | | |
| Young Boys | A | D0-0 | | 1 |
| Switzerland | W | 1-0 | og | |
| Sporting Lisbon | H | W1-0 | Creaney | 2 |
| Portugal | A | L0-2 | | |
| | | **1995-96 ECWC** | | |
| Dinamo Batumi | A | W3-2 | Thom 2, Donnelly | 1 |
| Georgia | H | W4-0 | Thom 2, Donnelly, Walker | |
| Paris St Germain | A | L0-1 | | 2 |
| France | H | L0-3 | | |
| | | **1996-97 UEFA CUP** | | |
| Kosice | A | D0-0 | | Q |
| Poland | H | W1-0 | Cadete | |
| Hamburg | H | L0-2 | | 1 |
| Germany | A | L0-2 | | |
| | | **1997-98 UEFA CUP** | | |
| Inter Cable-Tel | A | W3-0 | Thom pen, Johnson pen, Wieghorst | Q |
| Wales | H | W5-0 | Thom pen, Jackson, Johnson, Hannah, Hay | |
| Tirol Innsbruck | A | L1-2 | Stubbs | Q |
| Austria | H | W6-3 | Donnelly 2, 1 pen, Thom Burley 2, Wieghorst | |

| Opponents | Venue | Res | Scorers | Rnd |
|---|---|---|---|---|
| Liverpool | H | D2-2 | McNamara, Donnelly | 1 |
| England | A | D0-0 | | |
| **1998-99 EC** | | | | |
| St Patrick's | H | D0-0 | | P |
| Eire | A | W2-0 | Brattbakk, Larsson | |
| Croatia Zagreb | H | W1-0 | Jackson | P |
| Croatia | A | L0-3 | | |
| **UEFA CUP** | | | | |
| Vitoria Guimareas | A | W2-1 | Larsson, Donnelly | 1 |
| Portugal | H | W2-1 | Stubbs, Larsson | |
| FC Zurich | H | D1-1 | Brattbakk | 2 |
| Switzerland | A | L4-2 | O'Donnell, Larsson | |
| **1999-2000 UEFA CUP** | | | | |
| Cwmbran Town | A | W6-0 | Berkovic, Larsson 2, Tebily, | Q |
| Wales | | | Viduka, Brattbakk | |
| | H | W4-0 | Brattbakk Smith, Mjallby, Johnson | |
| Hapoel Tel Aviv | H | W2-0 | Larsson 2 | 1 |
| Israel | A | W1-0 | Larsson | |
| Lyon | A | L0-1 | | 2 |
| France | H | L0-1 | | |
| **2000-2001 UEFA CUP** | | | | |
| Jeunesse Esch | A | W4-0 | Moravcik 2, Larsson, Petta | Q |
| Luxembourg | H | W7-0 | Burchill 3, Berkovic 2, Riseth, Petrov | |
| HJK Helsinki | H | W2-0 | Larsson 2 | 1 |
| Finland | A | L1-2 | Sutton | |
| Bordeaux | H | D1-1 | Larsson pen | 2 |
| France | H | L1-2 (aet) | Moravcik | |
| **2001-2002 EC** | | | | |
| Ajax | A | W3-1 | Petta, Agathe, Sutton | Q3 |
| Holland | A | L0-1 | | |
| **FIRST GROUP STAGE** | | | | |
| Juventus | A | L2-3 | Petrov, Larsson | |
| Italy | A | W4-3 | Valgaeren, Sutton 2, Larsson | |
| Porto | H | W1-0 | Larsson | |
| Portugal | A | L0-3 | | |
| Rosenborg | H | W1-0 | Thompson | |
| Norway | A | L0-2 | | |
| **UEFA CUP** | | | | |
| Valencia | A | L0-1 | | 3 |
| Spain | H | W1-0 | Larsson | |
| (aet, Valencia won 5-4 on penalties) | | | | |

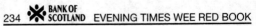

# DUNDEE

| Opponents | Venue | Res | Scorers | Rnd |
|-----------|-------|-----|---------|-----|
| | | **1962-63 EC** | | |
| FC Cologne | H | W8-1 | Gilzean 3, Wishart, Smith | P |
| W Germany | A | L0-4 | Robertson, Penman, og | |
| Sporting Lisbon | A | L0-1 | | 1 |
| Portugal | H | W4-1 | Gilzean 3, Cousin | |
| Anderlecht | A | W4-1 | Gilzean 2, Cousin, Smith | QF |
| Belgium | H | W2-1 | Cousin, Smith | |
| AC Milan | A | L1-5 | Cousin | SF |
| Italy | H | W1-0 | Gilzean | |
| | | **1964-65 ECWC** | | |
| Bye | | | | 1 |
| Real Zaragossa | H | D2-2 | Murray, Houston | 2 |
| Spain | A | L1-2 | Robertson | |
| | | **1967-68 FC** | | |
| DWS Amsterdam | A | L1-2 | McLean | 1 |
| Holland | H | W3-0 | Wilson, McLean 2, 1 pen | |
| FC Liege | H | W3-1 | Stuart 2, Wilson | 2 |
| Belgium | A | W4-1 | McLean 4 | |
| | | Bye in Round 3 | | |
| Zurich | H | W1-0 | Easton | QF |
| Switzerland | A | W1-0 | Wilson | |
| Leeds United | H | D1-1 | Wilson | SF |
| England | A | L0-2 | | |
| | | **1971-72 UEFA CUP** | | |
| Akademisk | H | W4-2 | Bryce 2, Wallace, Lambie | 1 |
| Denmark | A | W1-0 | Duncan | |
| Cologne | A | L1-2 | Kinninmonth | 2 |
| W Germany | H | W4-2 | Duncan 3, Wilson | |
| AC Milan | A | L0-3 | | 3 |
| Italy | H | W2-0 | Wallace, Duncan | |
| | | **1973-74 UEFA CUP** | | |
| Twente Ensch. | H | L1-3 | Stewart | 1 |
| Holland | A | L2-4 | Johnston, Scott | |
| | | **1974-75 UEFA CUP** | | |
| RWD Molenbeek | A | L0-1 | | 1 |
| Belgium | H | L2-4 | Duncan, Scott | |

# DUNDEE UNITED

| Opponents | Venue | Res | Scorers | Rnd |
|-----------|-------|-----|---------|-----|
| **1966-67 FC** | | | | |
| Bye | | | | 1 |
| Barcelona | A | W2-1 | Hainey, Seeman | 2 |
| Spain | H | W2-0 | Mitchell, Hainey | |
| Juventus | A | L0-3 | | 3 |
| Italy | H | W1-0 | Dossing | |
| **1969-70 FC** | | | | |
| Newcastle Utd | H | L1-2 | Scott | 1 |
| England | A | L0-1 | | |
| **1970-71 FC** | | | | |
| Grasshoppers | H | W3-2 | Reid I, Markland, Reid A | 1 |
| Switzerland | A | D0-0 | | |
| Sparta Prague | A | L1-3 | Traynor | 2 |
| Czechoslovakia | H | W1-0 | Gordon | |
| **1974-75 ECWC** | | | | |
| Jiul Petrosani | H | W3-0 | Narey, Copland, Gardner | 1 |
| Romania | A | L0-2 | | |
| Bursaspor | H | D0-0 | | 2 |
| Turkey | A | L0-1 | | |
| **1975-76 UEFA CUP** | | | | |
| Keflavik | A | W2-0 | Narey 2 | 1 |
| Iceland | H | W4-0 | Hall 2, Hegarty, pen, Sturrock | |
| Porto | H | L1-2 | Rennie | 2 |
| Portugal | A | D1-1 | Hegarty | |
| **1977-78 UEFA CUP** | | | | |
| KB Copenhagen | H | W1-0 | Sturrock | 1 |
| Denmark | A | L0-3 | | |
| **1978-79 UEFA CUP** | | | | |
| Standard Liege | A | L0-1 | | 1 |
| Belgium | H | D0-0 | | |
| **1979-80 UEFA CUP** | | | | |
| Anderlecht | H | D0-0 | | 1 |
| Belgium | A | D1-1 | Kopel | |
| Diosgyor | H | L0-1 | | 2 |
| Hungary | A | L1-3 | Kopel | |
| **1980-81 UEFA CUP** | | | | |
| Slask Wroclaw | A | D0-0 | | 1 |
| Poland | H | W7-2 | Dodds 2, Pettigrew, Stark, Hegarty, Payne pen | |
| Lokeren | H | D1-1 | Pettigrew 2 | |
| Belgium | A | D0-0 | | |
| **1981-82 UEFA CUP** | | | | |
| Monaco | A | W5-2 | Bannon 2, 1 pen, Dodds 2, Kirkwood | 1 |
| (France) | H | L1-2 | Milne | |

| Opponents | Venue | Res | Scorers | Rnd |
|---|---|---|---|---|
| Borussia M. | A | L0-2 | | 2 |
| (W. Germany) | H | W5-0 | Milne, Kirkwood, Hegarty, Sturrock, Bannon | |
| Winterslag | A | D0-0 | | 3 |
| (Belgium) | H | W5-0 | Bannon, Narey, Hegarty Milne 2 | |
| Rankicki Nis | H | W2-0 | Narey, Dodds | QF |
| (Yugoslavia) | A | L0-3 | | |

**1982-83 UEFA CUP**

| Opponents | Venue | Res | Scorers | Rnd |
|---|---|---|---|---|
| PSV Eindhoven | H | D1-1 | Dodds | 1 |
| (Holland) | A | W2-0 | Kirkwood, Hegarty | |
| Viking Stavanger | A | W3-1 | Milne 2, Sturrock | 2 |
| (Norway) | H | D0-0 | | |
| Werder Bremen | H | W2-1 | Milne, Narey | 3 |
| (W. Germany) | A | D1-1 | Hegarty | |
| Bohemians | A | L0-1 | | QF |
| (Czech) | H | D0-0 | | |

**1983-84 EC**

| Opponents | Venue | Res | Scorers | Rnd |
|---|---|---|---|---|
| Hamrun Spartans | A | W3-0 | Reilly, Bannon, Stark | 1 |
| (Malta) | H | W3-0 | Milne, Kirkwood 2 | |
| Standard Liege | A | D0-0 | | 2 |
| (Belgium) | H | W4-0 | Milne 2, Hegarty, Dodds | |
| Rapid Vienna | A | L1-2 | Stark | QF |
| (Austria) | H | W1-0 | Dodds | |
| AS Roma | H | W2-0 | Dodds, Stark | SF |
| (Italy) | A | L0-3 | | |

**1984-85 UEFA CUP**

| Opponents | Venue | Res | Scorers | Rnd |
|---|---|---|---|---|
| AIK Stockholm | A | L0-1 | | 1 |
| (Sweden) | H | W3-0 | Sturrock, Milne 2 | |
| ASK Linz | A | W2-1 | Kirkwood, Bannon pen 2 | 2 |
| (Austria) | H | W5-1 | Hegarty, Coyne 2, Gough Beaumont | |
| Man United | A | D2-2 | Hegarty, Sturrock | 3 |
| (England) | H | L2-3 | Dodds, Hegarty | |

**1985-86 UEFA CUP**

| Opponents | Venue | Res | Scorers | Rnd |
|---|---|---|---|---|
| Bohemians | A | W5-2 | Sturrock 3, Bannon 2 | 1 |
| Eire | H | D2-2 | Milne, Redford | |
| Vardar Skopje | H | W2-0 | Redford, Gough | 2 |
| (Yugoslavia) | A | D1-1 | Hegarty | |
| Neuchatel Xamax | H | W2-1 | Dodds, Redford | 3 |
| Switzerland | A | L1-3 | Redford | |

**1986-87 UEFA CUP**

| Opponents | Venue | Res | Scorers | Rnd |
|---|---|---|---|---|
| Lens | A | L0-1 | | 1 |
| France | H | W2-0 | Milne, Coyne | |
| Uni Craiova | H | W3-0 | Redford 2, Clark | 2 |
| Romania | A | L0-1 | | |

| Opponents | Venue | Res | Scorers | Rnd |
|---|---|---|---|---|
| Hadjuk Split | H | W2-0 | McInally, Clark | 3 |
| Yugoslavia | A | D0-0 | | |
| Barcelona | H | W1-0 | Gallacher | QF |
| Spain | A | W2-1 | Clark, Ferguson | |
| Borussia Munch. | H | D0-0 | | SF |
| W. Germany | A | W2-0 | Ferguson, Redford | |
| IFK Gothenburg | A | L0-1 | | F |
| Sweden | H | D1-1 | Clark | |
| **1987-88 UEFA CUP** | | | | |
| Coleraine | A | W1-0 | Sturrock | 1 |
| N. Ireland | H | W3-1 | Gallacher, Sturrock, Clark | |
| Vitkovice | H | L1-2 | Ferguson | 2 |
| Czechoslovakia | A | D1-1 | og | |
| **1988-89 ECWC** | | | | |
| Floriana | A | D0-0 | | 1 |
| Malta | H | W1-0 | Meade | |
| Din. Bucharest | H | L0-1 | | 2 |
| Romania | A | D1-1 | Beaumont | |
| **1989-90 UEFA CUP** | | | | |
| Glentoran | A | W3-1 | Clelland, McInally, Hinds | 1 |
| N. Ireland | H | W2-0 | Clark, Gallacher | |
| Antwerp | A | L0-4 | | 2 |
| Belgium | H | W3-2 | Paatelainen, O'Neill, Clark | |
| **1990-91 UEFA CUP** | | | | |
| Harnfjardar | A | W3-1 | Jackson, Cleland, og | 1 |
| | H | D2-2 | Connolly, og | |
| Arnhem | A | L1-0 | | 2 |
| | H | L0-4 | | |
| **1993-94 UEFA CUP** | | | | |
| Brondby | A | L0-2 | | 1 |
| Denmark | H | W3-1 | McKinlay, Crabbe, Clark | |
| **1994-95 ECWC** | | | | |
| Tatran Presov | H | W3-2 | Petric, Nixon, Hannah | 1 |
| Slovakia | A | L3-1 | Nixon | |
| **1997-98 UEFA CUP** | | | | |
| C E Principat | A | W8-0 | Zetterlund, Winters (4), McSwegan (3) | Q |
| Andorra | H | W9-0 | Olofsson, Zetterlund, Winters 2, McLaren, McSwegan 3 Thomson | |
| Trabzonspor | A | L0-1 | | Q |
| Turkey | H | D1-1 | McLaren | |

# DUNFERMLINE

| Opponents | Venue | Res | Scorers | Rnd |
|---|---|---|---|---|
| | | **1961-62 ECWC** | | |
| St Patrick's Ath. Eire | H | W4-1 | Melrose, Peebles, Dickson, Macdonald | 1 |
| | A | W4-0 | Peebles 2, Dickson 2 | |
| Vardar Skopje Yugoslavia | H | W5-0 | Smith, Dickson 2 Melrose, Peebles | 2 |
| | A | L0-2 | | |
| Ujpest Dozsa Hungary | A | L3-4 | Smith, Macdonald 2 | QF |
| | H | L0-1 | | |
| | | **1962-63 FC** | | |
| Everton England | A | L0-1 | | 1 |
| | H | W2-0 | Miller, Melrose | |
| Valencia Spain | A | L0-4 | | 2 |
| | H | W6-2 | Melrose, Sinclair 2 McLean, Peebles, Smith | |
| | N | L0-1 | | |
| | | **1964-65 FC** | | |
| Oergryte Sweden | H | W4-2 | McLaughlin 2, Sinclair 2 | 1 |
| | A | D0-0 | | |
| Stuttgart W Germany | H | W1-0 | Callaghan | 2 |
| | A | D0-0 | | |
| Athletico Bilbao Spain | A | L0-1 | | 3 |
| | H | W1-0 | Smith | |
| | A | L1-2 | Smith | |
| | | **1965-66 FC** | | |
| Bye | | | | 1 |
| KB Copenhagen Denmark | H | W5-0 | Fleming, Paton 2, Robertson, Callaghan | 2 |
| | A | W4-2 | Edwards, Paton, Fleming, Ferguson | |
| Spartak Brno Czechoslovakia | H | W2-0 | Paton, Ferguson, pen | 3 |
| | A | D0-0 | | |
| Real Zaragossa Spain | H | W1-0 | Paton | QF |
| | A | L2-4 | Ferguson 2 | |
| | | **1966-67 FC** | | |
| Frigg Oslo Norway | A | W3-1 | Fleming 2, Callaghan | 1 |
| | H | W3-1 | Delaney 2 Callaghan | |
| Dynamo Zagreb Yugoslavia | H | W4-2 | Delaney, Edwards, Ferguson 2 | 2 |
| | A | L0-2 | | |
| | | **1968-69 ECWC** | | |
| Apoel Cyprus | H | W10-1 | Robertson 2, Renton 2 Barry, Callaghan W 2, Gardner Edwards, Callaghan T | 1 |
| | A | W2-0 | Gardner, Callaghan W | |

| Opponents | Venue | Res | Scorers | Rnd |
|---|---|---|---|---|
| Olymp. Piraeus | H | W4-0 | Edwards 2, Fraser, | 2 |
| Greece | | | Mitchell | |
| | A | L0-3 | | |
| West Bromwich | H | D0-0 | | QF |
| England | A | W1-0 | Gardner | |
| Slovan Bratislava | H | D1-1 | Fraser | SF |
| Czechoslovakia | A | L0-1 | | |
| **1969-70 FC** | | | | |
| Bordeaux | H | W4-0 | Paton 2, Mitchell, Gardner | 1 |
| France | A | L0-2 | | |
| Gwardia Warsaw | H | W2-1 | McLean, Gardner | 2 |
| Poland | A | W1-0 | Renton | |
| Anderlecht | A | L0-1 | | 3 |
| Belgium | H | W3-2 | McLean 2, Mitchell | |

**ALEX EDWARDS
starred for
Dumfermline
against
Olympiakos in
the Cup-Winners'
Cup back in 1968**

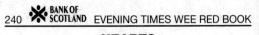
# HEARTS

| Opponents | Venue | Res | Scorers | Rnd |
|---|---|---|---|---|
| **1958-59 EC** | | | | |
| Standard Liege | A | L1-5 | Crawford | P |
| Belgium | H | W2-1 | Bauld | |
| **1960-61 EC** | | | | |
| Benfica | H | L1-2 | Young | P |
| Portugal | A | L0-3 | | |
| **1961-62 FC** | | | | |
| Union St Gilloise | A | W3-1 | Blackwood, Davidson 2 | 1 |
| Belgium | H | W2-0 | Wallace, Stenhouse | |
| Inter Milan | H | L0-1 | | 2 |
| Italy | A | L0-4 | | |
| **1963-64 FC** | | | | |
| Lausanne | A | D2-2 | Traynor, Ferguson | 1 |
| Switzerland | H | D2-2 | Cumming, Hamilton J | |
| | A | L2-3 | Wallace, Ferguson | |
| **1965-66 FC** | | | | |
| Bye | | | | 1 |
| Valerengen | H | W1-0 | Wallace | 2 |
| Norway | A | W3-1 | Kerrigan 2, Traynor | |
| Real Zaragossa | H | D3-3 | Anderson, Wallace, Kerrigan | 3 |
| Spain | A | D2-2 | Anderson, Wallace | |
| | A | L0-1 | | |
| **1976-77 ECWC** | | | | |
| Lokomotiv Leipzig | A | L0-2 | | 1 |
| East Germany | H | W5-1 | Kay, Gibson 2, Brown, Busby | |
| SV Hamburg | A | L2-4 | Park, Busby | 2 |
| West Germany | H | L1-4 | Gibson | |
| **1984-85 UEFA CUP** | | | | |
| Paris St Germain | A | L0-4 | | 1 |
| France | H | D2-2 | Robertson 2 | |
| **1986-87 UEFA CUP** | | | | |
| Dukla Prague | H | W3-2 | Foster, Clark, Robertson | 1 |
| Czechoslovakia | A | L0-1 | | |
| **1988-89 UEFA CUP** | | | | |
| St Patrick's Ath | A | W2-0 | Foster pen, Galloway | 1 |
| Eire | H | W2-0 | Black, Galloway | |
| FK Austria | H | D0-0 | | 2 |
| Austria | A | W1-0 | Galloway | |
| Velez Mostar | H | W3-0 | Bannon, Galloway, Colquhoun | 3 |
| Yugoslavia | A | L1-2 | Galloway | |
| Bayern Munich | H | W1-0 | Ferguson | QF |
| West Germany | A | L0-2 | | |

| Opponents | Venue | Res | Scorers | Rnd |
|---|---|---|---|---|
| | | **1990-91 UEFA CUP** | | |
| Dnepr | A | D1-1 | Robertson | 1 |
| | H | W3-1 | McPherson, Robertson 2 | |
| Bologna | H | W3-1 | Foster 2, Ferguson | 2 |
| Italy | A | L0-3 | | |
| | | **1992-93 UEFA CUP** | | |
| Slavia Prague | A | L0-1 | | 1 |
| Czech Rep | H | W4-2 | Mackay, Baird, Levein, Snodin | |
| Standard Liege | H | L0-1 | | 2 |
| Belgium | A | L0-1 | | |
| | | **1993-94 UEFA CUP** | | |
| Atletico Madrid | H | W2-1 | Robertson, Colquhoun | 1 |
| Spain | A | L0-3 | | |
| | | **1996-97 ECWC** | | |
| Red Star Belgrade | A | D0-0 | | 1 |
| Yugoslavia | H | D1-1 | McPherson | |
| | | **1998-99 ECWC** | | |
| Lantana | A | W1-0 | Makel | Q |
| Estonia | H | W5-0 | Hamilton, Fulton, McCann, Flogel, Holmes | |
| Real Mallorca | H | L0-1 | | 1 |
| Spain | A | D1-1 | Hamilton | |
| | | **2000-2001 UEFA CUP** | | |
| IBV | A | W2-0 | Severin, Jackson | Q |
| Iceland | H | W3-0 | McSwegan, Tomaschek, O'Neil | |
| Stuttgart | A | L0-1 | | |
| Germany | H | W3-2 | Pressley, Petric, Cameron pen | 1 |

**STEVEN PRESSLEY**
netted for Hearts in
the Tynecastle
club's 3-2 Uefa Cup
second-leg win over
Stuttgart back in
September, 2000

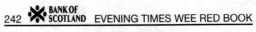
# HIBERNIAN

| Opponents | Venue | Res | Scorers | Rnd |
|---|---|---|---|---|
| **1955-56 EC** | | | | |
| Rot-Weiss Essen | A | W4-0 | Turnbull 2, Reilly, Ormond | 1 |
| West Germany | H | D1-1 | Buchanan J | |
| Djurgaarden | H | W3-1 | Combe, Mulkerrin, og | QF |
| Sweden | A | W1-0 | Turnbull pen | |
| Reims | A | L0-2 | | SF |
| France | H | L0-1 | | |
| **1960-61 FC** | | | | |
| Barcelona | A | D4-4 | McLeod, Preston Baker 2 | QF |
| Spain | H | W3-2 | Kinloch 2, 1 pen, Baker | |
| AS Roma | H | D2-2 | Baker, McLeod | SF |
| Italy | A | D3-3 | Baker 2, Kinloch | |
| | A | L0-6 | | |
| **1961-62 FC** | | | | |
| Belenenses | H | D3-3 | Fraser 2, Baird pen | 1 |
| Portugal | A | W3-1 | Baxter 2, Stevenson | |
| Red Star Belgrade | A | L0-4 | | 2 |
| Yugoslavia | H | L0-1 | | |
| **1962-63 FC** | | | | |
| Stavenet | H | W4-0 | Byrne 2, Baker, og | 1 |
| Denmark | A | W3-2 | Stevenson 2, Byrne | |
| DOS Utrecht | A | W1-0 | Falconer | 2 |
| Holland | H | W2-1 | Baker, Stevenson | |
| Valencia | A | L0-5 | | QF |
| Spain | H | W2-1 | Preston, Baker | |
| **1965-66 FC** | | | | |
| Valencia | H | W2-0 | Scott, McNamee | 1 |
| Spain | A | L0-2 | | |
| | A | L0-3 | | |
| **1967-68 FC** | | | | |
| Porto | H | W3-0 | Cormack 2, Stevenson | 1 |
| Portugal | A | L1-3 | Stanton pen | |
| Napoli | A | L1-4 | Stein | 2 |
| Italy | H | W5-0 | Duncan, Quinn, Cormack Stanton, Stein | |
| Leeds United | A | L0-1 | | 3 |
| England | H | D1-1 | Stein | |
| **1968-69 FC** | | | | |
| Ljubljana | A | W3-0 | Stevenson, Stein, Marinello | 1 |
| Yugoslavia | H | W2-1 | Davis 2 | |
| Lokomotiv Leipzig | H | W3-1 | McBride 3 | 2 |
| East Germany | A | W1-0 | Grant | |
| SV Hamburg | A | L0-1 | | 3 |
| West Germany | H | W2-1 | McBride 2 | |

| Opponents | Venue | Res | Scorers | Rnd |
|---|---|---|---|---|
| **1970-71 FC** | | | | |
| Malmo FF | H | W6-0 | McBride 3 Duncan 2, Blair | 1 |
| Sweden | A | W3-2 | Duncan, McEwan, Stanton | |
| Vitoria Giumaraes | H | W2-0 | Duncan, Stanton | 2 |
| Portugal | A | L1-2 | Graham | |
| Liverpool | H | L0-1 | | 3 |
| England | A | L0-2 | | |
| **1972-73 ECWC** | | | | |
| Sporting Lisbon | A | L1-2 | Duncan | 1 |
| Portugal | H | W6-1 | Gordon 2, O'Rourke 3, og | |
| Besa | H | W7-1 | Cropley, O'Rourke 3, | 2 |
| Albania | | | Duncan 2, Brownlie | |
| | A | D1-1 | Gordon | |
| Hadjuk Split | H | W4-2 | Gordon 3, Duncan | QF |
| Yugoslavia | A | L0-3 | | |
| **1973-74 UEFA CUP** | | | | |
| Keflavik | H | W2-0 | Black, Higgins | 1 |
| Iceland | A | D1-1 | Stanton | |
| Leeds United | A | D0-0 | | 2 |
| England | H | D0-0 | | |
| **1974-75 UEFA CUP** | | | | |
| Rosenberg | A | W3-2 | Stanton, Gordon, Cropley | 1 |
| Norway | H | W9-1 | Harper 2, Munro 2, Stanton 2, | |
| | | | Cropley 2 pens, Gordon | |
| Juventus | H | L2-4 | Stanton, Cropley | 2 |
| Italy | A | L0-4 | | |
| **1975-76 UEFA CUP** | | | | |
| Liverpool | H | W1-0 | Harper | 1 |
| England | A | L1-3 | Edwards | |
| **1976-77 UEFA CUP** | | | | |
| Sochaux | H | W1-0 | Brownlie | 1 |
| France | A | D0-0 | | |
| Osters Vaxjo | H | W2-0 | Blackley, Brownlie pen | 2 |
| Sweden | A | L1-4 | Smith | |
| **1978-79 UEFA CUP** | | | | |
| Norrkoping | H | W3-2 | Higgins 2, Temperley | 1 |
| Sweden | A | D0-0 | | |
| Strasbourg | A | L0-2 | | 2 |
| France | H | W1-0 | McLeod pen | |
| **1989-90 UEFA CUP** | | | | |
| Videoton | H | W1-0 | Mitchell | 1 |
| Hungary | A | W3-0 | Houchen, Evans, Collins | |
| FC Liege | H | D0-0 | | |
| Belgium | A | L0-1 | | |

| Opponents | Venue | Res | Scorers | Rnd |
|---|---|---|---|---|
| | | **1992-93 UEFA CUP** | | |
| Anderlecht | H | D2-2 | Beaumont, McGinlay | 1 |
| Belgium | A | D1-1 | Jackson | |
| | | **2001-02 UEFA CUP** | | |
| AEK Athens | A | L0-2 | | 1 |
| Greece | H | W3-2 (aet) | Luna 2, Zitelli | |

# KILMARNOCK

| Opponents | Venue | Res | Scorers | Rnd |
|---|---|---|---|---|
| | | **1964-65 FC** | | |
| Ein. Frankfurt | A | L0-3 | | 1 |
| West Germany | H | W5-1 | Hamilton, McIlroy, Sneddon McFadzean, McInally | |
| Everton | H | L0-2 | | 2 |
| England | A | L1-4 | McIlroy | |
| | | **1965-66 EC** | | |
| Nendori Tirana | A | D0-0 | | P |
| Albania | H | W1-0 | Black | |
| Real Madrid | H | D2-2 | McLean pen, McInally | 1 |
| Spain | A | L1-5 | McIlroy | |
| | | **1966-67 FC** | | |
| Bye | | | | 1 |
| Antwerp | A | W1-0 | McInally | 2 |
| Belgium | H | W7-2 | McInally 2, Queen 2 McLean 2, Watson | |
| La Gantoise | H | W1-0 | Murray | 3 |
| Belgium | A | W2-1 | McInally, McLean | |
| Lokomotiv Leipzig | H | L0-1 | | QF |
| East Gemany | H | W2-0 | McFadzean, McIlroy | |
| Leeds United | A | L2-4 | McIlroy 2 | SF |
| England | H | D0-0 | | |
| | | **1969-70 FC** | | |
| Zurich | A | L2-3 | McLean J, Mathie | 1 |
| Switzerland | H | W3-1 | McGrory, Morrison, McLean T | |
| Slavia Sofia | H | W4-1 | Mathie 2, Cook, Gilmour | 2 |
| Bulgaria | A | L0-2 | | |
| Dynamo Bacau | H | D1-1 | Mathie | 3 |
| Romania | A | L0-2 | | |
| | | **1970-71 FC** | | |
| Coleraine | A | D1-1 | Mathie | 1 |
| N. Ireland | H | L2-3 | McLean T, Morrison | |
| | | **1997-98 ECWC** | | |
| Shelbourne | H | W2-1 | Wright 2 | Q |
| Eire | A | D1-1 | McIntyre | |
| Nice | A | L1-3 | Wright | 1 |
| France | H | D1-1 | Reilly | |

| Opponents | Venue | Res | Scorers | Rnd |
|-----------|-------|-----|---------|-----|
| | | **1998-99 UEFA CUP** | | |
| Zeljeznicar | A | D1-1 | McGowne | P |
| Bosnia | H | W1-0 | Mahood | |
| Sigma Olomouc | A | L0-2 | | P |
| Czech Rep | H | L0-2 | | |
| | | **1999-2000 UEFA CUP** | | |
| KR Reyjkavic | A | L0-1 | | Q |
| Iceland | H | W2-0 | Wright, Bagan | |
| Kaislerslautern | A | L0-3 | | 1 |
| Germany | H | L0-2 | | |
| | | **2001-2002 UEFA CUP** | | |
| Glenavon | A | W1-0 | Innes | Q |
| Northern Ireland | H | W1-0 | Mitchell | |
| Viking Stavanger | H | D1-1 | Dargo | 1 |
| Norway | A | L0-2 | | |

# MORTON

| Opponents | Venue | Res | Scorers | Rnd |
|-----------|-------|-----|---------|-----|
| | | **1968-69 FC** | | |
| Chelsea | A | L0-5 | | 1 |
| England | H | L3-4 | Thorop, Mason, Taylor | |

# MOTHERWELL

| Opponents | Venue | Res | Scorers | Rnd |
|-----------|-------|-----|---------|-----|
| | | **1991-92 FC** | | |
| Katowice | A | L0-2 | | 1 |
| Poland | H | W3-1 | Kirk 2, Cusack | |
| | | **1994-95 UEFA CUP** | | |
| Hanvar | H | W3-0 | Coyne, McGrillen, Kirk | P |
| Faroe Islands | A | W4-1 | Kirk 2, Davies, Burns | |
| Bor Dortmund | A | L0-1 | | 1 |
| Germany | H | L0-2 | | |
| | | **1995-96 UEFA CUP** | | |
| My-Pa 47 | H | L1-3 | McSkimming | P |
| Finland | A | W2-0 | Burns, Arnott | |

# PARTICK THISTLE

| Opponents | Venue | Res | Scorers | Rnd |
|-----------|-------|-----|---------|-----|
| | | **1963-64 FC** | | |
| Glentoran | A | W4-1 | Hainey, Yard 2, Wright | 1 |
| N. Ireland | H | W3-0 | Smith 2, Harvey, pen, | |
| Spartak Brno | H | W3-2 | Yard, Harvey, pen, | 2 |
| Czechoslovakia | | | Ferguson | |
| | A | L0-4 | | |
| | | **1972-73 UEFA CUP** | | |
| Honved | A | L0-1 | | 1 |
| Hungary | H | L0-3 | | |

# RAITH ROVERS

| Opponents | Venue | Res | Scorers | Rnd |
|-----------|-------|-----|---------|-----|
| | | **1995-96 UEFA CUP** | | |
| Gotu | H | W4-0 | Dair, Rougier, Cameron | P |
| Faroe Islands | | | McAnespie | |
| | A | D2-2 | Lennon, Crawford | |
| Akranes | H | W3-1 | Lennon 2, Wilson | 1 |
| Iceland | A | L0-1 | | |
| Bayern Munich | H | L0-2 | | 2 |
| Germany | A | L1-2 | Lennon | |

COLIN CAMERON netted for Raith Rovers against Gotu, of the Faroe Islands, in the Uefa Cup of season 1995-96

# RANGERS

| Opponents | Venue | Res | Scorers | Rnd |
|---|---|---|---|---|
| | | **1956-57 EC** | | |
| Bye | | | | P |
| Nice | H | W2-1 | Murray, Simpson | 1 |
| France | A | L1-2 | Hubbard pen | |
| | N | L1-3 | og | |
| | | **1957-58 EC** | | |
| St Etienne | H | W3-1 | Kichenbrand, Scott, | P |
| France | | | Simpson | |
| | A | L1-2 | Wilson | |
| AC Milan | H | L1-4 | Murray | 1 |
| Italy | A | L0-2 | | |
| | | **1959-60 EC** | | |
| Anderlecht | H | W5-2 | Millar, Scott, Matthew, | P |
| Belgium | | | Baird 2 | |
| | A | W2-0 | Matthew, McMillan | |
| Red Star | H | W4-3 | McMillan, Scott, Wilson | 1 |
| Bratislava | | | Millar | |
| Czechoslovakia | A | D1-1 | Scott | |
| Sparta Rotterdam | A | W3-2 | Wilson, Baird, Murray | QF |
| Holland | H | L0-1 | | |
| | N | 3-2 | Baird 2, og | |
| Eintracht Frank. | A | L1-6 | Caldow pen | SF |
| West Germany | H | L3-6 | McMillan 2, Wilson | |
| | | **1960-61 ECWC** | | |
| Ferencvaros | H | W4-2 | Davis, Millar 2, Brand | P |
| Hungary | A | L1-2 | Wilson | |
| Borussia Munch. | A | W3-0 | Millar, Scott, McMillan | QF |
| West Germany | H | W8-0 | Baxter, Brand 3, Millar 2 | |
| | | | Davis, og | |
| Wolves | H | W2-0 | Scott, Brand | SF |
| England | A | D1-1 | Scott | |
| Fiorentina | H | L0-2 | | F |
| Italy | A | L1-2 | Scott | |
| | | **1961-62 EC** | | |
| Monaco | A | W3-2 | Baxter, Scott 2 | P |
| France | H | W3-2 | Christie 2, Scott | |
| Vorwaerts | A | W2-1 | Caldow pen, Brand | 1 |
| East Germany | H | W4-1 | McMillan 2 Henderson, og | |
| Standard Liege | A | L1-4 | Wilson | |
| Belgium | H | W2-0 | Brand, Caldow | |
| | | **1962-63 ECWC** | | |
| Seville | H | W4-0 | Millar 3, Brand | 1 |
| Spain | A | L0-2 | | |
| Tottenham | A | L2-5 | Brand, Millar | 2 |
| England | H | L2-3 | Brand, Wilson | |

| Opponents | Venue | Res | Scorers | Rnd |
|---|---|---|---|---|
| | | **1963-64 EC** | | |
| Real Madrid | H | L0-1 | | P |
| Spain | A | L0-6 | | |
| | | **1964-65 EC** | | |
| Red Star Belgrade | H | W3-1 | Brand 2, Forrest | P |
| Yugoslavia | A | L2-4 | Greig, McKinnon | |
| | N | W3-1 | Forrest 2, Brand | |
| Rapid Vienna | H | W1-0 | Wilson | 1 |
| Austria | A | W2-0 | Forrest, Wilson | |
| Inter Milan | A | L1-3 | Forrest | QF |
| Italy | H | W1-0 | Forrest | |
| | | **1966-67 ECWC** | | |
| Glentoran | A | D1-1 | McLean | 1 |
| Northern Ireland | H | W4-0 | Johnston, Smith D, Setterington, McLean | |
| Bor Dortmund | H | W2-1 | Johansen, Smith A | 2 |
| West Germany | A | D0-0 | | |
| Real Zaragoza | H | W2-0 | Smith, Willoughby | QF |
| Spain | A | L0-2 | | |
| Slavia Sofia | A | W1-0 | Wilson | SF |
| Bulgaria | H | W1-0 | Henderson | |
| Bayern Munich | N | L0-1 | | F |
| West Germany | | | | |
| | | **1967-68 FC** | | |
| Dynamo Dresden | A | D1-1 | Ferguson | 1 |
| East Germany | H | W2-1 | Penman, Greig | |
| FC Cologne | H | W3-0 | Ferguson 2, Henderson | 2 |
| West Germany | A | L1-3 | Henderson | |
| | | Bye | | 3 |
| Leeds United | H | D0-0 | | QF |
| England | A | L0-2 | | |
| | | **1968-69 FC** | | |
| Vojvodina | H | W2-0 | Greig pen, Jardine | 1 |
| Yugoslavia | A | L0-1 | | |
| Dundalk | H | W6-1 | Henderson 2, Greig Ferguson 2, og | 2 |
| Eire | A | W3-0 | Mathieson, Stein 2 | |
| DWS Amsterdam | A | W2-0 | Johnstone, Henderson | 3 |
| Holland | H | W1-0 | Smith, Stein | |
| Athletic Bilbao | H | W4-1 | Ferguson, Penman, Persson, Stein | QF |
| Spain | A | L0-2 | | |
| Newcastle Utd | H | D0-0 | | SF |
| England | A | L0-2 | | |

| Opponents | Venue | Res | Scorers | Rnd |
|---|---|---|---|---|
| **1969-70 ECWC** | | | | |
| Steaua Bucharest | H | W2-0 | Johnston 2 | 1 |
| Romania | A | D0-0 | | |
| Gornik Zabrze | A | L1-3 | Persson | 2 |
| Poland | A | L1-3 | Baxter | |
| **1970-71 FC** | | | | |
| Bayern Munich | A | L0-1 | | 1 |
| West Germany | H | D1-1 | Stein | |
| **1971-72 ECWC** | | | | |
| Rennes | A | D1-1 | Johnston | 1 |
| France | H | W1-0 | MacDonald | |
| Sporting Lisbon | H | W3-2 | Stein 2, Henderson | 2 |
| Portugal | A | L3-4 | Stein 2, Henderson | |
| Torino | A | D1-1 | Johnston | QF |
| Italy | H | W1-0 | MacDonald | |
| Bayern Munich | A | D1-1 | og | SF |
| West Germany | H | W2-0 | Jardine, Parlane | |
| Dynamo Moscow | N | W3-2 | Johnston 2, Stein | F |
| USSR | | | | |
| **1972-73 European Super Cup** | | | | |
| Ajax | H | L1-3 | MacDonald | |
| Holland | A | L2-3 | MacDonald, Young | |
| **1973-74 EC** | | | | |
| Ankaragucu | A | W2-0 | Conn, McLean | 1 |
| Turkey | H | W4-0 | Greig 2, O'Hara, Johnstone | |
| Borussia Munch. | A | L0-3 | | 2 |
| West Germany | H | W3-2 | Conn, Jackson, MacDonald | |
| **1975-76 EC** | | | | |
| Bohemians | H | W4-1 | Fyfe, Johnstone, O'Hara | 1 |
| Eire | | | og | |
| | A | D1-1 | Johnston | |
| St Etienne | A | L0-2 | | 2 |
| France | H | L1-2 | MacDonald | |
| **1976-77 EC** | | | | |
| Zurich | H | D1-1 | Parlane | 1 |
| Switzerland | A | L0-1 | | |
| **1977-78 ECWC** | | | | |
| Young Boys | H | W1-0 | Greig | P |
| Switzerland | A | D2-2 | Johnstone, Smith | |
| Twente Enschede | H | D0-0 | | 1 |
| Holland | A | L0-3 | | |
| **1978-79 EC** | | | | |
| Juventus | A | L0-1 | | 1 |
| Italy | H | W2-0 | MacDonald, Smith | |

| Opponents | Venue | Res | Scorers | Rnd |
|---|---|---|---|---|
| PSV Eindhoven | H | D0-0 | | 2 |
| Holland | A | W3-2 | MacDonald, Johnstone Russell | |
| FC Cologne | A | L0-1 | | QF |
| West Germany | H | D1-1 | McLean | |
| **1979-80 ECWC** | | | | |
| Lillestrom | H | W1-0 | Smith | P |
| Norway | A | W2-0 | MacDonald A, Johnstone | |
| Fortuna Dussel. | H | W2-1 | MacDonald A, McLean | 1 |
| West Germany | A | D0-0 | | |
| Valencia | A | D1-1 | McLean | 2 |
| Spain | H | L1-3 | Johnstone | |
| **1981-82 ECWC** | | | | |
| Dukla Prague | A | L0-3 | | 1 |
| Czechoslovakia | H | W2-1 | Bett, MacDonald J | |
| **1982-83 UEFA CUP** | | | | |
| Borussia Dort. | A | D0-0 | | 1 |
| West Germany | H | W2-0 | Cooper, Johnstone | |
| FC Cologne | H | W2-1 | Johnstone, McClelland | 2 |
| West Germany | A | L0-5 | | |
| **1983-84 ECWC** | | | | |
| Valetta | A | W8-0 | Paterson, McPherson 4 | 1 |
| Malta | | | MacDonald, Prytz 2 | |
| | H | W10-0 | Mitchell 2, MacDonald 3 Dawson, MacKay, Davis 2, Redford | |
| Porto | H | W2-1 | Clark, Mitchell | 2 |
| Portugal | A | L0-1 | | |
| **1984-85 UEFA** | | | | |
| Bohemians | A | L2-3 | McCoist, McPherson | 1 |
| Eire | H | W2-0 | Paterson, Redford | |
| Inter Milan | A | L0-3 | | 2 |
| Italy | H | W3-1 | Mitchell, Ferguson 2 | |
| **1985-86 UEFA CUP** | | | | |
| Osasuna | H | W1-0 | Paterson | 1 |
| Spain | A | L0-2 | | |
| **1986-87 UEFA CUP** | | | | |
| Ilves | H | W4-0 | Fleck 3, McCoist | 1 |
| Finland | A | L0-2 | | |
| Boavista | H | W2-1 | McPherson, McCoist | 2 |
| Portugal | A | W1-0 | Ferguson | |
| Borussia Munch. | H | D1-1 | Durrant | 3 |
| West Germany | A | D0-0 | | |

| Opponents | Venue | Res | Scorers | Rnd |
|---|---|---|---|---|
| | | **1987-88 EC** | | |
| Dynamo Kiev | A | L0-1 | | 1 |
| USSR | H | W2-0 | Falco, McCoist | |
| Gornik Zabrze | H | W3-1 | McCoist, Durrant, Falco | 2 |
| Poland | A | D1-1 | McCoist pen | |
| Steaua Buch. | A | L0-2 | | QF |
| Romania | H | W2-1 | Gough, McCoist pen | |
| | | **1988-89 UEFA CUP** | | |
| Katowice | H | W1-0 | Walters | 1 |
| Poland | A | W4-2 | Butcher 2, Durrant Ferguson | |
| FC Cologne | A | L0-2 | | 2 |
| W. Germany | H | D1-1 | Drinkell | |
| | | **1989-90 EC** | | |
| Bayern Munich | H | L1-3 | Walters, pen | 1 |
| W. Germany | A | D0-0 | | |
| | | **1990-91 EC** | | |
| Valetta | A | W4-0 | McCoist, Hateley, Johnston 2 | 1 |
| Malta | H | W6-0 | Dodds, Spencer, Johnston 3, McCoist | |
| Red Star Belgrade | A | L0-3 | | 2 |
| Yugoslavia | H | D1-1 | McCoist | |
| | | **1991-92 EC** | | |
| Sparta Prague | A | L0-1 | | 1 |
| Czechoslovakia | H | W2-1 | McCall 2 | |
| | | **1992-93 EC** | | |
| Lyngby | H | W2-0 | Hateley, Huistra | 1 |
| Denmark | A | W1-0 | Durrant | |
| Leeds United | H | W2-1 | og, McCoist | |
| England | A | W2-1 | Hateley, McCoist | |
| | | **GROUP STAGE** | | |
| Marseille | H | D2-2 | McSwegan, Hateley | |
| CSKA Moscow | A | W1-0 | Ferguson | |
| FC Bruges | A | D1-1 | Huistra | |
| FC Bruges | H | W2-1 | Durrant, Nisbet | |
| Marseille | A | D1-1 | Durrant | |
| CSKA Moscow | H | D0-0 | | |
| | | **1993-94 EC** | | |
| Levski Sofia | H | W3-2 | McPherson, Hateley 2 | 1 |
| Bulgaria | A | L2-1 | Durrant | |
| | | **1994-95 EC** | | |
| AEK Athens | A | L2-0 | | 1 |
| Greece | H | L0-1 | | |

**1995-96 EC**

| Opponents | Venue | Res | Scorers | Rnd |
|---|---|---|---|---|
| Anorthosis | H | W1-0 | Durie | P |
| Cyprus | A | D0-0 | | |
| **GROUP STAGES** | | | | |
| Steau Bucharest | A | L0-1 | | |
| Borussia Dort | H | D2-2 | Gough, Ferguson | |
| Juventus | A | L1-4 | Gough | |
| Juventus | H | L0-4 | | |
| Steau Bucharest | H | D1-1 | Gascoigne | |
| Borussia Dort | A | D2-2 | Laudrup, Durie | |
| **1996-97 EC** | | | | |
| Vladikavkaz | H | W3-1 | McInnes, McCoist, Petric | Q |
| Russia | A | W7-2 | McCoist 3, van Vossen Laudrup 2, Miller | |
| **GROUP STAGES** | | | | |
| Grasshoppers | A | L0-3 | | |
| Auxerre | H | L1-2 | Gascoigne | |
| Ajax | L | 4-1 | Durrant | |
| Ajax | H | L0-1 | | |
| Grasshoppers | H | W2-1 | McCoist 2, 1 pen | |
| Auxerre | A | L1-2 | Gough | |
| **1997-98 EC** | | | | |
| Gotu | A | W5-0 | Negri, Durie 2, McCoist 2 | Q |
| Faroe Islands | H | W6-0 | Durie, Negri 2, McCoist Albertz, Ferguson | |
| Gothenburg | A | L0-3 | | Q |
| Sweden | H | D1-1 | Miller | |
| **UEFA CUP** | | | | |
| Strasbourg | A | L1-2 | Albertz | 1 |
| France | H | L1-2 | Gattuso | |
| **1998-99 UEFA CUP** | | | | |
| Shelbourne | A | W5-3 | Albertz 2, 1 pen, | Q |
| Eire | | | Amato 2, van Bronckhorst | |
| | H | W2-0 | Johansson 2 | |
| PAOK Salonika | H | W2-0 | Kanchelskis, Wallace | Q |
| Greece | A | D0-0 | | |
| Beitar | A | D1-1 | Albertz | 1 |
| Israel | H | W4-2 | Gattuso, Porrini, Johansson, Wallace | |
| B Leverkusen | A | W2-1 | van Bronckhorst, | 2 |
| Germany | | | Johansson | |
| | H | D1-1 | Johansson | |
| Parma | H | D1-1 | Wallace | 3 |
| Italy | A | L1-3 | Albertz | |

| Opponents | Venue | Res | Scorers | Rnd |
|---|---|---|---|---|
| | | | **1999-2000 EC** | |
| FC Haka | A | W4-1 | Amoruso, Mols 2 | Q |
| Finland | | | Johansson | |
| | H | W3-0 | Wallace, Mols, Johansson | |
| Parma | H | W2-0 | Vidmar, Reyna | Q |
| Italy | A | L0-1 | | |
| | | | **GROUP STAGES** | |
| Valencia | A | L0-2 | | |
| Spain | H | 1-2 | Moore | |
| Bayern Munich | H | D1-1 | Albertz | |
| Germany | A | L0-1 | | |
| PSV Eindhoven | A | W1-0 | Albertz | |
| Holland | H | W4-1 | Amoruso Mols 2, McCann | |
| | | | **UEFA CUP** | |
| Bor Dortmund | H | W2-0 | Kohler og, Wallace | |
| Germany | A | L0-2 | | |
| | | | (Dortmund won 3-1 on penalties) | |
| | | | **2000-2001 EC** | |
| Zalgiris Kaunas | H | W4-1 | Johnston, Albertz, Dodds 2 | Q2 |
| Lithuania | A | D0-0 | | |
| Herfolge BK | A | W3-0 | Albertz, Dodds, Amoruso | Q3 |
| Denmark | H | W3-0 | Wallace, Johnston, Kanchelskis | |
| | | | **GROUP STAGES** | |
| Sturm Graz | H | W5-0 | Mols, de Boer, Albertz, | |
| Austria | | | van Bronckhorst, Dodds | |
| | A | L2-0 | | |
| Monaco | A | W1-0 | van Bronckhorst | |
| France | H | 2-2 | Miller, Mols | |
| Galatasaray | H | L2-3 | Kanchelskis, van Bronckhorst | |
| Turkey | H | 0-0 | | |
| | | | **UEFA CUP** | |
| Kaiserslautern | H | W1-0 | Albertz | 3 |
| Germany | A | L3-0 | | |
| | | | **2001-2002 EC** | |
| NK Maribor | A | W3-0 | Flo 2, Nerlinger | Q2 |
| Slovenia | H | W3-1 | Caniggia 2, Flo | |
| Fenerbahce | H | D0-0 | | Q3 |
| Turkey | A | L1-2 | Ricksen | |
| | | | **UEFA CUP** | |
| Anzhi | N | W1-0 | Konterman | 1 |
| Moscow Dynamo | H | W3-1 | Amoruso, Ball, de Boer | 2 |
| Russia | A | W4-1 | de Boer, Ferguson, Flo | |
| | | | Lovenkrands | |
| PSG | H | D0-0 | | 3 |
| France | A | D0-0 | | |
| | | | (aet, Rangers won 4-3 on penalties) | |
| Feyenoord | H | D1-1 | Ferguson pen | 4 |
| Holland | A | L2-3 | McCann, Ferguson pen | |

# ST JOHNSTONE

| Opponents | Venue | Res | Scorers | Rnd |
|---|---|---|---|---|
| | | **1971-72 UEFA CUP** | | |
| SV Hamburg | A | L1-2 | Pearson | 1 |
| West Germany | H | W3-0 | Hall, Pearson, Whitelaw | |
| Vasas Budapest | H | W2-0 | Connolly pen, Pearson | 2 |
| Hungary | A | L0-1 | | |
| Zeljeznicar | H | W1-0 | Connolly | 3 |
| Yugoslavia | A | L1-5 | Rooney | |
| | | **1999-2000 UEFA CUP** | | |
| VPS Vaasa | A | D1-1 | Lowndes | Q |
| Finland | H | W2-0 | Simao 2 | |
| Monaco | A | L0-3 | | 1 |
| France | H | D3-3 | Leonard og, Dasovic, O'Neil | |

# ST MIRREN

| Opponents | Venue | Res | Scorers | Rnd |
|---|---|---|---|---|
| | | **1980-81 UEFA CUP** | | |
| Elfsborg | A | W2-1 | Somner, Abercromby | 1 |
| Sweden | H | D0-0 | | |
| St Etienne | H | D0-0 | | 2 |
| France | A | L0-2 | | |
| | | **1983-84 UEFA CUP** | | |
| Feyenoord | H | L0-1 | | 1 |
| Holland | A | L0-2 | | |
| | | **1985-86 UEFA CUP** | | |
| Slavia Prague | A | L0-1 | | 1 |
| Czechoslovakia | H | W3-0 | Gallagher, McGarvey 2 | |
| Hammarby | A | D3-3 | Gallagher 3 | 2 |
| Sweden | H | L1-2 | McGarvey | |
| | | **1987-88 ECWC** | | |
| Tromso | H | W1-0 | McDowall | 1 |
| Norway | A | D0-0 | | |
| Mechelen | A | D0-0 | | 2 |
| Belgium | H | L0-2 | | |

*Ties finishing level on goals have been settled by: play-offs, toss of the coin, away goals rule (from 1966-67), penalty kicks, or golden goal (from 2000-2001).*

# SCOTTISH JUNIOR CUP

| 1886-87 | Fairfield (Govan) . . .3 | Edin Woodburn . . . . . . .1 |
|---|---|---|
| | (After protest) | |
| 1887-88 | Wishaw Thistle . . . .3 | Maryhill . . . . . . . . . . . . .1 |
| 1888-89 | Burnbank Swifts . . .4 | W Benhar Violet . . . . . . .1 |
| 1889-90 | Burnbank Swifts . . .3 | Benburb 1 . . . . . . . . . . . . |
| | (After protest) | |
| 1890-91 | Vale of Clyde . . . . . .2 | Chryston Ath. . . . . . . . . .0 |
| | (After a draw) | |
| 1891-92 | Minerva . . . . . . . . . .5 | W Benhar Violet . . . . . .2 |
| 1892-93 | Vale of Clyde . . . . . .3 | Dumbarton Fern . . . . . .2 |
| | (After a draw) | |
| 1893-94 | Ashfield . . . . . . . . . .3 | Renfrew V . . . . . . . . . . .0 |
| 1894-95 | Ashfield . . . . . . . . . .2 | West Calder Wan. . . . . .1 |
| | (After a draw) | |
| 1895-96 | Cambuslang Hibs . .3 | Parkhead . . . . . . . . . . . .1 |
| 1896-97 | Strathclyde . . . . . . .2 | Dunfermline Jun. . . . . . .0 |
| | (After protest) | |
| 1897-98 | Dalziel Rovers . . . . .2 | Parkhead . . . . . . . . . . . .1 |
| 1898-99 | Parkhead . . . . . . . . .4 | Westmarch XI . . . . . . . .1 |
| 1899-00 | Maryhill . . . . . . . . . .3 | Rugby XI . . . . . . . . . . . .2 |
| 1900-01 | Burnbank Ath. . . . . .2 | Maryhill . . . . . . . . . . . . .0 |
| 1901-02 | Glencairn . . . . . . . . .1 | Maryhill . . . . . . . . . . . . .0 |
| | (After a draw) | |
| 1902-03 | Parkhead . . . . . . . . .3 | Larkhall Th. . . . . . . . . . .0 |
| 1903-04 | Vale of Clyde . . . . . .3 | Parkhead . . . . . . . . . . . .0 |
| 1904-05 | Ashfield . . . . . . . . . .2 | Renfrew Vic. . . . . . . . . .1 |
| 1905-06 | Dunipace Jun. . . . . .1 | Rob Roy . . . . . . . . . . . .0 |
| | (After a draw) | |
| 1906-07 | Strathclyde . . . . . . .1 | Maryhill XI . . . . . . . . . . .0 |
| | (After two draws) | |
| 1907-08 | Larkhall Th. . . . . . . .1 | Q.P. Hampden XI . . . . . .0 |
| 1908-09 | Kilwinning R. . . . . . .1 | Strathclyde . . . . . . . . . .0 |
| | (After a draw) | |
| 1909-10 | Ashfield . . . . . . . . . .3 | Kilwinning R. . . . . . . . . .0 |
| | (After protest) | |
| 1910-11 | Burnbank Ath. . . . . .1 | Petershill . . . . . . . . . . . .0 |
| | (After a draw) | |
| 1911-12 | Petershill . . . . . . . . .5 | Denny Hibs . . . . . . . . . .0 |
| 1912-13 | Inverkeithing Un. . . . 1 | Dunipace Jun . . . . . . . . 0 |
| 1913-14 | Larkhall Th. . . . . . . . 1 | Ashfield . . . . . . . . . . . . .0 |
| | (After two draws) | |
| 1914-15 | Parkhead. . . . . . . . . 2 | Port Glasgow Ath. . . . . . 0 |
| 1915-16 | Petershill . . . . . . . . . 2 | Parkhead. . . . . . . . . . . . 0 |

| 1916-17 | St Mirren Jun. . . . . . 1 | Renfrew Jun. . . . . . . . . . 0 |
|---|---|---|
| | (After a draw) | |
| 1917-18 | Petershill awarded cup, no final tie. . . . . . . . . . . . . | |
| 1918-19 | Glencairn. . . . . . . . 1 | St Anthony's . . . . . . . . 0 |
| | (After a draw) | |
| 1919-20 | Parkhead. . . . . . . . . 2 | Cambuslang R. . . . . . . 0 |
| 1920-21 | Rob Roy . . . . . . . . 1 | Ashfield . . . . . . . . . . . . 0 |
| 1921-22 | St Roch's. . . . . . . . . 2 | Kilwinning R. . . . . . . . . 1 |
| | (After protest) | |
| 1922-23 | Musselb'gh Bruntonian . 2 | Arniston R. . . . . . . . . . . 0 |
| 1923-24 | Parkhead. . . . . . . . . 3 | Baillieston Jun. . . . . . . . 1 |
| | (After a draw) | |
| 1924-25 | Saltcoats Vics . . . . . 2 | St Anthony's . . . . . . . . 1 |
| | (After two draws) | |
| 1925-26 | Strathclyde . . . . . . . 2 | Bridgeton Wav. . . . . . . 0 |
| | (After a draw) | |
| 1926-27 | Glencairn. . . . . . . . . 2 | Cambuslang R. . . . . . . 1 |
| 1927-28 | Maryhill Hibs . . . . . 6 | Burnbank Ath. . . . . . . . 2 |
| 1928-29 | Dundee Violet . . . . . 4 | Denny Hibs . . . . . . . . . 0 |
| 1929-30 | Newtongrange Star . 3 | Hall Russell's. . . . . . . . 0 |
| 1930-31 | Denny Hibs . . . . . . . 1 | Burnbank Ath. . . . . . . . 0 |
| | (Replay ordered, Denny failed to appear) | |
| 1931-32 | Perthshire . . . . . . . . 2 | Rob Roy . . . . . . . . . . . 1 |
| 1932-33 | Yoker Ath. . . . . . . . 4 | Tranent Jun.. . . . . . . . . 2 |
| | (After a draw) | |
| 1933-34 | Benburb . . . . . . . . . 3 | Bridgeton Wav. . . . . . . 1 |
| 1934-35 | Tranent . . . . . . . . . . 6 | Petershill . . . . . . . . . . . 1 |
| 1935-36 | Benburb . . . . . . . . . 1 | Yoker Ath. . . . . . . . . . . 0 |
| | (After a draw) | |
| 1936-37 | Arthurlie. . . . . . . . . . 5 | Rob Roy . . . . . . . . . . . 1 |
| 1937-38 | Cambuslang R. . . . . 3 | Benburb . . . . . . . . . . . 2 |
| 1938-39 | Glencairn. . . . . . . . . 2 | Shawfield. . . . . . . . . . . 1 |
| 1939-40 | Maryhill . . . . . . . . . . 1 | Morton Jun. . . . . . . . . . 0 |
| 1940-41 | Perthshire . . . . . . . . 3 | Armadale Th. . . . . . . . . 1 |
| | (After two draws) | |
| 1941-42 | Clydebank . . . . . . . . 4 | Vale of Clyde . . . . . . . . 2 |
| 1942-43 | Rob Roy . . . . . . . . . 3 | Benburb . . . . . . . . . . . 1 |
| | (After two draws) | |
| 1943-44 | Perthshire . . . . . . . . 1 | Blantyre Vics.. . . . . . . . 0 |
| 1944-45 | Burnbank Ath. . . . . 3 | Cambuslang R. . . . . . . 1 |
| | (After protest) | |
| 1945-46 | Fauldhouse Un. . . . 2 | Arthurlie. . . . . . . . . . . . 0 |
| 1946-47 | Shawfield . . . . . . . 2 | Bo'ness Un.. . . . . . . . . 1 |
| | (After a draw) | |
| 1947-48 | Bo'ness Un. . . . . . . 2 | Irvine Meadow . . . . . . . 1 |

| 1948-49 | Auchinleck Talbot ..3 | Petershill ............. 2 |
|---|---|---|
| 1949-50 | Blantyre Vics .....3 | Cumnock............. 0 |
| 1950-51 | Petershill .........1 | Irvine Meadow........ 0 |
| 1951-52 | Kilbirnie Ladeside ..1 | Camelon ............. 0 |
| 1952-53 | Vale of Leven .....1 | Annbank Un .......... 0 |
| 1953-54 | Sunnybank ........2 | Lochee Harp .......... 1 |
| 1954-55 | Kilsyth R. .........4 | Duntocher Hibs ....... 1 |

(After a draw)

| 1955-56 | Petershill .........4 | Lugar Boswell Th...... 1 |
|---|---|---|
| 1956-57 | A'deen Bnks o' Dee .1 | Kilsyth R. ........... 0 |
| 1957-58 | Shotts Bon Accord .2 | Pumpherston.......... 0 |
| 1958-59 | Irvine Meadow .....2 | Shettleston ........... 1 |
| 1959-60 | St Andrew's .......3 | Greenock............. 1 |
| 1960-61 | Dunbar United .....2 | Cambuslang R. ....... 0 |

(After a draw)

| 1961-62 | Rob Roy ..........1 | Renfrew.............. 0 |
|---|---|---|

(After a draw)

| 1962-63 | Irvine Meadow .....2 | Glenafton Ath......... 1 |
|---|---|---|
| 1963-64 | Johnstone Burgh ...3 | Cambuslang R. ....... 0 |

(After a draw)

| 1964-65 | Linlithgow Rose ....4 | Baillieston ............ 1 |
|---|---|---|
| 1965-66 | Bonnyrigg Rose ....6 | Whitburn ............. 1 |

(After a draw)

| 1966-67 | Kilsyth R. .........3 | Glencairn............. 1 |
|---|---|---|

(After a draw)

| 1967-68 | Johnstone Burgh ...4 | Glenrothes............ 3 |
|---|---|---|

(After a draw)

| 1968-69 | Cambuslang R. ....1 | Rob Roy ............. 0 |
|---|---|---|
| 1969-70 | Blantyre Vics ......1 | Penicuick Ath......... 0 |

(After a draw)

| 1970-71 | Cambuslang R. ....2 | Newtongrange Star .... 1 |
|---|---|---|
| 1971-72 | Cambuslang R. ....3 | Bonnyrigg Rose....... 2 |

(After 1-1 draw)

| 1972-73 | Irvine Meadow .....1 | Cambuslang R. ....... 0 |
|---|---|---|

(After two draws)

| 1973-74 | Cambuslang R. .....3 | Linlithgow Rose....... 1 |
|---|---|---|
| 1974-75 | Glenrothes ........1 | Glencairn............. 0 |
| 1975-76 | Bo'ness Un........3 | Darvel ............... 1 |
| 1976-77 | Kilbirnie Ladeside .3 | Rob Roy ............. 1 |
| 1977-78 | Bonnyrigg Rose ....1 | Stonehouse Violet.......0 |
| 1978-79 | Cumnock .........1 | Bo'ness Un. .........0 |
| 1979-80 | Baillieston ........2 | Benburb ..............0 |

(After a draw)

| 1980-81 | Pollok ...........1 | Arthurlie ...............0 |
|---|---|---|

| 1981-82 | Baillieston | 0 | Blantyre Vics | 1 |
| 1982-83 | East Kilbride Th. | 2 | Bo'ness Un. | 0 |
| 1983-84 | Baillieston | 0 | Bo'ness United | 2 |
| 1984-85 | Pollok | 3 | Petershill | 1 |

(After 1-1 draw)

| 1985-86 | Auchinleck Talbot | 3 | Pollok | 2 |
| 1986-87 | Auchinleck Talbot | 1 | Kilbirnie Ladeside | 0 |

(After 1-1 draw)

| 1987-88 | Auchinleck Talbot | 1 | Petershill | 0 |
| 1988-89 | Cumnock | 1 | Ormiston Primrose | 0 |
| 1989-90 | Hill o' Beath | 1 | Lesmahagow | 0 |
| 1990-91 | Auchinleck Talbot | 1 | Newtongrange Star | 0 |
| 1991-92 | Auchinleck Talbot | 4 | Glenafton | 0 |
| 1992-93 | Glenafton | 1 | Tayport | 0 |
| 1993-94 | Largs Thistle | 1 | Glenafton | 0 |
| 1994-95 | Camelon | 2 | Whitburn | 0 |
| 1995-96 | Camelon | 0 | Tayport | 2 |

(After 0-0 draw)

| 1996-97 | Pollok | 3 | Tayport | 1 |
| 1997-98 | Arthurlie | 4 | Pollok | 0 |
| 1998-99 | Kilwinning Rangers | 1 | Kelty Hearts | 0 |
| 1999-2000 | Johnstone Burgh | 2 | Whitburn | 2 |

(aet, 2-2 full time. Whitburn won 4-3 on penalties)

| 2000-2001 | Renfrew | 0 | Carnoustie Panmure | 0 |

(aet. Renfrew won 6-5 on penalties)

| 2001-2002 | Linlithgow Rose | 1 | Auchinleck Talbot | 0 |

**Linlithgow Rose celebrate after winning the OVD Scottish Junior Cup with a 1-0 victory over Auchinleck Talbot**

# JUNIOR CONTACTS

## CENTRAL REGIONAL LEAGUE

**ARTHURLIE** .................................................J Docherty, 0141 881 3262
**ASHFIELD** ....................................................T Robertson, 0141 944 0571
**BAILLIESTON** ................................................G Kelly, 0141 643 0104
**BELLSHILL** .....................................................J Love, 01698 341172
**BENBURB** ......................................................I Pope, 0141 633 1853
**BLANTYRE VICS** ...........................................J Wylie, 01698 331078
**CAMBUSLANG RANGERS** ...............Ms E Lloyd, 0141 583 2979
**CARLUKE ROVERS** .........................Ms C Kay, 01555 772154
**COLTNESS UTD.** ...........................................T Sloan, 01698 383971
**CUMBERNAULD UTD** ....................................J McIntosh, 01236 720536
**DUNIPACE** ...................................................I Duncan, 01324 813463
**EAST KILBRIDE THISTLE** .............................B Kidd, 01355 227667
**FORTH WANDERERS** ....................................J Kelly, 01555 840861
**GLASGOW PERTHSHIRE** ..............D Preston 07932 487033
**GREENOCK** ..................................................B Barbour, 07944 329878
**JOHNSTONE BURGH** ....................................R Cantwell, 0141 561 6010
**KILSYTH RANGERS** ......................................J Ferguson, 01236 824306
**KIRKINTILLOCH ROB ROY** ...........J Robertson, 0141 776 3618
**LANARK UNITED** .........................................T Anderson, 01555 663796
**LARKHALL THISTLE** .....................................C Lenson, 01698 885472
**LESMAHAGOW** ............................................W McKinlay, 07901 980490
**MARYHILL** ....................................................G Anderson, 0141 563 0969
**NEILSTON** .....................................................H Blair, 0141 881 8282
**PETERSHILL** ................................................A Sideserf, 0141 552 9554
**POLLOK** ........................................................G Allan, 0141 639 8635
**PORT GLASGOW** .........................................P Galbraith, 01475 710951
**RENFREW** .....................................................J Barclay, 0141 884 6142
**ROYAL ALBERT ATHLETIC** ..........................P Higgins, 01698 888498
**RUTHERGLEN GLENCAIRN** ..............A Forbes, 0141 643 1406
**ST ANTHONY'S** ............................................F McKenna, 0141 641 9659
**ST ROCH'S** ...................................................C McLean, 0141 558 8976
**SHETTLESTON** .............................................M Scollan, 0141 554 8809
**SHOTTS BON ACCORD** ..................W Quilter, 01501 771165
**STONEHOUSE VIOLET** ...................................A Brown, 01698 792629
**THORNIEWOOD UTD** ...................................J Miller, 01236 421465
**VALE OF CLYDE** ...........................................J Wilson 0141 778 3340
**VALE OF LEVEN** ...........................................H Hamill, 01389 841050
**WISHAW** ......................................................J Nelson, 01236 754718
**YOKER ATH.** .................................................D Andrew, 01389 381308

## AYRSHIRE LEAGUE

| | |
|---|---|
| **ANNBANK UTD** | S McCroskie, 01292 520394 |
| **ARDEER THISTLE** | P McBlane, 07950 922034 |
| **ARDROSSAN WINTON ROVERS** | T Ferrie, 01294 604264 |
| **AUCHINLECK TALBOT** | H Dumigan, 01290 421785 |
| **BEITH** | R McCarter, 01505 503800 |
| **CRAIGMARK BURNTONIANS** | T Farrell, 01292 550093 |
| **CUMNOCK** | G Morton, 01290 423992 |
| **DALRY** | Ms L Daly, 01294 835808 |
| **DARVEL** | J MacLachlan, 01560 321487 |
| **GLENAFTON ATHLETIC** | T King, 01292 478568 |
| **HURLFORD** | W McMahon, 01563 821047 |
| **IRVINE MEADOW** | I McQueen, 01292 471884 |
| **IRVINE VICTORIA** | A Nicol, 01294 550120 |
| **KELLO ROVERS** | D Cowan, 01659 67168 |
| **KILBIRNIE LADESIDE** | D Gardner, 01505 683548 |
| **KILWINNING** | T Moore, 01294 557585 |
| **LARGS** | D Keenan, 01475 686342 |
| **LUGAR BOSWELL THISTLE** | K Young, 07967 907537 |
| **MAYBOLE** | A Meek, 01655 883419 |
| **MUIRKIRK** | A McKay, 01290 423022 |
| **SALTCOATS VICTORIA** | G Hunter, 01236 602828 |
| **TROON** | R Murray, 01292 476530 |
| **WHITLETTS VICTORIA** | I Dick, 01292 265402 |

**CENTRAL: Arthurlie** (Dunterlie Pk), **Ashfield** (Saracen Pk), **Baillieston** (sharing Provanmill Pk), **Bellshill** (Brandon Pk), **Benburb** (Tinto Pk), **Blantyre V** (Castle Pk), **Cambuslang Rangers** (Somervell Pk), **Carluke Rov** (Loch Park Stdm), **Coltness Utd** (Victoria Pk), **Cumbernauld Utd** (Guys Meadow), **Dunipace** (Westfield Pk), **East Kilbride Th.** (Showpark), **Forth Wand.** (Kingshill Pk), **Glasgow Perthshire** (Keppoch Pk), **Greenock** (Ravenscraig Stdm), **Johnstone Burgh** (Keanie Pk), **Kilsyth Rangers** (Duncansfield), **Kirkintilloch Rob Roy** (Adamslie Pk), **Lanark Utd** (Moor Pk), **Larkhall Th** (Gasworks Pk), **Lesmahagow** (Craighead Pk), **Maryhill** (Lochburn Pk), **Neilston** (Brig-O-Lea Stdm), **Petershill** (Petershill Pk), **Pollok** (Newlandsfield Pk), **Port Glasgow** (sharing Ravenscraig Stdm), **Renfrew** (Western Pk), **Royal Albert** (Robert Smillie Memorial), **Rutherglen Glen.** (Southcroft), **St Anthony's** (McKenna Pk), **St Roch's** (Provanmill Pk), **Shettleston** (Greenfield Pk), **Shotts Bon Accord** (Hannah Pk), **Stonehouse Violet** (Tilework Pk), **Thorniewood Utd** (Robertson Pk), **Vale of Clyde** (Fullarton Pk), **Vale of Leven** (Millburn Pk), **Wishaw** (Victoria Pk), **Yoker Athletic** (Holm Pk).

**AYRSHIRE: Annbank Utd** (New Pebble Pk), **Ardeer Th** (Ardeer Stdm), **Ardrossan Winton Rovers** (Winton Pk), **Auchinleck Talbot** (Beechwood Pk), **Beith** (Bellsdale Pk), **Craigmark Burntonians** (Station Pk), **Cumnock** (Townhead Pk), **Dalry Th** (Merskworth Pk), **Darvel** (Recreation Pk), **Glenafton Athletic** (Loch Pk), **Hurlford Utd** (Blair Pk), **Irvine Meadow** (Meadow Pk), **Irvine Vics** (Victoria Pk), **Kello Rovers** (Nithside Pk), **Kilbirnie Ladeside** (Valefield), **Kilwinning Rangers** (Abbey Pk), **Largs Th** (Barrfields Stdm), **Lugar Boswell Th** (Rosebank Pk), **Maybole** (Ladywell Stdm), **Muirkirk** (Burnside Pk), **Saltcoats Vics** (Campbell Pk), **Troon** (Portland Pk), **Whitletts Vics** (Voluntary Pk).

# FA CUP WINNERS

1872 Wanderers 1 Royal Engineers 0

1873 Wanderers 2 Oxford Uni 0

1874 Oxford Uni 2 Royal Enginers 0

1875 Royal Enginers 2 Old Etonians 0 (after 1-1 draw)

1876 Wanderers 3 Old Etonians 0 (after 1-1 draw)

1877 Wanderers 2 Oxford Uni 1 (aet)

1878 Wanderers 3 Royal Engiers 1

1879 Old Etonians 1 Clapham Rovers 0

1880 Clapham Rovers 1 Oxford Uni 0

1881 Old Carthusians 3 Old Etonians 0

1882 Old Etonians 1 Blackburn R 0

1883 Blackburn Oly 2 Old Etonians 1 (aet)

1884 Blackburn R 2 Queen's Park 1

1885 Blackburn R 2 Queen's Park 0

1886 Blackburn R 2 WBA 0 (after a 0-0 draw)

1887 Aston V 2 WBA 0

1888 WBA 2 Preston 1

1889 Preston 3 Wolves 0

1890 Blackburn R 6 Sheff Wed 1

1891 Blackburn R 3 Notts Co 1

1892 WBA 3 Aston V 0

1893 Wolves 1 Everton 0

1894 Notts Co 4 Bolton 1

1895 Aston V 1 WBA 0

1896 Sheff Wed 2 Wolves 1

1897 Aston V 3 Everton 2

1898 Notts Forest 3 Derby 1

1899 Sheff Utd 4 Derby 1

1900 Bury 4 Southampton 0

1901 Tottenham H 3 Sheff U 1 (after 2-2 draw)

1902 Sheff U 2 Southampton 1 (after 1-1 draw)

1903 Bury 6 Derby 0

1904 Man City 1 Bolton 0

1905 Aston V 2 Newcastle 0

1906 Everton 1 Newcastle 0

1907 Sheff W 2 Everton 1

1908 Wolves 3 Newcastle 1

1909 Man U 1 Bristol C 0

1910 Newcastle 2 Barnsley 0 (after 1-1 draw)

1911 Bradford C 1 Newcastle 0 (after 0-0 draw)

1912 Barnsley 1 West Brom 0 (aet, after 0-0 draw)

1913 Aston Villa 1 Sunderland 0

1914 Burnley 1 Liverpool 0

1915 Sheff U 3 Chelsea 0

1920 Aston V 1 Huddersfield 0 (aet)

1921 Tottenham 1 Wolves 0

1922 Huddersfield 1 Preston 0

1923 Bolton 2 West Ham 0

1924 Newcastle 2 Aston Villa 0

1925 Sheff U 1 Cardiff 0

1926 Bolton 1 Man City 0

1927 Cardiff 1 Arsenal 0

1928 Blackburn 3 Huddersfield 1

1929 Bolton 2 Portsmouth 0

1930 Arsenal 2 Huddersfield 0

1931 West Brom 2 Birmingham 1

1932 Newcastle 2 Arsenal 1

1933 Everton 3 Man City 0

1934 Man City 2 Portsmouth 1

1935 Sheffield W 4 West Brom 2

1936 Arsenal 1 Sheffield U 0

1937 Sunderland 3 Preston 1

1938 Preston 1 Huddersfield 0 (after extra time)

1939 Portsmouth 4 Wolves 1
1946 Derby 4 Charlton 1 (aet)
1947 Charlton 1 Burnley 0 (aet)
1948 Man Utd 4 Blackpool 2
1949 Wolves 3 Leicester 1
1950 Arsenal 2 Liverpool 0
1951 Newcastle 2 Blackpool 0
1952 Newcastle 1 Arsenal 0
1953 Blackpool 4 Bolton 3
1954 WBA 3 Preston 2
1955 Newcastle 3 Man City 1
1956 Man City 3 Birmingham 1
1957 Aston Villa 2 Man U 1
1958 Bolton 2 Man U 0
1959 Notts Forest 2 Luton 1
1960 Wolves 3 Blackburn 0
1961 Tottenham 2 Leicester 0
1962 Tottenham 3 Burnley 1
1963 Man U 3 Leicester 1
1964 West Ham 3 Preston 2
1965 Liverpool 2 Leeds 1 (aet)
1966 Everton 3 Sheff Wed 2
1967 Tottenham 2 Chelsea 1
1968 West Brom 1 Everton 0
     (aet)
1969 Man City 1 Leicester 0
1970 Chelsea 2 Leeds 1 (aet,
     first game a 2-2 draw)
1971 Arsenal 2 Liverpool 1 (aet)
1972 Leeds 1 Arsenal 0
1973 Sunderland 1 Leeds 0
1974 Liverpool 3 Newcastle 0
1975 West Ham 2 Fulham 0
1976 Southampton 1 Man U 0
1977 Man U 2 Liverpool 1
1978 Ipswich 1 Arsenal 0
1979 Arsenal 3 Man U 2
1980 West Ham 1 Arsenal 0
1981 Tottenham 3 Man City 2
     (after 1-1 draw)
1982 Tottenham 1 QPR 0
     (after 1-1 draw)
1983 Man U 4 Brighton 0
     (after 2-2 draw)

1984 Everton 2 Watford 0
1985 Man U 1 Everton 0 (aet)
1986 Liverpool 3 Everton 1
1987 Coventry 3 Tottenham 2
     (aet)
1988 Wimbledon 1 Liverpool 0
1989 Liverpool 3 Everton 2 (aet)
1990 Man U 1 Crystal P 0
     (after 3-3 draw)
1991 Tottenham 2 Notts Forest 1
     (aet)
1992 Liverpool 2 Sunderland 0
1993 Arsenal 2 Sheff Wed 1
     (aet, first game 1-1)
1994 Man U 4 Chelsea 0
1995 Everton 1 Man U 0
1996 Man U 1 Liverpool 0
1997 Chelsea 2 Middlesboro 0
1998 Arsenal 2 Newcastle 0
1999 Man U 2 Newcastle 0
2000 Chelsea 1 Aston V 0
2001 Liverpool 2 Arsenal 1
2002 Arsenal 2 Chelsea 0

**ARSENE WENGER holds
aloft the FA Cup trophy**

## ENGLISH LEAGUE CHAMPIONS

| | | | |
|---|---|---|---|
| 1888-89 | Preston NE | 1936-37 | Manchester City |
| 1889-90 | Preston NE | 1937-38 | Arsenal |
| 1890-91 | Everton | 1938-39 | Everton |
| 1891-92 | Sunderland | 1946-47 | Liverpool |
| 1892-93 | Sunderland | 1947-48 | Arsenal |
| 1893-94 | Aston Villa | 1948-49 | Portsmouth |
| 1894-95 | Sunderland | 1949-50 | Portsmouth |
| 1895-96 | Aston Villa | 1950-51 | Tottenham Hotspur |
| 1896-97 | Aston Villa | 1951-52 | Manchester United |
| 1897-98 | Sheffield United | 1952-53 | Arsenal |
| 1898-99 | Aston Villa | 1953-54 | Wolves |
| 1899-1900 | Aston Villa | 1954-55 | Chelsea |
| 1900-01 | Liverpool | 1955-56 | Manchester United |
| 1901-02 | Sunderland | 1956-57 | Manchester United |
| 1902-03 | The Wednesday | 1957-58 | Wolves |
| 1903-04 | The Wednesday | 1958-59 | Wolves |
| 1904-05 | Newcastle United | 1959-60 | Burnley |
| 1905-06 | Liverpool | 1960-61 | Tottenham Hotspur |
| 1906-07 | Newcastle United | 1961-62 | Ipswich Town |
| 1907-08 | Manchester United | 1962-63 | Everton |
| 1908-09 | Newcastle United | 1963-64 | Liverpool |
| 1909-10 | Aston Villa | 1964-65 | Manchester United |
| 1910-11 | Manchester United | 1965-66 | Liverpool |
| 1911-12 | Blackburn Rovers | 1966-67 | Manchester United |
| 1912-13 | Sunderland | 1967-68 | Manchester City |
| 1913-14 | Blackburn Rovers | 1968-69 | Leeds United |
| 1914-15 | Everton | 1969-70 | Everton |
| 1919-20 | West Bromwich Albion | 1970-71 | Arsenal |
| 1920-21 | Burnley | 1971-72 | Derby County |
| 1921-22 | Liverpool | 1972-73 | Liverpool |
| 1922-23 | Liverpool | 1973-74 | Leeds United |
| 1923-24 | Huddersfield Town | 1974-75 | Derby County |
| 1924-25 | Huddersfield Town | 1975-76 | Liverpool |
| 1925-26 | Huddersfield Town | 1976-77 | Liverpool |
| 1926-27 | Newcastle United | 1977-78 | Nottingham Forest |
| 1927-28 | Everton | 1978-79 | Liverpool |
| 1928-29 | Sheffield Wednesday | 1979-80 | Liverpool |
| 1929-30 | Sheffield Wednesday | 1980-81 | Aston Villa |
| 1930-31 | Arsenal | 1981-82 | Liverpool |
| 1931-32 | Everton | 1982-83 | Liverpool |
| 1932-33 | Arsenal | 1983-84 | Liverpool |
| 1933-34 | Arsenal | 1984-85 | Everton |
| 1934-35 | Arsenal | 1985-86 | Liverpool |
| 1935-36 | Sunderland | 1986-87 | Everton |

| 1987-88 | Liverpool | 1994-95 | Blackburn Rovers |
|---------|-----------|---------|------------------|
| 1988-89 | Arsenal | 1995-96 | Manchester United |
| 1989-90 | Liverpool | 1996-97 | Manchester United |
| 1990-91 | Arsenal | 1997-98 | Arsenal |
| 1991-92 | Leeds United | 1998-99 | Manchester United |
| **PREMIER LEAGUE** | | 1999-00 | Manchester United |
| 1992-93 | Manchester United | 2000-01 | Manchester United |
| 1993-94 | Manchester United | 2001-02 | Arsenal |

**Patrick Vieira, Ashley Cole and Sol Campbell celebrate Arsenal winning the Premiership title at Old Trafford**